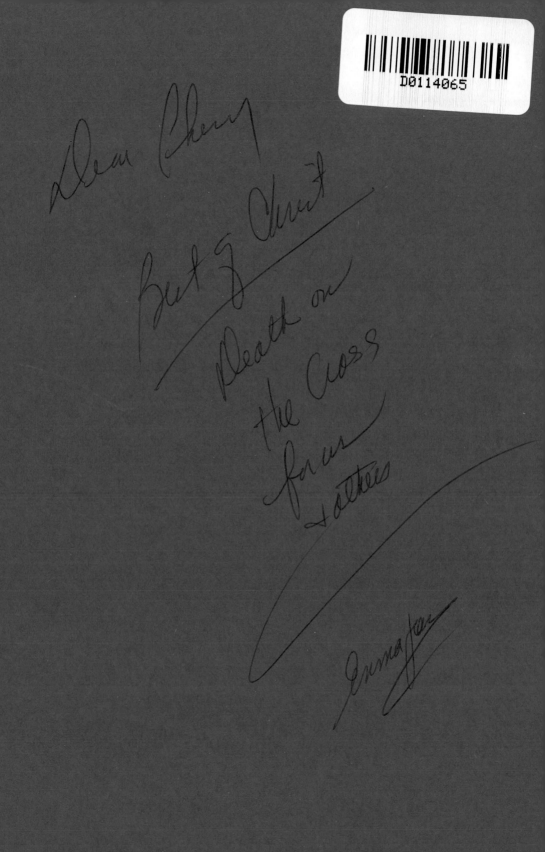

Dear Cheng

But of Christ
Death on
the Cross
for us
+ others

Emma Hen

High Call
High Privilege

Gail MacDonald

COMPLETELY REVISED & UPDATED

High Call High Privilege

A Pastor's Wife Speaks to Every Woman in a Place of Responsibility

Gail MacDonald

HENDRICKSON PUBLISHERS

Dedicated to

GORDON
my husband, pastor, teacher, and papa
to our grandchildren.
Your insistence that we both keep growing,
have more than a "ministry marriage,"
live as mercied people, and
move beyond commitment
to the enjoyment of solidarity
has made it possible for me to say,
It's still a high call and high privilege.
This truly is *our* book.

CONTENTS

PREFACE

It has been nearly twenty years since the first writing of *High Call, High Privilege*. At that time, I recall thinking, "This is a book that should be written by someone more seasoned in life and ministry than I." Now I smile as I realize that, for better or worse, I am seasoned. I have thirty-eight years of ministry behind me.

During those years my husband Gordon and I have served four congregations: one rural (as rural as you can get), two suburban, and one urban (as urban as you can get). And we have also had the experience of involvement with a parachurch organization. Today we find ourselves back at one of those four churches, thoroughly enjoying working with more than a few people with whom we have up to twenty-five years of history.

With such diversity in each of these settings, perhaps you appreciate that we have done more than our share of adjustment-making. The result? There's got to be something in this book that fits just about everybody's ministry world. If you're excited about where you are these days, I hope you'll find lots of excitement here. But if you're struggling and asking lots of hard questions, you'll find struggle here. There are blessings, and there are consequences.

I am grateful for the loving encouragement and writing expertise that my husband Gordon gave to this book. He never pushes but lovingly inspires me to believe I can write and then lends any support necessary toward completion. Our children and their spouses, Mark and Patty, Kristy and Tom, have prayed for this project and given their usual strong arms of affirmation to their mom. And they will honor me even more by reading it.

Over these past twenty years, I have come to believe even more that prayer is the main event, and so I thank those who have done the work of prayer: Joanna, Lourine, Lois W., Janet, Karen, Charlotte, and Lois F. I am ever in your debt.

There are others. Thanks, Jan, for your loving nudges that got me connected with Dan Penwell and Hendrickson Publishers. Your friendship of nearly forty years continues to be a shelter in a time of storm plus a laugh when I badly need one. And thank you, Joanna, for reading the manuscript, making helpful suggestions, and cheering me on so creatively..

To the four congregations we have served, Clough Valley, First Baptist, Grace Chapel, Trinity Baptist, as well as InterVarsity, my gratitude for receiving us and allowing me to serve you with such ease. Your gracious acceptance of and hospitality toward Gordon and me made it possible for us to grow and give even when we didn't always get it right.

A word of thanks to Dan Penwell who has encouraged me through these long months of rewrite. Your patience and flexibility have meant a lot, Dan. And to Judy Bodmer whose editing expertise as both an author in her own right and as a wife in ministry has helped immensely. I'm grateful for the gracious way you helped make this book easier to read, Judy. Finally, bless you Scott Pinzon for making *High Call, High Privilege* look so inviting. I appreciate you.

Gail MacDonald
Lexington, Massachusetts

INTRODUCTION

> How you can think so well of us,
> And be the God you are,
> Is darkness to my intellect,
> But sunshine to my heart.
> — *Frederick Faber, 1874*

The older I grow the more aware I am that I live under the grand umbrella of God's kindness, mercy, and leadership. St. Paul seemed to think this way too. He described the grand mystery of Christian ministry to the Corinthians in this way: "We have this treasure in earthen vessels" (2 Cor. 4:7 NASB). The treasure is the gospel of Jesus Christ. The earthen vessels are us: common clay pots, inexpensive, easily replaced, usually reserved for dirty work.

This is a book about how one woman, one of those earthen vessels, has tried to be faithful in handling the treasure. I'd like to pursue a balance in talking about both, for to emphasize one at the expense of the other would be to present an unhelpful story. Neither should be lost in the telling.

You should know that from the start I have loved the ministry. The regrets that have accumulated over almost four decades are but an anthill compared to the mountain of delights. Having been involved with four congregations and one parachurch organization,

Gordon and I have learned what it is like to be both givers and receivers. Like Paul the apostle who gave and received much from the churches, Gordon and I look gratefully at the journey we have shared with these distinctive groups of people. In each case we grew to love them and in turn felt deeply loved by them. It would, in fact, be difficult for me to calculate who did the most for whom. Have we given more to those we have led, or have they given more to us?

Throughout this book, I hope to take you on a tour through all these years of shared ministry. Each situation has been unique—set in a different cultural context. And to some extent, each has drawn from us a slightly different response. Each place has forced us to face new experiences and new growth. In the beginning it was impossible to see where everything was going to lead. Now in these latter years, I can see the finger of God which was always tracing the outline of the path for us to follow.

As the story unfolds, my hope is that you will see certain themes emerge with consistency. I believe that relationships need to be prioritized. For me, priority one focuses on my knowledge of and intimacy with God. If this relationship isn't vital and lively, all other connections are up for grabs. I have chosen to begin here.

And while it may sound odd, I believe that relational priority two is the one I have with myself. Am I experiencing the love of Christ enough that I can eagerly deny self and take up my cross, or is something dark in me screaming for center stage? Knowing who God has made me to be and how I am progressing in response to his love is absolutely essential.

Having placed those two relationships in such a deliberate order, I can then affirm my next relationship which is with Gordon, my husband of thirty-eight years (as of this writing). Priority four focuses on being a mother, a mother-in-law, and a grandmother.

The fifth priority takes me out of the home and into the life of our congregation and community where I join my husband in the disciplines and pursuits of the pastoral ministry.

The sixth and final priority has to do with those occasions when people have been kind enough to invite me to different parts of North America and to other countries of the world to speak to them from my perspective on faith. The most important audience in these travels are women married to pastors and missionaries. When I get into a room with such people, there is an almost instant rapport. A few candid words is all that is needed to bond through our common love for Christ and our commitment to the service of people in his name.

You'll see those priorities demonstrated through this book. After all these years, there is no doubt in my mind that when I put the congregation, the community, and travel before any of the previous priorities, I am soon in trouble.

In writing, I've tried to be honest—as much as possible. There are obvious lines of personal privacy which I observed. But I feel much more free to open up my life to people today than when I was younger. This, I think, is the challenge for those of us who are older if we are to be of any value to a younger generation who are anxious to profit from the stories of our blessings and our mistakes.

For many years now, I have had the joy of speaking to and spending large blocks of time with ministry wives. It's clear that most of them aren't interested in what I've done well; they want to know where I've struggled and how I've found wisdom and stamina to overcome the blows, the challenges, and the pressures. No doubt their interest has to do with sensing there is too little honesty and too much image polishing among leaders. Most of the women I meet don't want to play games. They want to be effective; they want to embrace a gospel that works; they want to be authentic. They don't want to whine, complain, or seek pity.

And those are the kinds of women I like to be with. As we share our insights and learning experiences with each other, we enhance our mutual effectiveness, and we minimize the possibilities of disappointment and failure. Never underestimate the synergy that comes from the sharing of book titles, quotes from the church fathers and mothers, thoughts from Scripture, and the practical stories of everyday life. That's what I have in mind as I write.

Because of my concern for the young and my belief that after the age of fifty I should pour my preponderant energies into the lives of the young, my writing is first directed to young women who are contemplating spiritual leadership, either as singles or married persons, then to young wives whose husbands are progressing through the rigors of a seminary curriculum and have been wondering what the world of Christian ministry will be like. Last but not least, I'm writing to a host of compatriots who, like myself, are in the heat of spiritual battle at this very moment. Among them are the exhilarated and the discouraged. They will doubtless relate to many of the feelings and events which I've described. It is my hope that each reader will see her own uniqueness in God's design, never trying to be anyone else but herself—the person God intended her to be.

Perhaps as you read this you are at a dark moment in your life; I pray you will find hope to see that the darkness need not prevail. Even in those cheerless times which will come, we can affirm that they are neither the terminus nor the norm of experience. Instead, they are points of growth from which can emerge a clearer vision of how to reflect the splendor of God and the joys of personal relationships. God means for us to finish strong.

Let me tell you how this book is written. Watch for chapters headed "The Journey Continues," for they will tell you my story in something of an autobiographical form: how and why we moved from one ministry to another and something of what we experienced along the way. The other chapters identify major themes of ministry life that came into focus as the years passed. I tried as best I could to place those chapters in the approximate time of life in which they became significant to me.

When you are finished reading, I hope you will have heard one unmistakable message: that a life of ministry in the church is indeed still a high call, a high privilege.

ONE

THE JOURNEY BEGINS

Come to the Fire

> Have your heart right with Christ, and He will visit you often, and so turn weekdays into Sundays, meals into sacraments, homes into temples and earth into heaven.   —*Charles Spurgeon*

S imple answers for tough questions! Years ago I believed they existed in abundance. In those days they called people like me easy believers. And that's what I was. As a young woman, I tended to sort events, people, and even God and his ways into neat little predictable categories. That way I protected myself from unwanted surprises in life and created a superficial sense of security. Today I am a different woman.

As a ministry wife, I live in a world that rejects easy answers. My domain demands that I think, make difficult choices, and face issues which often seem to have no precedent. This means that while life is exciting, it is fraught with complexities and challenges.

So while easy answers might be nice, what I've learned to seek are biblically based principles by which to think, to act, and to form my life. They've come to me as I've sat at the feet of mentors, asked questions of people I've admired, made a host of mistakes, and taken more than a few risks. I've learned to live with unpredictability, to avoid shortcuts and formulas, and to seek the truth no matter how tough the ultimate message.

I love this kind of life. Sometimes I get tired, make errors in judgment, and run into a bewildering brick wall. But I still love what I do, what I'm learning, and where it's taking me.

One morning many years ago, in those days when easy answers were still in my life, I found myself in an arena with thousands of other people. A retired missionary nearing his eightieth year spoke. His aged face and stooped shoulders evidenced the signs of a lifetime of spiritual warfare and the hard work of ministry. Perhaps a person more than twice my age would have some spiritual secret that I could press into my own life situation. And so I strained to hear every word from this quivering voice weakened by the years.

The man caught my attention with a simple word picture as he challenged people to seek something greater. He said, "*Untended fires soon die and become just a pile of ashes.*"

Sometimes you hear something so frequently that it loses its grip on you. Then someone rephrases it in a way that hits you like a bolt of lightening, and you are never the same. That's what that moment was like for me.

He said that the fire presumably burns in the heart of the one who follows Christ. It is a flame that cannot go unmanaged, for if it is allowed to dwindle into ashes, the outer person is destined to a life of coldness.

My life was altered by that simple statement. I'd heard the practical, personal, spiritual creed of a man who had eight decades behind him to support his claim. He proposed that we give serious attention to the condition of the "fire within." "Is it burning with force, or is it dying? Is it being fed or starved?" he asked. "Until this matter is addressed, understood, and resolved," he went on, "all attempts at finding one's way through the challenges of life will be relatively futile."

For a young woman in ministry, this was an insight of massive proportions. He could not have known that his words would mark me and who knows how many others for all these years since. I've often wondered if he had read the words of Walter Hilton of Thurgarton who once said:

> Fire shall always burn on the altar, which the believer shall nourish, putting wood underneath in the morning every day, so that the fire may not go out.[1]

Everything I have to share with you in this book is seen through the perspective of that simple statement: *Untended fires soon die and become a pile of ashes.* Nothing that I am about to tell you makes sense if you do not begin with this understanding.

☙ THEY CALL IT THE FISHBOWL

If you're like me, a woman in ministry or the wife of someone in ministry, you know something about life in the proverbial fishbowl. You know what it's like to live virtually every part of your life in the public eye. You know about pressure, applause, criticism, satisfaction, anger, joy, failure, and fulfillment. You know the excitement of mixing it up with the noblest and the neediest of people. You know laughter and tears, contentment and sorrow. You've felt the wonder of intimacy with God and the emptiness of spiritual dryness.

I've known this fishbowl for almost forty years, and I've grown to appreciate the challenges that thousands of women in the ministry lifestyle face daily. As I said, life in my own fishbowl, for the most part, has been an inspiring experience. I wouldn't exchange it for any other way of being. Admittedly, there have been occasions when I would have preferred to climb out for a spell, but mostly the experience has been one of great joy and thanksgiving. Almost weekly I hear from women who share my excitement.

But I am also aware that many of you live in similar fishbowls and don't agree with my enthusiasm. Some of you would say that fishbowl living has been painful and destructive, both spiritually and emotionally, and you'd gladly trade it for another way of life. Some of you feel you were pushed into the fishbowl, not called to it. And there are those who have met with nothing but disappointment. You keep wondering when the "fun" starts. I know you're there because you communicate such thoughts to me when I spend a few days with women in ministry at a conference or a retreat.

One woman wrote this to me:

My husband and I have been married five years. He has been in ministry six years. We are very happily married except for one problem that has reared its ugly head. I've decided I don't want to be a pastor's wife, and I don't feel I can handle it. I've been hurt and stomped on by so many people. I am intolerant of people's stupidity and judgmental attitudes and all-around childishness. Do I sound bitter? Well, I am. Please forgive me. If you ask anyone who has known me, they would tell you that I'm a normal, outgoing, considerate, even-tempered woman. I've probably fooled everyone into thinking I'm the model young, sweet pastor's wife, but I'm not. Nor do I want to be. So I'm torn. I love my husband, but I'm willing to give him up, as much as it would kill me, to get out of this life.

So this is us: those who are glad we're here and those who wish we weren't and a huge group in the middle of the extremes. Where can you start to think constructively about this style of life into which God in his providence put you? I suggest you go back to the words of that old man. It all begins with the *fire within* and your heart attitude.

I told you that this book begins and ends with that principle. So let me explain myself a bit further before I go on to life in the home and in the congregation for a woman in ministry.

From that day in the crowded arena to this one, the vitality of my inner fire has been my priority. Tending the fire within is another way of talking about being open to the presence of Christ. It is what makes me long for his likeness, offers direction and stability, establishes proper motives and responses. Here it is that the real issues of the Christian faith are thought out and pressed into action.

When I become aware that my attitude and conduct are drifting toward an un-Christlike perspective, I've learned to ask: "Have you been with Jesus at the fire, Gail? Have you allowed the fire to die down? Are there more ashes than flames?" Usually the alarming realization arises: He has been there at the fire within, waiting, but I've been a "no-show."

Fishbowl living forces a constant self-appraisal of the condition of the fire. When I find myself resisting the inner prompting to cross through a crowd of people in the fellowship hall of our church building to greet and encourage a person who may be rather demanding, what's the message? Does my reluctance stem from the quality of the fire within?

If I find myself instinctively resenting the ring of the telephone, what is being said? Is it a sign that I've been too long away from the fire?

When I've surrendered to my people-pleasing instinct rather than to say a strategic no, or when I find myself assuming the martyr's mind-set, is it time to realize that my fire time has been neglected?

The old missionary's picture of the fire has led me to remember that remarkable scene on the shore of Galilee. One morning Jesus invited a group of exhausted, dejected, and empty-boated fishermen to breakfast. As they gathered about his fire, several things happened. The men were fed (Jesus was very practical), they were reaffirmed in their relationships to him (he was sensitive to their uneasiness), and they were instructed and recalled to ministry (he would finish what he'd started with them). That morning on Galilee provides a great picture of what happens or should happen when you or I have fire time with the Lord.

You could say that after that moment, the fire on the shore was strangely transferred to their innermost beings. And as long as they were willing to keep that fire tended, it burned within. The feeding, the affirming, the instructing, and the sending went on and on.

Now having tested the validity of this thought for many years, I believe that every woman's life has to begin at that same sort of fire. It takes time to come to the fire, it takes effort to keep the fire burning, it takes a willingness to become quiet enough to hear what God might be saying, and it takes courage to snuff out competing sounds and demands that attempt to shorten or neutralize the effect of the fire time.

But here is the great choice that must be remade virtually every day. Do I give priority attention to tending the fire within, or do I surrender to the alternatives of busyness, hurry, people pleasing, or the seemingly urgent that slowly starves my spirit and my resolve to be the woman God wants me to be? If that fire burns brightly, I share the experience of the disciples; if it dwindles untended, I am gradually surrounded by a chill marking the onset of weakness and confusion.

One year our family gathered for the weekend to celebrate Gordon's birthday. We attended a play as the guests of a friend. The next morning at breakfast, I was feeling upset about parts of the play, and I made judgmental comments to my family that were neither kind nor thoughtful. I'd been a no-show at the fire that morning. When I realized what I had done, it was a moment for reflection, and later I wrote in my journal:

If only I had asked questions rather than made a judgment. As it was, it appeared more important for there to be a winner (me) and losers (others who didn't agree with me). Later, after the damage was done, I went back, humbled, to my neglected time with Christ only to be amazed that this was the admonition I would have read that morning: "Words from a wise man's mouth are gracious" (Ecc. 10:12). Thank heaven my speedy repentance was received well by these I love—but it's a shame that I brought a cloud over Gordon's special day.

Then I knew why the prophet Isaiah said:

But see here, you who live in your own light, and warm yourselves from your own fires and not from God's; you will live among sorrows (Isa. 50:11 TLB).

Jesus clearly appreciated the principle of the inner fire. A simple study of his earthly life and ministry shows the rhythm Jesus maintained: fire time first, then connecting with people, then back to the fire to commune with his Father. Only then would he reengage with people and their needs.

Neglect this rhythm, and love and courage falter. That is why I'm absolutely convinced that we cannot survive healthfully in the fishbowl if we don't stay close to the fire and keep it tended.

Each time I am on an airplane, I hear the flight attendant prepare passengers for a possible emergency. Her presentation goes like this:

Should there be a loss of cabin pressure, oxygen masks will be released automatically overhead. . . . Pull down the mask to your face,. cover both your nose and mouth, and breath normally. *If you are traveling with or seated next to a small child, place your mask on first, then assist the child.*

Interesting! "Place your mask on first, and then assist the child." Each time I hear this I am reminded that we who would bring help and hope to others must tend to our fires *first.*

∾ WHOSE FIRE?

My own pilgrimage to that fire has been a lifelong experience. Since earliest childhood days, I possessed both a general hunger to be in touch with God and a strong compulsion to help people. I didn't understand what I was searching for until, as a young teenager, l was invited by a boyfriend to a youth prayer meeting. I'll never forget my first impression when I saw a group of my peers on their knees, speaking personally to the God whom I'd been seeking. Soon after, I made a quiet, youthful commitment to Jesus Christ.

But what Christians often call conversion does not by any means imply completion, and that soon became evident in my experience of spiritual growth. The young man who'd invited me to that prayer meeting became a steady boyfriend. Our relationship was a good one in that it caused me to pursue deeper Christian growth. But there was an unhealthy side to it.

I came to confuse commitment to Christ with dependence upon this unusually committed young man whom I deeply admired. Without realizing it I fell into the trap of drawing spiritual vitality from him rather than from the Christ whom I'd accepted as Lord and Savior.

Looking back on our relationship, I now realize that I had relied upon a human being to give me something that was humanly impossible for him to give. I was looking for a man to start my spiritual fire and to tend it for me. He couldn't, and no one else could have either. The more I missed that point through immaturity, the more I clung to him in the hope of finally tapping a strength I thought he could transfer to me.

Understanding my unreasonable demands upon him has helped me appreciate what happens when people attempt to gain that same kind of strength from me. Surely, they reason, Gail has something (she's the pastor's wife, isn't she?) from which we can profit—if we draw close enough to her to get it.

I guess one might feel complimented by the fact that there are those who seek such strength. The reasoning behind the effort is faulty—just as mine once was when I tried to live off someone else's fire. But for those who are admired or reverenced for their spiritual vitality, it can be a heady experience . . . and a destructive one.

When someone attempts to seek that kind of courage from me, even if the person's motive is good, the reasoning is faulty—just as mine once was. It cannot be forgotten: Jesus is out to start a fire within *each* of us.

Henri Nouwen wrote:

> When we expect a friend or a lover to be able to take away our deepest pain, *we expect from him or her something that cannot be given by human beings.* No human being can understand us fully, no human being can give us unconditional love, no human being can offer constant affection, no human being can enter into the core of our beings and heal our deepest brokenness. *When we forget that and expect from others more than they can give, we will be quickly disillusioned; for when we do not receive what we expect, we easily become resentful, bitter, revengeful, and even violent.*[2] (italics mine)

What happened to me in those early Christian years dramatically illustrates what Nouwen has expressed. I was warming my soul at another person's fire, seeking a secondhand empowering. What I was doing was unfair to him and unhealthy for me.

Today I am slow to criticize people who make that same error in judgment because I know that this faulty thinking once threatened to destroy me. I faced the temptation to become, as Nouwen warns, bitter, resentful, and revengeful.

The wonderful story of my conversion and my romance took what seemed at the time an unhappy twist. After graduating from high school, the young man who had helped me find Christ and I became engaged. We went off to college together. At the end of our first year, we decided that I should drop out of school for a while to earn the money that would make both marriage and his continuing education a possibility. So he returned to the campus, and I went to work.

Soon both a bank account and a hope chest began to fill. There were wedding plans and honeymoon reservations. Wedding invitations were printed; showers were given. Everything was moving along smoothly. My little easy-answers world was in perfect order. Everything was under control.

But one day, as the wedding date approached, a shocking letter came from my fiancé. He wanted to terminate the relationship. And he did so: abruptly, decisively, and without explanation. The dream was over! My simple little world collapsed. And I never saw him again.

Loss, confusion, rejection, and self-pity engulfed me as I retreated to the privacy of my bedroom. Mom and Dad did their best to be sensitive and to allow me to grieve (for it was a death-like moment). Three years of life suddenly seemed null and void.

The turning point came a few days later when my father poked his head into my room and said, "Well, honey, I guess we're going to find out whether or not this Jesus is really all you've been trying to tell us he is to you."

If Dad's words did little to comfort, they certainly challenged. They were exactly what I needed. My dad was still on his way to asking Christ to be Lord of his life. How I handled this crisis mattered. Would I drown in self-pity or make this an opportunity for growth?

From that moment I resolved that I was going to build a fire of my own (using words I would hear many years later from the old missionary). I'm not sure what my father's intent was when he spoke as he did, but I will be forever thankful for his intrusion into my mood. His words motivated me to act on my own for once.

Immediately, I sprang into motion. I returned wedding gifts, canceled honeymoon reservations, and offered necessary explanations to a bevy of friends. It was all tough medicine, but it was an important beginning to the process of personal renewal. For the first time, I was abandoning an easy-answer world, renouncing reliance on the fire of others, and learning what it was like to receive my own strength and direction from the Christ of the inner fire.

In those days I learned that despair, depression, and a generalized sense of confusion could often be handled when I set out to create a corner of life filled with resolve and purpose. Once a beachhead of that sort has been established, it is a matter of simply extending it into other parts of life. It worked for me. I went on and did three other seemingly strange things.

First, I began a prayer meeting in our church, which hadn't had one since the 1890s. Secondly, I began to visit lonely people in the hospital once a week. Hospitals had an ironic way of making me feel ill; I knew I had to overcome that psychosomatic reaction before I could really help anyone. Thirdly, I resolved to go back to college and finish my degree.

I must mention that the young man who broke our engagement went on to become a man of God. I'm not sure that he would have ever achieved the levels of maturity and accomplishment he attained had we fulfilled our intentions to be married. I also am not certain that I would have ever participated in his growth. Rather, I suspect that if there had not been a crisis of the sort I'd faced, I would have become a serious negative influence, something of a drag upon his life. I would have drained power from him that he would have needed for himself. Ironically, my pain was his release.

But my pain was also my release. Those simple resolves filled my life with a new sense of meaning. As I made small, steady steps forward, I began to see spiritual progress—the growth of my own fire. The final three years at the University of Denver flew by quickly. The challenges of being a student and a resident assistant in the dormitories while holding a part-time job in a local church shaped my future.

Drawing closer and closer to the fire Jesus Christ had started, I gained insights that have remained with me throughout the years of my adulthood. Of course there were the usual hurts, disappointments, and failures. But through it all God was shaping me into a woman who knew how to draw strength at Christ's fire so that serving others became a joy. I hoped that one day I would link heart and hand with a man similarly committed, but if not, I would love what I was doing.

It is no surprise now when I look back and see that God had a perfectly prepared timetable for my inner growth and future relationships. After only five years of lessons and experiences, circumstances occurred that brought me into contact with the man destined to become my husband.

❖ MEET YOUR FUTURE

I became acquainted with a man who happened to share an apartment with Gordon during Gordon's final years of college. One night he said, "Gordon, I think I've met a woman who would make *you* a terrific wife. Her name is Gail."

He had Gordon's attention. A day later the two of them stopped at my college apartment for an introduction. Within minutes Gordon and I were locked in conversation. Perhaps I enhanced the possibility that we would be attracted to each other when I served him homemade apple pie. Before he left, we made a date. It would be a Russian history lecture at the University of Colorado where Gordon attended. (He was not financially extravagant.)

Three weeks later we were engaged; four months later we were married. Not a strategic plan we would recommend. But it worked for us. How could we know so quickly that this was the lifelong commitment we wanted to make? It's quite impossible for me to adequately convey the mysterious joy that sprang up within me when I learned that Gordon had been called to ministry in the same way that I had been.

What we were to form was not simply *his* ministry, a kind of bandwagon upon which I could jump. Instead, it was the merger of two ministries independently commissioned by the Christ of the inner fire.

Christ starts the fire and invites us to join him. My experience tells me that he is more than willing to keep the fire burning brightly for a time, but that a process is soon set into motion in which he begins to hand over the responsibility of tending the fire to us. And if there is a flaming, tended fire, he will continue that heavenly whisper of comfort and challenge, of gentle rebuke and affirmation.

It's sobering to realize that many woman all over the world have entered this fishbowl of life as leaders or as wives of men who are in Christian leadership. Each of us is unique, and it would be a mistake to assume that all of us should conform to one set "image."

But one thing these women should share is the joy that erupts from knowing that God has privileged each of us to be a part of a life marked by serving. The fact is that many women do not have that kind of joy, either because they lost it or because they never found it.

In the early days of our shared ministry, the wife of a pastor told me, "Gail, you're going to learn to hate the ministry." That comment shocked me! It seemed to clash with all the idealistic, romantic notions of what I'd thought life with my husband, the pastor, would become. Why would a woman, thirty years ahead of me, admit to such bitterness and distaste for something I'd been dreaming about for such a long time?

Why did she want to pour cold water on the vision Gordon and I had sought so fervently as together we worked his way through seminary? Sadly she was not the last woman from whom I was to hear that familiar theme during the passing years.

Many things, of course, could have been implied in a statement like that. Here and there the wives of some Christian leaders have been victimized by circumstances and situations both painfully agonizing and unfair. They have been joined to husbands who were less than sensitive to them as persons and who often left them to fend for themselves. Such women have faced congregational problems that tore at the human spirit. And perhaps there are those who've lived with hardships which were the result of the sins of other people.

I believe that the majority of women for whom ministry has been an unhappy experience share a common dilemma. They have perceived neither the principle of the inner fire nor its potential. They have consigned themselves to trying to make life work according to structures and external standards, but that's not the way to reach the fire. Thus, having missed the energy and the direction which comes from that fixed, centered experience, they attempt to live on an energy that comes from other sources. Rules and innate talents, personal knowledge and observations accumulated while growing up in Christian homes, or guidelines and examples set by seminary professors will help them only so long.

Sooner or later, stresses mount, crises occur, and temptations arise. They find themselves facing the lot of fishbowl lives and saying, "We've learned to hate it." Be assured that ministry is far too draining to be sustained without the experience of the inner fire.

Returning to the fire (where Christ is to be found), tending it, and learning to listen to his voice have not been easy for me. As long as I live, I fear there will be times when a part of me will resist coming back because it is all too often a place which costs me my pride. There are times when I think I can do it all alone. And I'm not always keen to face up to the aspects of my being which are not reflecting the nature of God. Admitting wrong within myself before blaming others, speaking out before I've taken the necessary time to think through my response, or being impatient with the growth rate of others are all things his fire exposes and he means to purge in me.

Conversation at the fire tends to point us in directions that we might like to avoid: unlikable people, responsibility, and mature inner attitudes. But when I am faithful to my trek to the fire, he has brought light-giving discoveries, my homesickness for something beyond this barren land is satisfied, and I discover that this audience of One is enough to carry me through any experience life can throw my way.

The journey from being an easy-answers *girl* to a fire-oriented *woman* has not been filled with ease. But it has made sense to me ever since I heard an old man put it so plainly: *Untended fires soon die and become a pile of ashes.* Knowing that has made all the difference.

TWO

THE JOURNEY CONTINUES

Sainty

Men are lonely because they build walls instead of bridges.
— *Anonymous*

In the extreme northwest corner of the state of Kansas is the town
of St. Francis. It sits astride U. S. Route 36. If you ever get to Sainty
(as it is called by the locals), drive twenty miles further to the west
and then seven miles north on a dirt road. There you'll find the
Clough Valley Baptist Church. Clough is pronounced "clue" by locals.
We spent two-and-one-half important years of our lives there. From
the air the Kansas countryside has the appearance of a checkerboard.
In each of the squares farmers and ranchers either sow winter wheat
every September or graze cattle. If you find the church, you'll see our
former parsonage, an old remodeled farm home on the other side of
the road. The nearest neighbor is a long way down the road.

We came to love that simple home of five rooms. Our water was
drawn from the ground by windmill power. Most of our food was
grown in a large garden out back or provided by farmers who often
brought baskets and boxes of meat, eggs, and potatoes when they
came to church on Sunday. Our congregation either raised crops or

cattle. On a normal day, they streamed by our crossroads location on huge tractors or beefed-up farm trucks and always gave a toot on the horn or a big wave. For the most part, they were contented, determined people who'd learned to survive in a tough agricultural world.

From the moment we came to Clough Valley, we felt loved and warmly appreciated. But, if the people were hospitable, the elements were not. The summers were hot, and hail storms and tornadoes were a frequent threat. Rattlesnakes made occasional appearances on our front lawn, and coyotes sometimes kept us awake at night with their howling. Winters brought brutal winds and occasional paralyzing snowstorms.

If we had listened to the counsel of most of our friends, I suspect we would never have passed through Clough Valley. It was a time when Gordon was pursuing his divinity degree in seminary, and the prevailing opinion of the day was that one ought to give maximum attention to study and little else. But neither Gordon nor I believed that. We shared a conviction that study ought to be matched by practical experience.

A few days after we married, Gordon became a youth pastor in a Denver church. We worked as a team pouring ourselves into high school young people. At first it was a happy experience, but then things turned sour. When Gordon looks back on those first ministry days, he often admits to a string of mistakes which he charges up to inexperience and immaturity. And we often sheepishly recall the moment when he prematurely resigned in total discouragement.

We were bewildered. This had been our first attempt at ministry, and we saw ourselves as failures. It became a time for self-examination. Were we really suited for ministry? Were our dreams, our sense of call, our assessment of our gifts unrealistic? Was it possible that we didn't have what it took to stick it out over the long haul?

In our desire to be sure of God's purposes, we made ourselves available to speak and sing (I was a vocalist) wherever anyone would have us. There was no glamour in what we did. We didn't charge fees, hoped that people would cover our expenses, and stayed in people's guest rooms. It usually meant long automobile trips at the end of the school week to small towns in Wyoming or Nebraska or the western parts of Colorado.

More than once we drove three hundred miles through the night to be with fifty or sixty people the next day. Our criteria for saying yes to invitations was simple: If they asked us, we were willing to go. And so we went, eager to serve in whatever ways we believed would bring a word of hope or a touch of encouragement. The result was preaching experience and an increased understanding of people and what they were looking for when they participated in church life.

I liken those weekend trips to the times when Jesus sent out his disciples to learn the hard way what serving was all about. When they returned, they were tired but excited. Full of questions, they were far more teachable. The same was true of us. Slowly, our confidence in God's call returned as our experience in ministry deepened.

It was that pursuit of more preaching/pastoring encounters that brought us to Clough Valley one Sunday morning. The friendly, farming families of that area had lost their pastor and were in pursuit of a new one. Gordon had been invited to preach. When the Sunday morning service ended, the people entertained us at one of the nearby farms with the typically delicious cooking that farm wives are known for. When we left that tiny church the next morning, we had been entranced by the simple but determined lifestyle of people who worked desperately hard to make a living from the soil. It was more than a one-time visit, however, because a call soon came to our home in Denver, asking if we would consider candidating for the pastorate at the Clough Valley church. Gordon was in his second year of seminary, but it didn't take either of us long to make up our minds. We'd do both: graduate school and ministry. Within a couple of months, he was pastoring his first congregation in "Sainty."

Our first child, Mark, who is now thirty-four, was only ten days old when we began our ministry at this little church 176 miles east of Denver. Moving into the parsonage across the road, we commenced a lifestyle that seems unbelievable and almost impossible when I look back at it. The schedule hardly varied for two years. Each Tuesday morning at 4:00 A.M., Gordon would climb into our little Volkswagen and begin a three-hour drive against the prevailing headwinds and tumbleweed of the Colorado prairie. Arriving in Denver by 7:15 A.M., he would attend a full four days of school and return to us by supper time on Friday.

Here was another one of those life-altering crossroads. In these surroundings I faced one of the first great lessons that a woman has to master if she is to be effective as a Christian woman, a wife, and a mother: Submit to the fact that *God is in control and is able to bring good out of every circumstance.* I had a choice to make, and it had to be made quickly. I could enter each circumstance of life, anticipated or unanticipated, draw strength from the Lord, and find character lessons from the experience. Or I could let the circumstances at Clough Valley make me resentful and restless, which could easily have happened.

The first alternative would make me into a more useful person for the kingdom, while the second would make me into a bitter woman who had to be carried and coddled and who would ultimately become an obstacle to her husband's life and ministry. I chose as best I could—the first of the two choices.

You may recall the words of the pastor's wife which I quoted in the last chapter. "You're going to learn to hate the ministry," she had said. Now I was in a challenging situation where I could easily have permitted that to happen.

A test of my choice came quickly. Mark was only a few weeks old when he came down with a serious intestinal infection. Gordon was in Denver at school, and I was alone with a very sick baby. His fever reached the danger point, and he became increasingly dehydrated. I had no transportation, we were twenty miles from the nearest town, and I knew of no local physician.

I remember pausing to think through the situation. I was going to have to draw strength from God and rely on people I hardly knew, people who would be watching closely. Moments like these were not unusual for them; they'd lived under such conditions all of their lives. If I had the slightest twinge of anxiety, it would be obvious to them.

If I was to be a spiritual leader among them as a young woman, it would have to start here in this situation. My credibility in trusting God was on the line. But even beyond this, I saw that how I handled this bad moment might set in place a pattern of how I would respond in the future to varying kinds of crises and struggles. I remember praying not only for God's care for our son but also that I would learn patience and calmness.

God answered my prayer with grace. People in the congregation responded to my need by checking on us frequently when Gordon was at seminary. They were eager to help me with transportation without making me feel like I was imposing on them. Together we made our way through the scary moments. As a result, the women in the church began to bond to me, and we were on our way to relationships of trust.

A couple of months later, Mark again became the instrument for a second test of my resolve. Riding about our small farmhouse in his walker, he had apparently decided to see whether he was ready to descend the cellar steps on his own. He wasn't ready! In fact, rather than walk down those steps in his walker, he somersaulted the length of the stairway and landed on cold, hard cement. The hematoma on the top of his head was horrific. And I learned a second time that God could be in control of me in *every circumstance*. I phoned the same doctor who had helped me earlier. He asked me questions to ascertain if I would need to make another emergency trip to town. Were his eyes dilated? Was he vomiting? Could I keep him from falling asleep for several hours? I prayerfully waited it out alone. On both occasions, it was encouraging to be able to roll with the punches and not disintegrate under pressure.

If I thought I was alone in the parsonage when Gordon was gone, I was wrong. Before the first winter had fully set in, I discovered that mice felt free to enjoy pastoral hospitality. One week alone, according to Gordon's journals, I killed six of the little visitors. I confess that mice have a disturbing effect upon me, and my feelings of antipathy were accelerated one night when I walked into our bathroom during Mark's 4:00 A.M. feeding only to find one of them in our bathtub.

I grabbed a broom and swung wildly. He scrambled frantically to scurry up the sides of the slippery tub. It was a grand contest to the end (his). I remember physically shaking from the violence and the strange fear I had throughout the episode. Why a mouse would be such a problem surprises me today. Perhaps he symbolized other feelings and stresses I was experiencing, and I took my frustration out on him. But again, I learned that God was in control, and this incident soon became a source of great laughter.

In subsequent years, having been given the privilege of traveling abroad and seeing firsthand the sorts of things that missionaries face on a daily basis, my bout with a mouse in a bathtub seems a tame affair, although at the time it certainly didn't seem so. The apostle Paul often talked about contentment under all circumstances; he also mentioned that in addition to contentment, one should be thankful for everything that happens. Was that possible during a cold, blustery Kansas winter when I was alone and the windmill froze? At that moment, flexibility meant calling a farmer's wife down the road and asking for instructions on how to free up a windmill. I quickly learned the routine, and it didn't take long for me to become an expert in thawing windmills.

If it was windmill demands in a Kansas winter, it was snakes in the summer, some harmless, some rattlers. All big, all ugly, all very frightening. We killed more than one rattler on the church steps, and they died regularly under the wheels of our car. One day a large one slithered into our front yard where Mark and several other small children were playing while a bunch of women were meeting in our living room. I watched a brave woman from our group calmly grab a hoe and kill the snake.

Afterwards I asked her, "Do you ever worry about letting your children play outdoors when there are so many snakes around?"

"You could worry about a lot of things," she said, "but a Christian has to put his or her children in the hands of the Lord and believe that the little ones are never out of God's sight. But of course we're always keeping a cautious eye on things," she added. It was one more time when those wonderful people of the earth would underscore what I was learning: *If you believe that God is in control of everything, then worry, panic, and resentment have no place in your life.*

If I needed any proof of that, it came when Gordon and I saw farmers plant (they called it "drilling") wheat in the fall. They waited patiently for it to grow under the winter snows, oversaw its maturing in the spring sun, and then faced the threat of June hailstorms when the vulnerable golden wheat was just about to be harvested. Yearly hailstorms seemed inevitable. Someone in the congregation would get "hailed out" by the random storms that could suddenly cross the afternoon sky, destroy one crop, and leave another untouched across the road. We never saw a farmer panic under such conditions. But we did see more than one plow a destroyed crop back under the soil and trust God for another better year.

We could not have known when we accepted the call to this small church that they would show us how to plod through life when we were "hailed out" by failure or immaturity. After our brief experience in youth ministry, we needed someone to model dogged determination and perseverance so we could see the beauty of graciously taking the easy with the tough. Without realizing it, they showed us that there are moments when we cannot control everything, that we must entrust ourselves to the one who judges righteously. We quickly learned that if we opened our eyes, our ears, and our hearts, the people of Clough Valley would have much to teach us in their own quiet way. We became conscious of the importance of listening and observing.

I also learned *flexibility*. During most of our worship services, I played the piano. At the rear of the church was a small "cry" room with cribs for Mark and other infants. If our son began to cry while I was up front participating in the service, it was perfectly natural for me, as a nursing mother, to leave the front row for a matter of higher priority. That was life, and no one seemed to be offended or startled by it. I instinctively felt embarrassed, but no one else was. And so I slowly learned to respond to matters in a more easy-mannered way.

Most of my life, I have preferred to be on the giving end. But the people at Clough Valley graciously taught me the *grace of receiving*. They eagerly shared material things as part of our salary. For example, a family would butcher a steer; then someone would stop by with steaks, hamburger meat, and a roast or two. A garden would yield fresh vegetables, and ears of corn, tomatoes, and cucumbers would make their way to our table. We regularly received two to three dozen eggs (complete with chicken droppings and feather-bits still attached) each Sunday. There were never hidden messages or strings attached to these love gifts.

We received when it came to being taught a new way of life. Many of our city ways were a source of amusement to the folk at Clough Valley. They had a different sense of what was really important. Thus, like missionaries, we had to acculturate, taking on their ways, not grudgingly but lovingly. It became important for us to watch, to listen, and to ask questions. I learned new gardening and canning techniques; I learned how to go to farm auctions and buy secondhand things which we could use in our family.

We learned how to share clothes. People did not have garage sales at Clough Valley. What God had given them, they gave to one another when they had ceased to use it. All of us in the MacDonald family learned how to accept gifts of used clothing and to wear them with grace and appreciation. A five-year-old once said, "All of my clothes have had someone else in them." That was certainly true of our family's wardrobe.

To the uninitiated, receiving can be misunderstood in at least two ways. There are those who resist receiving, thinking it to be demeaning. Their pride is hurt. But we knew that since the church couldn't afford to pay us much, this type of giving was to be part of what would make it possible for us to stay. Furthermore, to receive from them meant that we loved what they had to offer and how they offered it. Had we been too proud to receive, we would not have been loving them, and that would have short-circuited the promised provision of the Lord.

A second misunderstanding is the exact opposite: There are those who think that life is to be an excess of receiving. Gordon and I are increasingly concerned for the younger generation of people entering into Christian service. We hear a great deal of talk centering on security for one's career, guaranteed salary packages, and demands for better and more comfortable situations.

We are convinced that the effectiveness of ministry is drastically curtailed the minute people get the impression we are in it for the money or for any kind of gain. Gordon and I are God's responsibility. We have chosen not to negotiate financial arrangements; rather it has seemed best in this life of faith to simply receive with gratitude what was given. We lived that way then, and we live that way today.

We learned other things in Sainty country: the importance of *building bridges instead of walls.* Did we know what was important to these people? How else could we be all things to all people in order that we "might win some," as the apostle Paul said?

There was a presidential election during our Sainty years, and Gordon felt rather strongly about one of the candidates. Unfortunately, most of Cheyenne County (where we lived) had even stronger convictions about the other candidate. So when Gordon put a bumper sticker on the back of our VW which declared his sentiments, it drew a bit of notice. Gordon's father happened to be visiting us at the time and had a thought for us. "Is this an issue that you're prepared to alienate people on?" Gordon's father asked. "If they are going to turn against you, is this the issue you want it to be predicated upon?"

The "youthfulness" in us wanted to protest that we had a right to speak out on political matters, but my father-in-law's insight on this point was wiser than ours. He was helping us to understand that those of us who lead have to carefully evaluate the signals we send to people. We must indeed pay the price of a conviction, but "before you go to the wall," Gordon now tells students, "make sure that this is the topic you're ready to die for."

That principle also extended to the way I dressed in Sainty. The farm people were by no means prudes, but their standards of taste and decency were a bit different from those that we had known in Denver. In those days hemlines were climbing to ridiculous heights above women's knees, and many of the young wives of seminary students found it easy to go along with the trend. But I soon realized that those hemlines would have needlessly offended the men and the women whom my husband and I were trying to love in the name of the Lord. Dress styles were not a big enough issue for which to "go to the wall." There were other things that were far more important, and we wanted to build bridges that would help reach the people whom we loved so dearly.

We have heard about and seen pastors and missionaries who took different positions on everything, demanding their rights on every occasion. But in most cases we have also seen them lose the people whom they were called to serve. There is obviously a thin line between bridge building and total capitulation to the whims of people—only wisdom can draw that line. But in looking back, I can now see that whenever there was a conflict in Sainty, it was over the larger spiritual issues that should concern a church.

Gordon and I learned that bridge building ought to be a factor in virtually every decision we make about our lifestyle. To this day what we learned in Sainty has meant that we dress in clothes that are tasteful but not attention getting. It has meant that we have chosen a quality of living in our choice of cars, furniture, and decor which meets the standards of our people but does not exceed them. If people want to break away from our church or us, let it only be for an issue of supreme importance but not because they are jealous of our possessions or our appearance.

I remember one day when we visited the lovely home of a friend. Mark was a toddler, and Gordon and I were painfully aware that the woman hardly heard a word we were saying because she was so anxious that Mark might hurt or scratch her exquisite furniture. Although we did our best to keep him from touching anything, it was clear that he was a source of anxiety for her. When we left, Gordon and I discussed the importance of never having anything in our home that we were worried about losing through the mistreatment of a visitor.

The importance of the decision was reinforced the day that Mark etched a contemporary design in our coffee table with his toy truck. Naturally, I was horrified, but my feelings were quickly checked when I remembered that I had already pledged not to feel angry if someone else's child did that kind of thing. Why not the same treatment for our own child? Besides, I thought, the apostle Peter told us that it was all going to burn up someday anyway, so the important thing was to center in on the type of person I am. In that case, the key was what kind of mother I was going to be for Mark.

And so there in Sainty, I resolved that everything we owned would be *tools* and nothing more. For others who came to visit, our possessions would be tools of hospitality. For us, they would simply be items of convenience. Things would not matter; *people would.* And while we taught our children to respect the property of others, they both grew up repeating their mom's song, "Never mind; it's all going to burn up when Jesus comes."

Thomas á Kempis' words ring true: "Do not seek to have what may be a hindrance to you and may deprive you of inward liberty." Perhaps that is why during those days when we lived in parsonages, it didn't bother me. The houses simply have not belonged to us; they have been on loan. We have been able to part with them without too much emotion when the Lord has called us to a different place.

Learning how to adapt to people meant *ministering to them where they were.* Change comes slowly in rural communities, especially in a place like Sainty. People there have known each other since birth. And when you see the same people every day of the week, there is less likelihood of dramatic changes in matters spiritual and otherwise. Gordon and I had to accept the fact that our people had a hard time believing in the possibility of each other's transformation.

It would have been pastoral suicide for Gordon to have preached and pushed people to embrace dramatic changes of direction overnight. I would have lost credibility with women had I pressed them too hard. Thus I learned to accept their cautious manner of spiritual travel, which was capable of slight curves but rarely ready for the sharp, angular turns that we as young people tended to think were so necessary.

I learned to build bridges in the face of death. In the space of six short months, our tiny congregation on the prairie faced the sudden deaths of two young people—one in a motorcycle accident, the other from a broken neck when falling from a horse which had been spooked by a rattler.

In both cases the grief and the horror of the accidents was overwhelming. Here I was in my early twenties attempting to give leadership and spiritual stability to people who were twice my age and more. Neither Gordon nor I had experiences from the past upon which to draw. I could only love the people and stand by them. Gordon and I discovered that *presence is far more important than words.*

I watched the rural culture express its grief when the farmers came and dug the graves. At the end of the funeral services, the congregation formed double lines from the church sanctuary to the cemetery, standing silently as the grieving families walked between them to the open holes in the ground. The men each took the shovel in turn and poured dirt on the lowered caskets. Then the people wept and reminisced. I learned and loved by simply being there. It was clear that the certainty of the faith of the farming families expected God to use even the tragedies of life for good.

I found that children would be bridge builders for a pastor's family. Clough Valley was made up of mostly older couples—babies were in short supply. As a result, the people loved Mark, and he responded to them. I dragged him along to about everything. All he knew from the earliest days was being with loving people. That also meant that he was able to learn flexibility by being in different homes regularly and by being held in the arms of many different types of people.

One evening Gordon and I visited the mud-brick home of a family of ten. The eight children had been raised by their father because the mother had been institutionalized after the birth of their last child. The father, Ben Trembley, was a deacon in our congregation and had become one of the most cherished people we'd ever known. His gentle spirit in the face of adversity was extraordinary, and his children grew in turn to be men and women who loved Christ.

Ben taught us that the wealthiest people in church are not necessarily those who have money but rather those who have the Spirit. We never heard him speak a discouraging word. His face always had a smile when he climbed out of his dilapidated International Harvester pickup truck. On Sunday he was usually the first to arrive (and always with a dozen eggs for me) for any service. Ben Trembley taught us how to be rich while being poor.

The two of us, in turn, taught our farmers a thing or two about how to laugh. Not that they had to wait until Gordon and I arrived to learn that, but their lives were often so serious and intense that they had a difficult time relaxing and enjoying one another. One evening we took everyone thirty miles away to Wray, Colorado, where we'd reserved the back room of the Wray Cafe. At the end of the meal, Gordon spontaneously passed a soup spoon around the enormous table. He asked each person to put a small crumb of food on the spoon and then pass it to the next person. The instructions were simple. The person holding the spoon had to eat everything on it if something dropped off. We'd learned this silly little game when we'd worked with young people.

The tension rose as those gnarled farming hands began passing the spoon from person to person. Unrestrained laughter erupted when someone had to eat the combinations of food piled high on the soup spoon. Once into the game, they didn't want to stop.

It was in Sainty that I learned another important lesson. You could call it simply the lesson of *vision*. Today Gordon and I serve a relatively large congregation and have enjoyed opportunities to give spiritual leadership at a much broader level. Sometimes younger pastors will confess that they envy our present situation because their worlds are so much smaller and the people they serve do not seem to be interested in going anywhere in terms of growth and expansion.

I suspect that Gordon and I once had many of those same feelings. It was not because we didn't love and appreciate the people of Clough Valley, but after all, how much of the world could we change when church attendance hardly surpassed thirty-five or forty? But in our youthful enthusiasm to be effective, Gordon and I needed to learn how to be content with where we were. We would have to treat jealous thoughts ruthlessly.

Miriam, the sister of Moses, reminds me of the necessity of keeping envy from ever gaining a foothold in my spirit. A secret dissatisfaction once possessed her heart, and she began to compare her place with that of Moses and of others. God's judgment upon Miriam was leprosy. Later she repented and admitted that she had sinned and had acted foolishly. But the growth of the entire nation of Israel was stalemated until Miriam was restored. If God is sovereign, how could Gordon or I envy anyone else's success? Frankly, it was an important battle to fight when our vision seemed so limited. Now I realize what younger couples go through, since we are a few years away from Sainty and its rural limitations.

Ralph Turnbull relates the story of the late F. B. Meyer and his struggle in this same area of spiritual ambition and competition. When Meyer first went to the Northfield Conference in Massachusetts, he attracted a large crowd of people who came to hear him preach. However, G. Campbell Morgan also went to Northfield and lured the people by his brilliant Bible studies. The result was that Meyer's crowd began to dwindle while Morgan's grew. Meyer confessed a tendency to envy as he ministered to the smaller group. "The only way I can conquer my feeling," he said, "is to pray for Morgan daily, which I do." [1] This was a lesson that Gordon and I have also had to learn.

One afternoon while walking down our long gravel road, Gordon was thinking about the future. The Lord seemed to be speaking to his heart, "If you'll not be faithful over little, I'll never trust you with much." When Gordon shared that insight with me, we discussed the importance of living for today, regardless of the circumstance. We determined to serve the people of Sainty as if we were going to for the rest of our lives.

God vindicated that decision by making it possible for us to hold a Bible study for high school young people in the nearby town of St. Francis. We'd agreed to meet with them on Monday mornings at 7:00 A.M. before the school day began. Two families offered their living rooms so that Gordon could teach the boys and I could teach the girls. Though relatively close geographically, the people of Sainty lived on central standard time, while the people of Clough Valley to the west lived on mountain standard time. That meant that since it was actually 6:00 A.M. our time when we met, we had to rise at 5:00 A.M. in order to be ready for those young people!

Each Monday morning we would drop Mark off at a local farm home, drive to Sainty, go through our Bible studies, and then return for breakfast and the day's chores. "Is it worth it?" we asked again and again.

Yes, we thought on the final Sunday before we left Clough Valley. *Yes*, we thought when we subsequently met two of the original twelve who had entered some form of full-time Christian service. Each came up to us while we were speaking at different conferences in Europe and Latin America many years later. The initiative, they told us, for their being in Christian service began from those Bible studies held so early on Monday mornings. God does have a way of turning things upside down. The world, even in a little town like St. Francis, could be affected by our meager offering.

When the Billy Graham Association produced its first major film, *The Restless Ones*, Gordon convinced a BGA representative to preview the film in Sainty. The local pastors formed a committee, and a layman Gordon had discipled became the chairman of the film crusade. *Fifty people* were trained as counselors. We prayed, raised money, rented the high school auditorium, and got the publicity out. For each of three nights the film was shown to a packed house of one thousand. And each night *fifty people* came forward to profess faith in Christ. I have often wondered: If we would have trained more counselors, would we have seen more seekers?

As the years have passed, Gordon and I have become increasingly aware of the importance of those first three years of ministry. What we learned has had incalculable value. How forgiving the congregation was when we made mistakes! For example, I remember how impatient we were to make this church more than it was capable of being. And there was a tendency on our part to think more highly of the value of our education than we should have. Our degrees might mean something in the city, but to farmers, life's experiences were far more valuable. But, in spite of our immaturity, they supported us when they saw God giving us new and wider dreams. Adapting to the people and decoding their lifestyle was important. But even more important was that we leave these things intact with their farming culture rather than to change them and leave.

Now thirty-four years later, the people of Clough Valley Baptist Church continue to be a viable congregation. Many have gone to be with Jesus, but those who are still alive write to and pray for us. We have gone back for treasured visits to let them know once again of our gratitude for the grace they gave to us. They were the first big chapter in our ministry, and we grew because of them.

꧁ THREE ꧂

THE JOURNEY CONTINUES

Learning to Love, Loving to Learn

> Am I prisoner of people's expectations or liberated by Divine promises?
> —*Henri Nouwen*

Pastoral ministry has more than a few tense moments. One of them comes when you wait for a phone call from a congregation asking you to be its pastor. During our years of ministry, we've anticipated four such calls.

One of those occasions had to do with a Baptist congregation in the Midwest. They had met to vote on a recommendation that Gordon be invited to be their spiritual leader. A thousand miles away, we waited almost without breath to learn of their decision.

Gordon had just graduated from seminary. We had said good-bye to our farm church, and we were ready to throw ourselves into whatever was God's next choice for us. Like countless pastors and their spouses, we were consumed with anticipation: What door of ministry was God going to open up where we could invest ourselves in the enlargement of his kingdom?

So we waited for the phone to ring and hoped that the news would be positive because we had sensed a mutual affinity to this congregation during a recent visit. The Baptists call such a weekend "candidating," but I'm tempted to call it torture. The candidate and family are under intense scrutiny.

As with Clough Valley, some of our friends advised us against accepting such a call. The concern this time was Gordon's youth and inexperience (he was only twenty-eight). The church, it was reported, had been badly wounded in its previous experience with a pastor. There was serious division in the congregation, and the people were fresh from some bitter moments. A few who knew the situation thought that perhaps the church needed an older, wiser man who understood congregational healing. They were probably right.

But when the phone finally rang, and we were told of a unanimous vote (there was some unity after all), we soon found ourselves on our way to Collinsville, a suburb of St. Louis, to join the people of First Baptist Church. Gordon and I sought the counsel of a number of veteran pastors: we asked, What does a divided congregation need? And of course, we prayed a lot, asking for wisdom, for sensitivity, and for boldness. Our concern? To identify an overarching theme as we began to minister.

We could easily have missed the right focus if we'd gone there determined to make the church into something we wanted—something we'd learned at some conference or from somebody's book. But the central question was: *What did God desire for First Baptist . . . now?*

❧ LESSON ONE: GIVE LOVE WITHOUT CONDITION

The theme that was to be most important came to us, how or where I cannot remember. We concluded that the people of First Baptist *needed to be loved, not changed.* Youth always seems to want to change things, but sometimes love is the more important goal.

Love, biblical style (*agape* love), is something that any healthy Christian man or woman can give. Today when I hear so many ministry wives put themselves down as inadequate and untalented, I am reminded of this simple truth: *Anyone—regardless of talent or gift— can love if she or he asks God for the power and the will.* I believed it then, as I believe it now.

So our immediate goal was to accept and love the Collinsville congregation *without condition*. We would challenge the people to deal with the past and move ahead. This seemed simple enough.

The first implication was that Gordon would avoid making any significant alterations in the life of the congregation for the first year or two. He wouldn't come with an ambitious program. No easy decision for a visionary like Gordon but definitely, in retrospect, the best way to rebuild mutual respect and trust. I assumed responsibility for pressing patience and encouragement into Gordon when he wanted to try new things. Beyond that, I loved showing women what they could do—things they never dreamed they were capable of. One took on the challenge of pulling together a large missions event we had. To her surprise, it had long-term, life-changing consequences for many, and seeing what her gifts made possible changed her forever.

The congregation, we learned, had passed through a demoralizing time under a pastor who had become harsh and divisive. Some people had left the church. Among those who had stayed were many who were not sure they could ever trust a minister again. If the people were going to get back on track, a new pastor would have to restore their belief in what God could do through them—if they would forgive the past. We thought that was more than possible if we concentrated on loving them.

We were welcomed with great warmth when we drove into Collinsville. And we let the congregation know what their greeting meant to us. The home provided by the church seemed a mansion to us, and we said so. The people were surprised and relieved because the previous pastor had complained that the home was not good enough for him. But it was certainly nicer than anything we'd ever lived in.

Families brought in meals, helped us get things unpacked and cleaned, and made sure that we had everything we needed. It wasn't hard to respond gratefully to such hospitality. I soon realized that expressing genuine appreciation to the people was something for which I could take the lead on behalf of both of us. Gordon was naturally busy in the early stages of getting the ministry started and was therefore apt to overlook many of the things that deserved recognition and affirmation.

So I began to increase the output of notes and verbal expressions of praise to people—for the smallest of reasons. Is there anything that rebuilds our sense that God loves us and wants to use us than for others to be specific in giving thanks to us? This discipline of expressed appreciation became a cornerstone of our ministry. I cannot exaggerate its worth.

∾ LESSON TWO: MASTER THE LITTLE THINGS

I also decided to work hard at *remembering names.* Collinsville was considerably larger than Clough Valley, and it was not a simple thing to remember everyone I met in those first few weeks. But it occurred to me that one way we could convince the people that we cared about them was to take their names seriously.

Over the years women have asked me how I remember names. It may encourage you to know that while I work at it, it's easier for a person with my personality type. People like me latch on to details easier than others. When I'm involved in an introduction, I often ask for a name to be repeated, or, if difficult, I may even ask for it to be spelled. Sometimes I'll ask about its national origin and what the name means. "Did it come from your family background? Does it have biblical significance?" Questions of that type help me remember names; they also let people know that I'm interested in them.

Furthermore, when someone begins to talk about her name, she often reveals things about herself which will help me get to know her better. What fascinating conversations have ensued when I've asked someone whether she's always enjoyed her name or whether she thinks it describes what she knows about herself.

To help me remember, on the way home I might recall where people sat in the room by reviewing their names. Word association also helps. But I try not to make the error one woman did when she met a friend of ours whose name is Mrs. Swearingen. The next time she saw our friend she said, "How are you, Mrs. Cussingen?"

In addition, I began to write down the birthdays of people in the church leadership. Names and dates were kept in a birthday book; today they might be kept more easily in a computer. On weekends Gordon and I would fill out cards with words of greeting and specific affirmations so that our church's leaders would have a word from us on their special day.

An additional value of keeping a journal comes from recording the names of people met during the day. Many times I've returned to my journal to retrieve the names of children in a family so that when I sent a note or a gift, I could include the smallest children in the greetings. Haven't you told people that you truly care when you even recall their children's names? It was in Collinsville that I began to send crisp one dollar bills to the older children in a family when a baby had been born. I would wait for a few weeks and then send big sisters or big brothers cards with money suggesting they take mom or dad out for ice cream cones. Being able to thank the children for being a help to their mommy and daddy while stressing that I knew babies take lots of care was important to me. Of course, I underscored the fact that their parents gave them the same care when they were babies. And Jesus is pleased when we help.

LESSON THREE: BE HOSPITABLE

I also began to love the people by extending hospitality. As soon as the house took on a reasonably ordered appearance, we held an open house. Most of the membership had not been in the parsonage for years. This was their chance to meet us as real people in the context of our home. I was eight months pregnant with our daughter Kristy, but the help I recruited from several willing women in the church made hosting the open house an easy thing to do.

Later on we decided to use our home as a tool for an ambitious hospitality project. Setting aside money in our budget and clearing every Thursday night for ten weeks, we set out to serve every adult member of First Baptist Church—thirty of them at a time. Our objectives were multiple. Of course, Gordon and I wanted to know people better and to serve them. But more than that, we wanted to serve them *together*. We were hoping that people would be drawn to one another as a result of being in our home. Many of them had been hurt by broken relationships in the past, and they needed an experience of wholeness to heal past memories.

Many things happened during those delightful evenings. People felt like the congregation suddenly became "small" because they got to know some rather nostalgic things about twenty-eight other folks. Walls of resentment and misunderstanding seemed to fall before our eyes.

With the cost of living as it is, and the little time people have for hospitality, it has become a rare and precious gift. I recall hearing our friend, Dr. R. Judson Carlberg, the president of Gordon College, address the difference between hospitality and entertainment:

> Hospitality is a safe place; entertainment is a show place. Hospitality focuses on people; entertainment focuses on things. Hospitality creates an open atmosphere; entertainment can be neat and closed. Hospitality exudes a warm attitude; entertainment can degenerate to being cool and calculated. Hospitality puts one at ease; entertainment implies competition. . . . Hospitality involves making people feel good in God's world. God created a hospitable world; sin made the world inhospitable. By our supportive action, we can dispel the sinful atmosphere.

As the years have passed and our congregations have grown larger, I miss those nights. They added a warmth and an acceptance in many people's hearts that would not have happened had we not developed such close contact.

We have entered the congregational life of four different churches during our ministry. Each time Gordon has been careful to tell people prior to our coming that I would need six months or so to settle and discover where I was needed and best able to use my spiritual gifts. And he has gently reminded the lay leadership that they had hired him, not me. It's a relief when our husbands do this.

But as you can see from how quickly I became involved in serving at Collinsville, I didn't give myself the necessary time to stand back and say, "Where does God want me to make my key contribution?" Every place I looked I saw wounds, and I probably leaped too fast in too many directions with the hope that I could make a difference. Perhaps I should have remained a bit quieter—like Nehemiah who carefully studied the broken walls of Jerusalem before he sprang into action.

ᘒ LESSON FOUR: MAKE STAFF RELATIONSHIPS A PRIORITY

Everywhere I looked, there were new and different things happening to us. First Baptist was the first congregation where Gordon worked with staff associates. As time passed, the ministry began to grow, and it became necessary to add an associate pastor for Christian Education. Later, a pastor for youth joined us. Each, of course, came with a family, and soon we were enjoying the camaraderie of fellow servants in the Lord. We worked in the church together, raised our children together, and played together. Because we all had musical abilities, we were able to offer occasional concerts on Sunday evenings which the congregation loved. We enjoyed lots of laughter and tremendous mutual support.

But what Gordon and I began to learn was that healthy relationships with those we work with cannot be assumed. Even the best of people can fall into conflict and misunderstanding. There are those in every congregation who look for hints that their pastoral staff may not be happy with each other and for cracks in relationships. We came to see that our connections with colleagues demanded constant maintenance and that sooner or later the quality of loyalty and teamwork would be tested. Because of these realities, Gordon and I saved large blocks of time for staff. At times we felt robbed of time with the people in the church. But, diligence in this paid off.

It has made me more patient with myself and others to realize that such relational challenges date back to the Tower of Babel when God judged his people for their arrogance and pride by giving them different languages, none of which others understood. Since then, there has been a *discordant spirit* just under the surface of all relationships. Whether a marriage, family, business, or church, people find it challenging to get along. I never underestimate the importance of this.

❧ LESSON FIVE: ADAPT TO CHILDREN'S NEEDS

Working at building strong relationships was something Gordon and I loved doing together. We felt made for it. At first, we would take our children everywhere with us. But as our son Mark entered his fourth year of life, his preschool teacher approached us and commented on his restlessness in the classroom. Perhaps she was nervous about offending us, but she was wise enough to press the issue. "What time does Mark go to bed at night?" she asked.

"Depends upon what night you're talking about," I answered. "Mark and Kristy are often with us when we go to different homes and meetings. So their bedtime varies from night to night."

"I'd advise you to rethink this kind of a schedule," she said. "Mark needs to be in bed the same hour every night of the week. Make that happen, and you'll see a huge difference in his demeanor."

If we were to follow her advice, it meant that I would have to stay home much more. This was not the kind of change either of us wanted to make. But as we talked, we agreed that the children had to come first. If this was best for them, then we had to heed this admonition and rethink our options.

Because of this teacher's wise rebuke, I withdrew from weeknight church activity for the next few years. Within a week or two, Mark's teacher was on the phone to say that his conduct in preschool was vastly improved. But for me, it was a significant loss. I loved being a part of Gordon's world. I adapted partly because he reminded me that he missed having me alongside and gave me needed breaks from the children.

On Fridays he arranged his schedule so that he could spend a large part of the day at home. "I want you to feel that you own Friday mornings," he said, making it clear that I was free to use those hours in any way I wished, to meet a friend, find a quiet place to feed my soul, catch up on things, or go to the city to shop. It was my time, no questions asked. Gordon would be with the children, and I could feel secure that they were in good hands. That simple gift on his part made a strong statement to me of devoted love at a time when I needed it.

God gave Gordon and me a wonderful gift during the Collinsville days. I came to know Lynn, an unusual teenager. At the time, her parents were on the verge of divorce, and she came to me for counsel. We hit it off, and she immediately connected with and loved our children. They in turn responded to her as a big sister.

One day Lynn came to me and said, "Why don't you give me your calendar for the month, and I'll plan to be with the children whenever you need to be away?" She seemed to know exactly what our children needed and was easily as strict and directive (as well as caring and loving) as we might be. The result was that the children never felt a significant sense of change if Gordon and I were gone from the home for an evening. Lynn was a part of our family, and we all profited from her generosity and love.

Years later Lynn went on to be an expert on abused children, adopting a number of them and giving them a wholesome way of life.

A few years ago Lynn succumbed to cancer and went to be with the Lord. But her memory is very much with us. Even though our own children are long gone from our home and well into adulthood, we still see characteristics of Lynn's personality in theirs.

I have often been asked, "Where do you find Lynn's?" Obviously I don't know the answer for sure. All I can say is this. Lynn seems to have entered our lives because I first entered hers. Having poured a lot of love into her, it seemed only natural for her to respond by pouring love into our family. Perhaps that's the way "Lynns" are found. For me it was the first of many times I would see this truth realized in our lives, "He who refreshes others will himself be refreshed" (Proverbs 11:25).

◐ LESSON SIX: BE HONEST ABOUT YOUR WEAKNESSES

Lynn's gift of time no doubt made me feel a little freer to get involved in the lives of others again. Frankly, I began to say yes too often. In my enthusiasm to serve, I allowed some people to depend on me too much. This sort of frenetic pace on the part of those of us in ministry may look like a caring thing on the surface. It can actually be selfish and destructive. I was there to direct people's questions, affections, and first connection to Christ's presence, not mine. I'm not confident that I always did that at Collinsville. I found myself wanting to please everyone— an impossibility. My inability to make sound judgments about the use of my time and energy caused me to enter quickly into a schedule of activities and relationships which could only be maintained because I was still young enough and had the physical energy.

I was often complimented and gained a sense of value from the fact that other women wanted my advice, desired my presence at their showers and parties, and sought me out to shop and have lunch with them. The phone was constantly ringing with callers interested in my opinions on various decisions they had to make. A healthy way to live? Hardly. There were times when this way of life fed my pride and starved my humility.

Some probably didn't help the situation as they applauded what they perceived to be my eager availability. I guess I permitted them to believe, inadvertently, that I had the capacity to live up to their *ever-increasing expectations.*

In fact, I was getting up earlier, staying up later, and probably, on many occasions, not giving myself the adequate rest and refreshment to be all that my family needed in a wife and a mother. We have all reasoned at one time or another, This is the Lord's work, and people have unending needs.

This kind of grind not only drained my physical makeup, but also sapped my inner spirit. I began to feel as if no matter what I gave, it wasn't enough. I compared my life with the needs of women around me and said, like the disciples who had a small boy's lunch, "But what is this among so many?" Too often I lived with a sense of inadequacy and guilt.

Joan Jacobs, in her book, *Feelings*, is absolutely correct when she says that we are often captured by a *false* sense of guilt. True guilt occurs when we've broken God's laws. False guilt erupts when we or others set up unattainable or superficial expectations of ourselves that even our Lord would not have attempted. Frankly, that's exactly what I was doing. I had the growing inner sense of being trapped. I was, in Henri Nouwen's words, becoming "a prisoner of people's expectations rather than being liberated by the Divine promises."

The dilemma of those Collinsville days came to mind when a friend wrote:

> What do I do about people who hope that I will be their "best friend," confidante, in fact, almost their "Jesus"? These people have genuine, sometimes horrendous, needs, and yet, if I try to be their "Holy Spirit"—making judgments, asking questions, and giving advice—am I not also in danger?

In retrospect, I can see that the answer lies in a balance of such things as: timely disengagement, speaking the truth in love, sensing where the whole story has yet to be told, and of course, knowing our own mental, spiritual, and physical limits.

I remember one overly dependent woman who discovered important inner growth and later broke the pattern of dependence. She was very needy and had to overcome the habit of manipulating people through pity and sympathy. It took the determination of a team of four of us to help her set limits on her expectations of me and other leaders. Today you would never know she once had this character flaw. She is loved and useful to her church family.

You may conclude that ministry life is far too crowded with opportunities for disaster and error. That simply isn't true. Mistakes? Of course. But as I recall our days in Collinsville, the great moments and experiences quickly blot out the instances of difficulty and stress. The people were lovable, and there was much shared affection. As we taught them, they also taught us.

© LESSON SEVEN: LEARN, FORGIVE, AND RECEIVE

Shortly after Kristy was born, I spent six weeks in bed with a tough case of mononucleosis. I became completely dependent upon my husband and several women in the congregation who carried on my chores for me. I remember that Gordon and I took some of our greatest marital strides forward during those weeks of illness because we had time to talk without interruption. Occasionally in an afternoon, he would sit on the edge of our bed, and we would share in depth matters that had often been put on the shelf for want of better times to talk.

I learned so much about the helpful and not-so-helpful ways to care for people—lessons I no doubt would not have learned in any other way. During that time, for example, I discovered that I should not call someone and ask, "What can I do?" and "Do you need anything for dinner?" Most people in a difficult strait will answer that they really don't need anything—even if they actually do. The sick often feel that being sick is in itself an imposition. Far more comforting were the times women called and said, "I'm planning to bring supper for you and your family. Which night this week would be the best, Tuesday or Thursday?" A direct and defined plan of action is far superior to an innocuous question that leaves the burden or response on the one who needs the help. Beyond this I found it an enormous gift when people used disposables which eliminated the stacks of dishes and containers that would have to be returned at a later date.

On another occasion, I learned a wonderfully creative way to minister. When my younger brother died, a dear friend gave me a handful of envelopes marked with the days my family and I would be away for the funeral. Every morning I was to open the appropriate envelope and find an encouraging note containing a word of Scripture and an affirmation of my ability to handle the sorrow of the situation if I would lean on

Christ for help. What a ministry! Not only was I deeply blessed by it, but over the years I have enjoyed imitating my friend's thoughtful gesture.

One other crisis taught us how to minister to others and bonded us to the people of Collinsville forever. One day our three-and-a-half-year-old daughter Kristy was rushed to the hospital with a stomach full of turpentine which she had accidentally swallowed. We didn't know it at the time, but she had been born without the sense of smell. Thinking the milky white substance in the jar was milk, even though I had told her otherwise, she placed it to her lips and began to drink.

The first twenty-four hours in the hospital were terrifying. The doctors had warned us of the possibility of kidney, lung, and even brain damage. They made no promises that Kristy would even survive. Gordon and I were like so many others we'd seen who had faced grim emergencies while sitting in the waiting room of the intensive care unit. Now Gordon couldn't march in and announce that he was a pastor visiting a patient. This time he was restricted by the rule that parents could have only five minutes of visiting time every two hours.

As we sat helpless, wondering what the future might bring, we learned what would have been impossible without such a crisis: the sustaining power of prayer. We'd often been on the intercessory end of prayer for others; now we were on the other end. It was a Wednesday night; the church had gathered to pray for Kristy's complete recovery. Only those who have been prayed for in such times know what I mean when I say there is no peace like it.

Many of Gordon's colleagues stopped by as we waited. Some of the deacons from our church followed. Each one embraced us, prayed, and spoke the comforting words of Scripture and loving affirmation. They brought us words of hope when we sorely needed them. Later when we were alone, Gordon said, "No matter what happens, this experience will remain with us for a lifetime. We've gone to the bottom and found that God is there." That fact remains etched into our spirits, but it came to us because others ministered to us.

Kristy healed without any bad aftereffects. Today she is the healthy wife and mother of three. I remain grateful for what that experience taught me about being cared for by heaven and earth and what it feels like to be given a word of hope. Neither Gordon nor I would have ever grappled with such issues had we not first been reduced to helplessness in those early years of our ministry.

Things do not always work out as one would wish. In Collinsville we had another lesson to learn: *how to respond when others find your vision isn't in alignment with theirs*. New programs that will mean adding more people to an already full sanctuary can be threatening to some. Or others might fear risking the challenges of building new buildings. When things don't go according to *our* "script," it's too easy to fall into the trap of whining. Being a leader can easily command sympathy and morbid attention. While it's important to share feelings at appropriate times, more often the mature response is to keep hurt, frustration, and sorrow to ourselves. Brigid Herman, a pastor's wife of many years, said something I've often found convicting:

> Sorrow may be among God's mightiest angels, but it does not necessarily, and in itself, do angels' work. A time of sorrow is often a time of moral and spiritual relaxation, of weakening self-pity, and of incontinent demands upon the sympathy of others. It breeds self-importance rather than heroism. And the selfishness of sorrow feeds upon speech. Small wonder that the masters of the spiritual life have always held up as the ideal what all writers used to call "the virginity of suffering"—the habit of keeping silence concerning our sorrows to all except God! There is of course a limit to such counsel.
>
> Human sympathy of the right kind is sacramental, and God comforts his servants, as he comforted St. Paul, "by the coming of Titus." *But while past ages tend to deny the divine nature of sympathy and fellowship, our own tends to idolize them. We again and again weaken ourselves and others and miss the divine consolation, by running to this person and to that before we make our need known to God. In the joy of our discovery of the sacredness of human affection, we forget that it remains unshakably true that whatever be the power of human sympathy, the soul of man is created for direct, immediate communion with its God. Nothing, however lovely and true in its own order, can take the place of that immediate touch. And that touch will not be experienced by a soul that has exposed itself to every well-meaning hand, in its feverish search for comfort.*[1] (italics mine)

Her words also apply to the times when you face criticism from people in the congregation. Involvement with people means that there are going to be times when men and women with good or bad motives will comment on things that are important to a leader, and their statements will not always be pleasant.

One woman wrote, "My children, family, house, every aspect of our lives needs to be perfect. And we're supposed to be perfect. We don't have problems." This woman's perception of the congregation's expectations are demoralizing to her.

Most pastoral experiences begin with a so-called "honeymoon" period between leader and congregation. But sooner or later the pastor and his wife discover that not everyone is pleased with what they are doing. With that discovery comes an important moment: handling the unpleasant feedback.

A. W. Tozer once wrote that the mark of a person of God was that he or she would elect never to fight back when attacked for any reason. It's a simple principle, but Gordon and I chose to adopt it at any cost. We pledged to the Lord and to one another that we would seek justice only on those occasions when God's truth had to be defended or the rights of others were being jeopardized. *We would not knowingly ever defend ourselves.* In subsequent years this slowly acquired discipline became a godsend.

We learned this first from Christ of whom it was said, "And the chief priests accused him of many things; but he answered *nothing*" (Mark 15:3 KJV). One of our mentors and Gordon's lifelong friend, Vernon Grounds, modeled this well. When Dr. Grounds first became president of Denver Seminary, he had some angry critics, but he refused to retaliate or defend his decisions and choices. Beyond that Vernon didn't hold grudges against these people either. It was as though, like a duck, he had oil on his wings to which resentment wouldn't cling. That is why now in his eighties he's the godly, tenderized, loving, sharp-minded man he is.

Over these years I have learned to gently but firmly take a person who had a complaint either to an elder, staff member, or Gordon so that no one would be tempted to use me as a conduit to my husband. This is a trap to which young wives especially are apt to succumb. I've learned so much from Gordon's choice to use a soft answer. It does turn away wrath.

I must admit that there were times in each of our churches when it was almost impossible for me to keep my mouth shut when someone spoke out of ignorance or from an improper motive. But slowly I've learned that it's more important for us to embrace the art of draining every criticism of the tiniest element of truth than to appear right. I had to school myself to see things as others might be seeing them and thereby gain insight into their perspectives or frustrations. Learning to contextualize people's criticisms has made a great difference in my attitude toward comments and people. It's helped me see that there were times when what Gordon or I had said or done was not exactly what people had heard or seen. We learned by listening.

When Gordon or I were wrong, we tried to acknowledge it and express appreciation to the critic, especially if a person had come directly to Gordon to voice his or her concern. As people noticed that he and I could take criticism, they became willing to level with us. In that healthy atmosphere, all of us grew.

I believe that part of my role is to encourage Gordon to listen as carefully as possible to his critics—lest I become a part of the problem and not a part of the solution. I speak to many women for whom this seems to be difficult. A man in the public eye needs his wife to stand resolutely with him. But she is also the best one to encourage him to listen—assuming of course, that he is willing to do so.

I'll write more of this later, but the choice to forgive when maligned has been essential for me, day by day by day. It has helped me to remember that part of my role in ministry is to absorb the anger of other people. Those whom Gordon and I have been called to serve were often themselves the targets of experiences and frustrations in their daily lives over which they had no control. Sometimes they simply took their feelings out on the first person they met, especially if they sensed that the person would not fight back. In a strange way, when they trusted Gordon and me with their anger, they were saying, "I know you won't desert me, even after this." And when I have been tempted to fight this part of ministry, I have to recall that Jesus also absorbed my hostilities on the cross.

The apostle Paul's awareness of his role among the Thessalonian believers greatly encouraged me. He saw himself as a nurse-comforter and a father-encourager. When you or a few people assume that role, there can be healing and restorative love in a congregation. Strength is built, and there is a chance for a new start instead of the raising of walls and the cry of battle among people.

Slowly, through the acts of forgiving and of absorbing anger, Gordon and I began to recognize that our role in relationships was often that of peacemakers. The world has enough warriors. It can certainly use a few more peacemakers. When Thaddeus Stevens, a Massachusetts congressman who bitterly wished to crush the South at the end of the Civil War, heard President Lincoln stress the importance of binding up the wounds of the nation—forgiving and reconciling—Stevens pounded the cabinet table and shouted, "Mr. Lincoln! I think enemies ought to be destroyed!"

Those present reported that Lincoln quietly responded, "Mr. Stevens, do not I destroy my enemy when I make him my friend?" That attitude is totally Christian and is the context in which people can grow to be more like Christ.

Some six years after coming to Collinsville, both Gordon and I sensed that we had reached a crossroads in our ministry among those wonderful people. It would be hard to describe all of the elements that make up an awareness that a decisive moment has come, but one knows when it is there.

We realized that it was either time to dig in for a number of years or else turn the work over to somebody else who could perhaps take it in a slightly different direction. We wrestled with that choice for several months. The decision was complicated by our affection for the people who had poured so much into our lives. Besides, our children were happy with their home and their congregation. For each member of our family, the thought of having to say good-bye seemed unbearable.

Do you believe that a life submitted to God has no chance occurrences? If you do, then you would have to ask the meaning of three men, unknown to one another, calling within a short time to say that they had recommended the name of Gordon MacDonald to a New England church seeking a pastor. It seemed uncanny to us that these men could have known that for the first time in years both Gordon and I were open to a possible change. That was the backdrop for the evening when a strange voice on the telephone identified himself as a representative of Grace Chapel, an interdenominational congregation in Lexington, Massachusetts. We later learned it was a beautiful suburban community saturated in American history outside of Boston.

There had been other invitations over the years. But there was something different about the query from Grace Chapel. A spiritual magnet was drawing us, it seemed, to Lexington by way of the voice on the phone and later through letters. We prayed, asking God to close or open this door as he saw fit. We were ready to leave or stay. But the door remained widely open and the inner witness said yes.

Is there a good way to leave a church? Good-byes are hard for most of us. And if people don't believe your reasons for leaving, they make up their own. Leaving the less-than-mature Christians was the hardest, especially those I had allowed to become too dependent on me. However, the more spiritually perceptive and mature members of the congregation seemed to understand Gordon's decision and gave us their blessing. Soon the final good-byes had been said, and the last service had been held. The moving van had come and gone.

I was comforted by the words of the missionary Helen Roseveare about the necessity of saying good-byes. She reminded me that you cannot be the last link in everybody's chain of experience. For some in Collinsville, we had been the first link in giving them an opportunity to find Christ and begin new lives. For others we were the middle link, urging them on to maintain their earlier commitments. And, to our delight, we were for a few others the last link helping them to accelerate into maturity and the joys of life grounded in Jesus Christ until they went to meet him. Links in a chain. A humbling thought.

In one sense, we have never closed this chapter of our lives We have both returned to visit several times and been delighted to see old friends persevering. Until this day, whenever a letter arrives from Collinsville, we open it eagerly, hoping to hear news about the people. We're happy as we read about the ones who are getting married or who are having their first children; these are people we knew as infants and toddlers in the Sunday school departments. Some have headed to the mission field or accepted positions of leadership within the Collinsville congregation.

What made our memories of Collinsville so precious? Our primary goal to love the people—without condition. They in turn had loved us, and together we all learned to love Christ a bit more.

SERVING AN AUDIENCE OF ONE

Am I now trying to win the approval of men, or of God? Or am I trying to please men? If I were still trying to please men, I would not be a servant of Christ.   (*Gal. 1:10*)

Every major change in life, a relocation, loss, success, or failure, ought to be accompanied with a time of reflection lest its lessons be squandered. We should be careful to take time to assess things such as: What have I learned from this experience? What weaknesses were revealed? What strengths did I acquire, or what do I need to acquire? What things about myself should I renounce or reaffirm? Where am I spiritually? And where does God want me to go from here?

The change from Collinsville in the Midwest to Lexington in the Northeast was an occasion for such reflection. I was thirty-two, and I had a lot of growing to do.

For example, this *people-pleasing* thing hung about my neck like dead weight. A favorite cartoon depicts it well. A couple is seated in a restaurant two thousand miles away from home, but they aren't relaxing because they suffer from *transcontinental congrephobia*, the fear that no matter how far from home they are, one of their parishioners is eavesdropping on their conversation. "Will what they hear please them?" the couple asks. I laughed nervously when this cartoon was shown because it struck a familiar chord.

Serving people in the name of Jesus is a joy, even fun. But worrying about who I am pleasing can be a curse. It was time for me to be sure that I knew the difference. During this transition time, a string of words entered my life and brought a new focus to my spiritual perspective: *Live as if you are playing to an audience of One.*

I'd often heard Gordon talk about athletes who wisely ignore the crowd and "play it to the coach." In my case, the coach was Jesus. I had been a sometime musician and a soloist. I'd sung before large and small audiences. Now it came to me: The most important audience in the scope of my personal reality is Jesus. He was my audience of One.

I've met more than a few women who are living for multiple audiences, striving frantically to hear the applause of each one of them. And there were times when I had done the same thing. Someone once said, "At twenty we worry about what *everyone* thinks of us. At forty we don't care what *anyone* thinks of us. And at sixty we realize *no one* was even thinking about us!" To some extent I was still in the first of those three phases.

During the transition between Collinsville and Lexington, it was important for me to think and pray and talk about how, with God's help, I was going to get serious about focusing on how Jesus thought and responded as seen in Scripture.

At a recent conference of ministry wives sponsored by Focus on the Family, women were asked what they thought was their greatest challenge in ministry-leadership. Seventy-eight respondents were consistent in identifying these five top areas:

- Loneliness and feelings of isolation. (I need a good friend.)
- Balance of family and church. (There isn't any.)
- Expectations of church members. (Feeling like everyone has a great plan for my life.)
- Criticism. (Needing affirmation but receiving "you-don't-measure-up" messages.)
- Finances. (If I don't work, we can't make it.)

This list held no surprises. These were legitimate concerns. But I was impressed with what was missing. Only five out of the group said that their greatest challenge was loving and pleasing Christ in such a way that he would receive praise from how they lived. As I studied the points that the ministry wives had prioritized, I realized that there were times when I too have been far too interested in the people-centered issues. What has come to me is that the more I've focused on playing all of life to Jesus, what characterizes him, what pleases him, what points others to him, the more these other issues have found their proper place.

The years in Collinsville taught me that if I did not beat the dilemma of who I was serving, life as a ministry wife was going to become an increasingly unhappy experience.

Oswald Chambers stated it clearly:

> Our LORD's first obedience was to the will of His Father, not to the needs of men; his obedience brought the outcome of the saving of men. If I am devoted to the cause of humanity only, I will soon be exhausted and come to the place where my love will falter; but if I love Jesus Christ personally and passionately, I can serve humanity though men treat me as a doormat.[1]

St. Paul understood this struggle. "I care very little if I am judged by you, . . ." he wrote. "I do not even judge myself. . . . It is the Lord who judges me" (1 Cor. 4:3–4). I had not always lived that way in Collinsville. The judgment of others *had been too important to me.* I had something to repent of—mixed motives. I longed to help bring others nearer to Christ, but also needed to please them.

Why this inner battle? Because my personality and spiritual gifts all point to wanting to help people by lifting them up—through teaching, encouraging, and being merciful. If I think I have failed at using these gifts, I feel guilty and try to do more.

Since we are born with our personalities (or temperaments) and the Holy Spirit gives us our spiritual gifts as *he* sees fit, then thankfully he must understand where our challenges will be. Whenever I try to please people at the expense of asking what would Christ do or be, I find it necessary to return to Paul's focus: "We make it our goal to please him" (2 Cor. 5:9).

The challenges which the Focus on the Family survey pointed out affect us all. People and their needs are ever with us. As I have gone through seasons, even since the Collinsville days, when the people challenges seemed to engulf me, I've found myself turning to

Scripture to find someone there who could be a straightedge for me when I was tempted to give in to the whims of others instead of doing what I knew was best in God's eyes.

❧ MEET MY FRIEND HANNAH

It was in such a biblical search that I met a wonderful ancient friend. Her name was Hannah. My first surprise was that she too was a ministry wife. Her husband Elkanah was a priest from the central highlands of what we call Israel. The more I got inside of Hannah's life, the greater strength I gained as I wrestled with the question of whom I was serving. Today I talk about Hannah whenever I am with women in leadership.

Our first glimpse of Hannah has to do with her problem with infertility. She not only lived with the ache of being childless, but she had to cope with Peninnah, Elkanah's other wife, who had no trouble becoming pregnant and seizing every opportunity to flaunt her good fortune. Peninnah's derision of Hannah was remorseless. But Hannah's focus was on God alone, and while she felt the deep pain of her inability to conceive, she nevertheless retained her composure.

There was an interesting tension between the two women. Peninnah had the children, but Elkanah, the husband, loved Hannah more. This fact kept Peninnah in Hannah's face (as they say). Both women had something to be jealous about: Hannah about Peninnah's ability to conceive, Peninnah about Hannah's position of affection with Elkanah.

Sooner or later most of us in ministry find ourselves the target of someone's jealously. I would do almost anything to avoid this in my world. But it seems to come with the territory. Today Gordon and I live a very contented life. He encourages me to use the full scope of my spiritual gifts and opportunities for Christian service. Not every woman is as fortunate to receive such encouragement. I have felt their envy at times. Hannah taught me that I would have to live with that. I concluded, If she could live through having another woman in her home who bore children to her husband and still keep her heart with diligence, I can live quietly and kindly with my few irritations.

Three times a year Elkanah was required to offer sacrifices at Shiloh, and he took his wives with him. Talk about a fishbowl! We have little appreciation of the shame an infertile Jewish woman felt. If God didn't "open the womb," the sense of disgrace was almost intolerable. An heir was a necessity. Offspring were one's social security; they perpetuated the family business.

Hannah comes to mind every time we dedicate newborn babies at Grace Chapel. Many women who are infertile simply don't come to worship on such days because it's too painful. Gordon will sensitively remark about how aware he is that there are those in the congregation or those listening by way of radio who find it hard to enter into the joy of these couples. Perhaps they have been unable to conceive, or they may have lost a child recently. Some grieve over the ways of a rebellious youth or regret the choice to have aborted an unborn child some time in the past.

Hannah could easily have joined the thinking of such women. Why go to the tabernacle when all it did was intensify her own sense of loss? Why? Because Hannah played life to an audience of One. Period.

Remind yourself of the things Hannah was living with. She needed to guard her heart from reacting to the scorn of Peninnah who provoked her until she would not eat. She had to live with the fact that, when it came to her sorrow, her husband, Elkanah who loved her dearly, simply didn't get it. "Why is having a baby so important? Aren't I enough?" he asked. Try as he might, he couldn't understand his wife's need to bear a child. (Women and men are different.) Then when she arrived at what should have been a "safe place," the tabernacle, she found that the priest, their elder colleague Eli, wasn't a bit more sensitive than anyone else. He totally misjudged her.

This short poem would have done all three—the pitiless Peninnah, the undiscerning Elkanah, and the indiscreet Eli—a world of good:

> Lord, give me eyes
> That I may see
> Lest I, as people will,
> Should pass someone's Calvary
> And think it just a hill.
> —*Unknown*

The days at the tabernacle were Hannah's lowest points in life. We're told that she quietly poured her anguished heart out to God. "In bitterness of soul Hannah wept much and prayed."

Eli jumps to a wrong conclusion. "How long will you keep on getting drunk? Get rid of your wine" (1 Sam 1:10, 14). Her response to Eli's censure was amazing. No defensiveness or need to protect herself. She simply told him why she came to pray. And she did it without anger. Both the depth of her connection with God and her seeming lack of self-consciousness while being humiliated by a peer move me deeply. She was focused on her primary audience.

Oswald Chambers explains what must happen deep within us if we are to fulfill God's larger purposes when faced with such bleak moments:

> When you are in the dark, listen, and God will give you a very precious message for someone else when you get in the light. . . . Now he gives you the gift of *humiliation* which brings the softness of heart that will always listen to God *now*.[2]

Such softness of heart doesn't "just happen." It is borne out of a soul that has been diligently monitored at the fire with Christ. A heart that says yes to whatever God allows. We know Hannah permitted the Spirit to do this work in her because she was able to receive God's peace and Eli's blessing—leaving with a changed countenance . . . and an eagerness to eat.

What a picture of the fact that we have Christian bodies— whether we live like Christians or not. David Seamands once pointed out that when we allow hate, resentment, anger, or distrust to have free reign in our bodies, it is like pouring sand into a machine. The machine grinds to a halt. But when we choose forgiveness, love, grace, kindness, and understanding , it is like pouring oil into a machine. It purrs along well. Frederick Buechner writes:

> To lick your wounds, to smack your lips over grievances long past, to roll your tongue over the prospect of bitter confrontations still to come, to savor the last toothsome morsel of both the pain you are given and the pain you are giving back—in many ways it is a feast for a king. The chief drawback is that what you are wolfing down is yourself. The skeleton at the feast is you.[3]

Several years ago I was asked to help two women who had a conflict that was beginning to affect their families. They had been close friends for a long time but had very different personalities. When I arrived at the home of the friend who had gotten them together out of concern for them, she had homemade muffins waiting for us. But they said they didn't feel like eating. And I wasn't about to eat in front of them!

But after we talked it through and they were hugging and telling each other how sorry they were for misinterpreting things—you are ahead of me—yes, they wanted those muffins. It's true. When we are in the presence of the ones about whom we feel resentful, we aren't hungry. Hannah left Eli ready to eat her muffins. She was not holding a grudge even though he called her a drunk. And beyond that, she was free to prepare her heart to one day leave her much-prayed-for son in the care of this man who had once said such a despicable thing to her. Put simply, Hannah was not playing her life to, nor deriving her pleasure from, people.

Three or four years later, when Samuel, her long-awaited son was weaned, she was able to find the courage to leave him in Eli's care—forever. The very next verse finds her worshipping her God with a deep prayer of acceptance and faith. It is an amazing prayer of a woman whose heart is free from past hurts, regrets, and future grief. The focus is not on Hannah or the fact that she had just left her child. No, the focus is on how great her God was and how he turned everything upside down.

Hannah's heart attitudes set the stage for God's great plan that this praying ministry-mom would one day see her son become the king's spiritual director. "The LORD . . . revealed himself to Samuel through his word" (1 Sam. 3:21).

The reason this has meant so much to me personally is that I realized how far I was from having this heart-set during the Collinsville years. Hannah's *first* call was to the Lord, not people. And even when Peninnah and Eli used her as a doormat, she was undaunted because they weren't who she was trying to please. She found her strength and solace first and foremost from her fire-starter audience of One.

I find myself returning often to Hannah and her strength of soul to remind me that we are called to a cross, not ease, and I'd better fall in line, not whine, when life seems sour for a spell. Like us, you have no doubt had periods of humiliation in your life. Hannah stands tall before you, showing you how to live, pulling you back to the audience of One.

This is why most of my mentors are dead people in books who lived one hundred or two hundred years ago. Yes, like Hannah, they intimidate me by appearing to be far more mature than I. But they call me higher—away from whining or an attitude of entitlement. Too often books today encourage self-centeredness. "Poor us. We're all victims. You can't know how bad I'm hurting. . . . If you only knew you would understand why I am so self-centered." No, life is difficult.

A few short years ago, two of our younger Grace Chapel missionaries, Sindia and Stuart Foster, lost their six-year-old daughter to an illness that hit so hard and fast that she was dead in four days. The Fosters lived in Mozambique when their little Belva became violently ill. They buried her in the soil of the country they'd gone to serve. When they returned to the U. S., Gordon and I asked if we might visit with them.

During our conversation Stuart said that they were thankful that Belva hadn't died in the U.S. That comment caught my attention, so I asked him to tell us what was behind it. He explained that when Belva was buried, flanked on all sides of him were four African brothers who also had laid their young in that soil. They were bound to each other forever by their mutual losses. If it had happened in the States, he feared that people would have said, "How cruel of God to take your daughter when you have given your life to missionary service. You are entitled to better treatment than that."

Stuart and Sindia went on to tell us that that kind of misguided thinking didn't touch them in Africa. They received comfort and care but were also challenged to accept it. They observed that North American Christians tend to think that God owes them a full life without ailments or death. That is not the perspective of their loved ones in Africa. They preferred being called to higher responses. Gordon and I were cut to the heart. These are the kind of models we need today. I long for more of such people who call us back to the audience of One. May their tribe increase.

But I have gone ahead of my story. What seems so obvious to me today was almost a blur twenty-five years ago. I had left Collinsville with a mixture of feelings: deep gratitude, happiness, love for the people, and sorrow at having to say good-bye. Yet, I left with a sense of relief. I had a chance to start all over again and to find that appropriate distance in relationships so that I had a reasonable amount of control over time, choices, and priorities. I had some growing to do, and I had to do it as quickly as possible. The most pressing issue had to do with audiences. And I decided it would be an audience of One.

 FIVE

TO BE OR TO DO

That Is the Question

Let me do nothing today without calmness of soul.
—*John Wesley*

Collinsville, Illinois, and Lexington, Massachusetts, are separated by a thousand miles: two days hard driving or a two-hour plane flight. We made the trip in just under three weeks.

It was not just a vacation we needed. Gordon and I had to push the reset button of our lives. We had to make sure that we were ready for a totally different kind of challenge. Life in the southern Midwest was busy, predictable, and pleasant. Life in the Northeast, New England, would be like moving to a totally new country. Just how new and just how different, we were yet to learn.

What we needed most of all was an opportunity to reflect on both the recent past and the immediate future. For me, it was a time not only to face my lifelong battle with people-pleasing and commitment to an audience of One but also some things about my temperament, *my way of being*. I would have to learn how not to take myself so seriously and to become a calmer, more reflective kind of person. I would have to cultivate a quieter spirit.

That took me back to Hannah. Study her life, and you get the strong impression of a woman at peace with herself. A heartbreak, an inner anguish? She took it quietly before the Lord. That was her nature. But not mine. By nature, I am a "talker-doer." When in anguish, my first instinct would be to talk it to death in order to make sense of it. I had even more to learn from Hannah.

Hannah's prayer at the altar over which Eli presided was unusual because it was inaudible. Most tabernacle prayers were not. Perhaps this drew Eli's attention: moving lips, no sound. He wondered if she were drunk.

It seems clear that Hannah was very much at home in an inner world known only to herself and the Lord. It was a world so private that no one else was privy to its inner culture. Doubtless, living with a woman like Peninnah drove Hannah even deeper inside herself.

♢ MR. INSIDE AND MRS. OUTSIDE

Today I think we'd call Hannah an introvert, one who *thinks before* she speaks—not having to explain things she didn't say. We're talking about a person much unlike me. In contrast, I am an extravert who often *speaks as I think*. Introverts, like Hannah, draw their strength from within themselves, while we extraverts draw our strength from people and the things outside ourselves.

Introverts can teach us much about deep waters and quiet streams (assuming they fill their inner thoughts with the right stuff). Even though they do not speak as quickly as extraverts, many introverts are fast on their "thinking feet." Before their thoughts are voiced, they prefer to practice how it will sound inside themselves. We extraverts have a lot to learn from introverts if we would give them time to process their thinking before we give our opinions.

As an extravert, I love connecting with people. I like to use others to test my thoughts—to see if what I'm thinking makes sense. I'm what you call a *noisy thinker*. The good news is that you'll always know what I'm thinking; the bad news is that you will struggle to know which thought is my last, my final conclusion on a matter. People like me can annoy an introvert who wants to say, "Why doesn't she remain quiet until she figures out what she wants to say?"

Here was Hannah "in bitterness of spirit" in the tabernacle praying about her infertility. And here was Eli speaking too quickly. She's drunk, he thought. His instinct was to rebuke her, to demand an explanation. Only then did he discover her more noble purpose.

Too often, people like Eli push those who aren't ready to say things publicly deeper inside themselves by forcing the issue. They say, "Tell me what you're thinking." Meaning, *now*.

When I left Collinsville in the Summer of 1972, I had only developed the extraverted part of my personality. My tendency was to speak first and ask questions later; my habit was to act without adequate reflection. I was tired, feeling the need for more control in my life. It was time to come to grips with my extraverted temperament which had its value but which needed greater discipline.

Now perhaps you can understand more fully why keeping my inner fire is so important to me. It became much more so after the Collinsville years.

As an extravert I prefer that my prayers end in action. Often as I pray, thoughts of something I can do for someone will come to mind, and I have to force myself not to do it now but to do the inward work *first*.

I live with an introvert. In the same way that I've described Hannah, Gordon has a very large inner world. He can retreat into it and be quite at home with himself. I had come to admire, even long for that capability. My inner world needed enlargement; it needed to become a more hospitable place for me . . . and for the Lord. That became a primary commitment for me on our way to Lexington.

I would need to work on proactively deepening my inner world, an acquired introvertedness for many years to come. For example, here's a comment out of my journal on the day I learned that my father had cancer. It was written fourteen years *after* the first journey to Lexington:

It's a time to go inward. To walk through the pain instead of drowning it in busyness. The fact remains that because I live in a world filled with fallenness, I must come to those places of inner refreshment, or my soul will shrivel up. How thankful and comforted I am to be *homesick* for these quiet moments of inner rest.

This morning I read about the role dew plays in nature. "I will be like the dew to Israel" (Hosea 14:5). Dew is God's provision for renewing the earth. Quietness and absorption bring the dew. But the experts say it will never gather in a wind. The temperatures must fall, wind must cease, and both come to still point—before it can yield its invisible particles of moisture to revive flowers and me. Why do I so often need to be forced to still point when it is such a rewarding experience? Lord, I know you will bring meaning out of all of this. I rest in you.

Guilt is a counterproductive response to Christ's call to the fire. *Homesickness* for Christ's presence is far better. This alone will keep calling us back to him. Perhaps young mothers may read what I've just written and be frustrated. I can hear them protest, "We can't find any minutes to do these things, Gail! Give us a break! We feel swamped by so many expectations from husband, children, church, job, and home. There simply is no time for tending our own spirits."

I hear you. I've been there, done that! But I'm not going to back off. I'll concede that there are times in life when we have to be content merely to *snatch moments* when we simply "chew" on the strength of a word, a sentence from Scripture, or a refreshing thought from a friend who challenges us to keep becoming more like Christ. Just one insight that we can own, that will get us through the day. In fact, that is why I've included many "snatch books" in the bibliography in the back of this book. Sometimes Christ will take a word, a sentence, or a thought and multiply it to our souls like he once did with bread and fish.

A friend once reminded me that this is why it is so important to memorize Scripture so that in any idle moment, whether we are waiting for children, trains, or cabs, we can meditate on his truth day and night. Think of memorization as a way of packing a spiritual lunch that can be nourishing at another time.

Ruth Graham, mother of five, used to leave books open around her home so that if she was near one while holding a baby or playing with a child, she would be more apt to look down at the book if it were open than if it were closed. Ruth would agree with Francois Fenelon who, though writing in the 1600s, seemed very contemporary when he said:

You must learn, too, to make good use of chance moments: when waiting for someone, when going from place to place, or when in society where to be a good listener is all that is required—at such times it is easy to lift the heart to God, and thereby gain fresh strength for further duties. The less time one has the more carefully it should be managed. If you wait for free, convenient seasons in which to fulfill real duties, you run the risk of waiting forever: especially in such a life as yours. No, make use of all chance moments.[1]

🐌 HOCKEY PUCKS?

In any day, too many opinions, attitudes, and options come at us which can either be God's gift, something to distract, or something perverse. Years ago, Gordon and I used to enjoy an occasional hockey game. During the warm-up period, players line up and shoot pucks at the goalie, one coming at him every two or three seconds. I found myself commiserating with the goalie. I wanted to tell him that I knew just how he felt as he moved almost violently from side to side, thrashing out at every puck with his stick. I wanted to say, "Your pucks are like my phone calls, my mail, my visitors, the demands of children and husband, the questions, the criticisms, the decisions. I love it all, or most of it anyway, but must they keep on coming, so many, so fast?"

Try picturing yourself as the goalie behind that ugly mask with pucks coming at you. How do you feel as you adjust to their speed and force? Are you ready for the next one? Because it's coming.

How many "pucks" will you stop today? Have you the wisdom? The patience? The sense of thankfulness? Do you know where your strength will come from?

The lives of the spiritual masters suggest that there is only one way we can be adequate to the task. And it is not found in the way of the extravert with his/her many words. It is found in the quiet, moving lips of Hannah where we learn to take life's "pucks" into the presence of God. Amy Carmichael understood this when she wrote:

Too much of your nature is exposed to the winds that blow on it. You and I both need to withdraw more and more into the secret place.[2]

As I journeyed from Collinsville to Lexington, I knew I would have to acquire that spiritual skill.

Now many years later, I am much more confident of a balance between extraversion and introversion in my life.

On weekends, we have four worship services at Grace Chapel. Two of them happen on Sunday morning. At the end of the first service recently, I went to Gordon and told him that I had to go home. In a sense I felt like the distressed Hannah, and I needed a quiet place to seek God. My emotions were frayed; I was living with a deep inner sadness brought on by too many of those flying pucks. I couldn't even be specific about what they were, which was one reason I needed to ferret it out in silence.

Gordon sent me on my way. Soon I was in a place of quiet where I could expose my heart to Scripture, to some of my favorite writings, and my journal. That morning I wrote:

> I had to leave after the first service today because of feeling so vulnerable emotionally. I felt like my head was going to burst. I knew if I stayed, I would blubber, and today I can't stand the fish-bowl feeling of being watched. There is deep sadness in me, and I'm confused as to why it is so deep. I think it may be important for me to list the myriad of emotions so God can have the freedom to show me how to handle the pucks—those I know are getting to me and those I may not be owning up to.

In the ensuing hour, the "stuff" I was dealing with came pouring out in my writing—an accumulation of experiences and impressions that had come in my direction over the past few days:

- A sense of isolation: The men and women on Gordon's staff can process a criticism that has been launched by a church member. But to whom does a pastor's wife speak?

- Meeting an old friend at a banquet but feeling a mystifying distance in the coolness of her response.

- A Sunday school class I'd taught that seemed to have ended poorly because of a discussion which turned counterproductive.

- What to say to the person who wanted to use me as a conduit to Gordon because he doesn't have the courage to talk to Gordon directly.

- Maybe there is a part of me clamoring for attention—making much of little, pity-pot stuff. I loathe the complaining spirit that seems too free right now. I want to renounce self, but I also have to call these things by name and understand why I feel like I'm dying inside and why my need to weep is so great.

There were ten such comments in all that day. What I discovered by the end of that redemptively quiet hour was that I needed to stop and get off the merry-go-round. I needed to repent of my small thinking and desire for attention and control. God was in control. He would give me what was needed when I needed it.

And when the time had ended, I felt awash in a fresh peace. I think of the words of Scripture when the harried, frenzied Hannah found quietness in the tabernacle and heard the final well-wishes of a more sensitive Eli: "Then she went her way and ate something, and her face was no longer downcast" (1 Sam. 1:18).

Frankly, I've often wondered how honest we are with ourselves, starting with me, when it comes to living out what we say we believe. If I truly believe that God works most supremely in my life when I come to him in quietness and receive his thoughts and strength, then why don't I place a higher priority on it? Perhaps there are times when I need to pay someone to watch our child so I can have an hour of solitude. Some pay a sitter to go to the shopping mall for an hour ... but to the "tabernacle"?

Understanding this part of me that needed ruthless management before arriving in Lexington made all the difference in our years there. God meant for me to develop a part of my personality that didn't come as naturally. This is how I learned to love "being."

It's interesting to me that both Hannah and Mary, the mother of our Lord, were people who worked from the inside out. Scholars tell us that Mary's *Magnificat* (Luke 1:46–55) is fashioned after Hannah's. The two women, living centuries apart, clearly understood each other.

Imagine what would have happened if Mary had been an extravert and received the word from the Lord that she was going to bear the Messiah by the power of the Holy Spirit. Phones would have been ringing all over Israel! "You'll never believe what happened to me!" But no, instead it is said of her, "*Mary treasured up all these things, pondering them in her heart*" (Luke 2:19).

When Mary needed the comfort of a friend during this time of humiliation and joy in her life, she went to one person, Elizabeth, not a crowd or group. When God picked a woman for the most unique task of all time, he picked someone with a quiet spirit.

For Gordon and me, an awareness of temperament (particularly introversion and extraversion) also led to greater discoveries not only of our spiritual lives but also of the way we meshed with one another.

For the first ten years of marriage, we often lived with a certain amount of tension when it came to the way we both related to the congregation. For example, Gordon was at home with crowds of people if he was in his role as a pastor and leader. But the minute his tasks were completed, I would watch him quickly withdraw into solitude or seek the company of a few people with whom he felt most comfortable. On the other hand, I could not get enough of people.

"Why do you have to be the last person out of church?" Gordon would sometimes ask as he waited for me to have one more conversation on Sunday morning.

"Why do you want to get away so quickly when *you* are their pastor?" I asked in response.

What we did not realize was that there was great significance behind those questions. Our marriage underwent an important adjustment when we discovered this.

☘ So That's Why You're So Strange!

One day we attended a lecture introducing the Myers-Briggs temperament indicator. Earlier that morning Gordon had resisted going to a breakfast where he knew he'd be among strangers. "I can't stand going into a room full of people I don't know and talking about things that are so trivial," he'd said to me. But I'd convinced him to go.

Now we were at the lecture. "Introverts are people who are extremely uncomfortable in large crowds, being among people they don't know, making small talk about things that they don't think count," the lecturer said. "Put an introvert into such a situation and he/she gets quickly fatigued."

Gordon looked at me and whispered, "Did you tell this guy about me?"

No, I hadn't. But it helped us understand why some things I did irritated him and why things he did ruffled my feathers. Suddenly we began to understand why I was the one who wanted to have more nights for hospitality in our home and why Gordon so badly wanted the evenings to be quiet, why I loved being immersed in relationships and Gordon preferred the companionship of a few trusted friends.

We came to appreciate for the first time one of the hidden reasons we'd been attracted to one another years before. Opposites attract, and we certainly were opposites. *But we were too often trying to "convert" the other to be just like we were.* I wanted Gordon to come out of his inner world and get engaged like I did. He wanted me to embrace "aloneness" as he had done.

Our "oppositeness" even explained our differing view of personal space. Gordon loves his quiet space and privacy. I never realized that I was violating that part of him when I barged into his study and launched into a conversation. It would never have occurred to me to seek permission to interrupt his deep thoughts. Why? Because at the time, I didn't understand his temperament.

Since our husbands make their living by reading and studying, it's their work and therefore should not be minimized. Even now, I have to stop and think before I simply begin talking in a stream of consciousness instead of waiting for the right moment.

Or what about our prayer times? I love to do prayer-walks, praying as we go. If my husband is going to walk, he wants to get lost in thought, enjoy the scenery, and talk very little. So when we pray together, we are more apt to sit still and concentrate on prayer alone. Gordon is much more likely to enjoy praying alone or with one other person (thank heaven for that!), while I enjoy praying with others in conversational prayer.

Even interruptions are seen differently by people who derive their energy from different sources. The telephone is a wonderful connector for me, but for Gordon, it interrupts concentration and is therefore undesirable. Writing projects like this one are pure joy to my husband. Sitting deep in thought all day is heavenly. For me, I have to push myself hard to concentrate for ten to eleven hours—with no phone calls in between.

We laugh because I will go away to be quiet and gain soul-strength from Christ. But more often than I like to admit, the minute I arrive I'll find myself picking up the phone to connect with Gordon or one of our children to check on things.

The changes have not all been one way in our marriage. As I have worked hard to develop an introverted side to my life, so Gordon has worked equally hard to develop his extraverted self. Both of us have covered a lot of distance. We've learned the rhythms of engaging and disengaging with each other and with those in our larger world. The irritations, once so prevalent, hardly exist today, because we understand what each of us needs and when and how one reaches into the other's life.

Extraversion and introversion are neither good nor bad. One temperament is not superior to the other. We are all in need of relationships with people who bring both perspectives to us. The healthiest thing, however, is to work hard at developing oneself so that there is freedom to be comfortable with people or comfortable alone.

You and I must guard against the tendency to use our personality strengths as whipping blocks to make a point. "If you really loved Christ, you would find it easy to sit for an hour each morning and be still." "If you really loved him, you would care more about people, even if you are tired." "Why don't you get off your duff and do something!" "I wish just once you would think before you talk!" No, we must learn to celebrate each other rather than chip away.

As we made our way toward Lexington and the Grace Chapel congregation, I found myself deep in such thinking. We had almost twelve good years of ministry behind us. We were young; we were healthy; we hoped to have a lot of years ahead of us. But like my husband, I wanted every year to be better because we had drained the past of all its lessons. And I knew the two things I needed to understand most if the next years were to be fruitful: I needed to know who my real audience was, and I needed to find a comfortable way to bring inner restfulness into my life.

Note: To read more about personalities look at *Please Understand Me*, by David Keirsey and Marilyn Bates, Prometheus Nemesis Books, 1978, and *Your Personality and the Spiritual Life*, by Reginald Johnson, Victor Books, 1995. Other books on this topic are included in the bibliography.

SIX

GIVING GIFTS TO EACH OTHER

To love is to find pleasure in the happiness of the one loved.
—*Unknown*

In 1812, Adoniram and Ann Judson became the first couple to leave New England as missionaries. For Ann this journey would be an enormous leap of faith, an act of devotion first to Christ and then to her husband. She would be surrendering the comforts of home, close friends, and life in a familiar culture and exposing herself to the possibility of persecution and even death.

The Judsons, supported by New England Congregationalists, were headed for Burma. The voyage was long and arduous. And it wasn't long before there was an unexpected tension between them due to their differing temperaments. Each day Adoniram, ever the intense and searching student, buried himself in his New Testament, studying the subject of baptism. You could say he was truth-driven, passionate to find it and to act upon it.

Ann, on the other hand, was people-driven. She cared deeply about relationships: how people felt, keeping the peace, and being supportive.

So all was not at ease when they arrived in Burma. It became apparent that Adoniram had changed his views on baptism and had become convinced of a different doctrinal position than the supporting Congregationalists back home. This, of course, meant he could not serve with integrity under their sponsorship.

For Ann all of this was unthinkable, and it presented great inner conflict. She was concerned about the relationships she would lose if they became Baptists. What would her family think? The denomination? The fellow missionaries with whom they'd sailed? By contrast, this was no problem for Adoniram. After all, truth was truth; relationships came after.

To Ann's credit, she did her own in-depth study and eventually embraced Adoniram's viewpoint. What could have been a severe marital tension was resolved. After being baptized, she wrote:

> We feel like we are alone in the world, with no real friends but each other, no one on whom we can depend but God.[1]

They were able to resolve such differences without dividing. The Judsons went on to become a rare and unique team. The depth of the gifts they brought to their ministry-marriage far outweighed any disagreement. Each knew how to bring varied strengths to play in the life of the other, and *because those gifts were gladly received by the partner*, they shared an amazing life in spite of untold stress, torture, imprisonment, illness, resistance, and loneliness.

I've already noted that I married a man who is temperamentally opposite. When we were dating, these differences often seemed amusing. Take it from me: it's not so amusing *after* the wedding.

☙ MADE IN HIS IMAGE, NOT OURS

When it comes to temperament, more than a few of us make a vain attempt to remake our spouses into our images. But maturity suggests that we encourage our marriage partners to grow in their uniqueness *as God made them*. Maturity suggests we become something of a gift to them, complementing their weaknesses with our strengths. And that is what we have slowly learned to do. Our contrasting ways of looking at reality have helped to sharpen us over our thirty-eight years.

Earlier I spoke of a beloved friend who had brought Gordon and me together. Asians would call him an "introducer." One day our "introducer" told Gordon, "When God brings people together, he means for each of them to bring gifts to the other." Reflecting on our pending marriage, he said, "Gordon, God has given you a *thoroughbred* [did I really want to be known as a thoroughbred?]. Be careful never to squelch Gail's gifts, but encourage them, celebrate them, and your own life will be enhanced."

Gordon embraced those words and chose to follow his advice from day one. It's a story I love to tell.

🐚 Some Gifts for You

When Gordon speaks of the time we met, he often reflects on his own tendency to be self-centered. I think I would prefer to say that he lacked a sensitivity about people, their feelings, their wounds, and their aspirations that you normally learn in family life. But Gordon had gone off to prep school when he was in his early teens, and there was little opportunity for him to grow in this area of his life.

Since my earliest years as a teenage Christian, I had prayed for a sensitive heart that would see beneath words and deeds. God in his kindness gave me an overabundance of sensitivity to what people were *not* saying, and doing something to uplift them. Today we would no doubt call it the gift of mercy/encouragement. I was much more aware of the unspoken things, that level of reality that Gordon may have been tempted to overlook. I found it natural to discern the messages of people in body language, eye contact, silences, facial expressions, and tones of voice. Gordon was not yet in touch with this dimension of listening.

My husband could have destroyed this giftedness of mine if he had minimized, criticized, or competed with it. And that would have been an easy thing to do. Early on there were times when we would leave a meeting, and I would ask him if he noticed what someone was *really* saying. And he would reply with a little impatience, "No, I didn't hear what she was *really* saying." Later he would make a point of checking to see if I was correct and come back and tell me.

What a present this was. *He saw my sensitivity as a gift* which would add to and not detract from his ministry. Over the years I've watched this gift be graciously given to Gordon as well. It's important because people long for us to notice when they are inwardly shouting what they can't outwardly say.

The sensitivity I'm describing works in many ways. It spots the person who is withdrawing from fellowship. It notices the acts of a person who is in great personal struggle. It picks up on pain, guilt, despair, resentment, and fear. And it latches onto the need for affirmation, encouragement, and love. Remember Eli berating the sobbing Hannah in the tabernacle? He lacked sensitivity. Remember Mary of Bethany when she anointed the feet of a sorrowing Jesus? She had it.

I tried to bring a second gift to Gordon. I wanted to offer him *a place of rest* in our home and in our relationship. Our husbands often feel hassled and fragmented because of the many hats they wear in a day. I wanted our life together to be a distinct contrast from all of that.

Years ago I was challenged when I read that Sarah Edwards, wife of the great preacher Jonathan Edwards, was said to be "a resting place for Jonathan's soul." Before he died, Jonathan spoke of their "uncommon union." These became rich words to my own heart.

Being a source of rest for my husband meant, of course, that he would be willing to be transparent, to share his real self with me. So often when I speak with ministry wives today they tell me their husbands can't admit that they have weaknesses. That means that these wives cannot offer the resting place I wanted to make for Gordon.

Looking for those who understood the gift of a resting place brought me to Catherine Booth who became a remarkable resting place for her husband William. While traveling, he wrote to her:

> I wish I were in a more satisfactory state spiritually. I feel almost *dead; powerless*. Consequently my preaching and praying in public has but little effect on the people. But wishing produces no improvement. O that God would come and give me some new light or some new power. Will you pray for me? I never felt less emotion and power in prayer in my life. And I am sure I don't know what to do . . . You far exceed me in the influence you can command in a service. I should much like to spend the evening with you all alone, far away from all

excitement and disturbance, where we could commune with each other's heart and be still.[2]

Is there any doubt as we read this that Catherine was a gift to him? She was not only a source of rest, but she also knew how to enter William's heart and provide the spiritual challenges he frequently needed. And he didn't become defensive. Rather, he embraced each of her thoughts with appreciation.

At the young age of twenty-four, Catherine wrote to William:

> Oh, my love, I have felt acutely about you, I mean *your soul*. I rejoice exceedingly to hear how the Lord is blessing your labors, but as I stand at a distance and contemplate the scene of action and all the circumstances attending it, I tremble. . . . I know how possible it is to preach and pray and sing, and even shout while the heart is not right with God. I know how popularity and prosperity have a tendency to elate and exalt self, if the heart is not humble before God. I know how Satan takes advantage of these things to work out the destruction (if possible) of one whom the Lord uses to pull down the strongholds of his kingdom, and all these considerations make me tremble, and weep and pray for you, my dearest Love, that you may be able to overcome all his devices, and having done all to stand not in your own strength but in humble dependence on Him who worketh "all in all." [3]

In response William was grateful, prayerful, and open. Perhaps this is one of the reasons why together they changed their world, and one hundred years later the Salvation Army remains strong and purposeful across the known world.

I have tried to offer Gordon a third gift: *protection*. For years I saw myself as the family meteorologist. I have tried to be sensitive to the pressures of the calendar, to sense the health of Gordon's emotional and spiritual life, and to be aware when our priorities are being ignored. I've looked for the signs of overstimulation when he might be getting mesmerized by applause or reacting to events rather than initiating them. I've watched to see if we are becoming jaded, uncaring, caught up in organizationalism. But most of all, I've found it important to make sure that the outside world didn't become unbearably intrusive on Gordon's need to find soul time.

I have not always been successful at this. We paid a terrible price when the need to protect was neglected. But let me emphasize once again that these gifts are only useful if one of us is willing to take the necessary time to give and the other is willing to receive.

One more gift that I believe our husbands need in abundance is that of being their *source of physical affection and pleasure.* Ministry can become sensual. We have to accept this as part of the territory.

Many Christian leaders have pointed out that there is a close parallel between the spiritual and sexual drives within us. The result is that when one works closely with people in a caring, emotional context, the implications of sexual overtones are more likely to increase. Speaking as a woman, if I choose to become defensive, suspicious, or resentful about these realities, I cripple my husband, and I do damage to myself. As I watch Gordon moving among people from day to day, I find myself frequently reminded that *he picked me thirty-eight years ago to be his partner in life; I'm going to make him glad that he did.*

I know that many women live in terror that their husbands could be susceptible to bad choices in this area. There are too many tragic stories for them to feel at ease. Some write to me of their fears. They say, "He sees other women at their best—too often he sees me at my worst. I'm at home wiping baby bottoms and folding clothes. How can I match the beautiful, competent, energetic kind of person he's apt to meet out there?"

A wise husband understands this fear and does not mock it. He is careful to communicate his constant commitment, reassurance, and appreciation. He is wise if he reminds his wife that he looks forward to their times together, and that she ascends above all others in his esteem and affection. As wives, we must proactively make ourselves and home such a desirable place to be so that from the time he leaves in the morning he is looking forward to when he can return.

I honestly do not have many helpful answers for the woman who wants to or must have her own career separate from her husband's ministry. I do not suggest that she is wrong in this aspiration, but I am quick to warn her that there is a price to be paid. Few vocations are as emotionally and spiritually draining as the parish ministry, and replenishment of spirit has to come from someplace. When both husband and wife go separate directions each day to differing kinds of work, they are not likely to find as much resource in one another at the end of the day. Bottom line: Expectations in terms of what each can give the other may need to be lowered.

In 1995 Gordon and I spent the better part of a day with Kathleen Chambers, daughter of Oswald and Biddy Chambers, in her north end London home. At the time of our visit, Kathleen was eighty-four years old. She had invited us to visit her because Gordon had written a preface for one of Oswald's books, and I had written about her mother's role in Oswald's writing. Apparently few have taken adequate notice of Biddy's contribution to Oswald's writing ministry, and Kathleen wanted to tell us even more about her mother.

Almost everyone is familiar with Oswald Chambers. But what do you know about his wife Biddy? Let me offer a brief biographical sketch. Biddy was a person of frail health. She decided to become a stenographer and to pursue a proficiency level that might attract the attention of the prime minister of England. She reached her goal of excellence, but before the prime minister heard about her, she met and married Oswald. Instead of taking down the words of the prime minister in shorthand, she began to record every one of Oswald's sermons and Bible lessons—*word for word.* Seven years after they married, Oswald suddenly died.

Biddy spent the next thirty-five years raising Kathleen, their only child, and transcribing Oswald's words into book form. If you've profited from Oswald Chambers' *My Utmost for His Highest,* you have Biddy to thank. And if you've ever read the many dozens of titles over Oswald's name, remember Biddy. She made it all possible.

But when you pick up an Oswald Chambers' book, try and find Biddy's name and a reference to her contribution. You won't find it. It's not there. Biddy refused to accept recognition. She was only interested in giving herself as a gift to Oswald's vision to serve and build people for Jesus Christ. Unspeakable devotion!

The same month we were with Kathleen, I received notice that a book I had written in 1989, *A Step Farther and Higher,* was going out of print. For a moment I had to pause and rethink my own personal commitment. Would I be sad because something with my name on it was going to disappear from bookshelves? Biddy's perspective grabbed me and brought me back to my own commitment to be

Gordon's partner and helpmeet. I will not permit anything to deter me from that goal as long as I am able.

ᴀ AND SOME GIFTS FOR ME

One of the truly unique teams in Scripture that Gordon and I love to think and talk about is the A&P team: Aquila and Priscilla. They were generous, good listeners, flexible, willing to change or relocate, mature, able to teach, and even ready to risk their lives. But what I honor the most about Aquila is the way he encouraged Priscilla to work in concert with him. In fact, in Scripture, they are never mentioned separately. Sometimes Priscilla's name even comes first. Aquila understood how to encourage his wife to flower to all of her God-given potential, and he did it in a day when such values were not encouraged.

I have lived with such a man. Allow me to enumerate the three major gifts Gordon has given me which have made me want to be *even more* of a gift to him. I have often been heard to say that 75 percent of why I have continued to love ministry over these four decades has its seeds in the way my husband treats me.

The first of these gifts was Gordon's willingness to *live a repentant lifestyle* before me in the first nine years of our marriage. From him I learned that we must always be ready to acknowledge our brokenness. This was especially important to me because I found this difficult and needed to see it modeled. The gift has three sides to it. First, when other's criticize him, I know his first instinct will be to go inside of himself and ask the Holy Spirit for insight. By the time he reaches me with it, he has already gotten rid of defensiveness.

Criticism has never been easy for either of us, but over the years we have worked hard to receive it with grace. I can remember when we read how Dawson Troutman, the founder of Navigators, responded to faultfinding. He removed himself from the company of others and lay the criticism before the Lord to see if there was a *kernel* of truth there. Since reading that, Gordon and I have tried to do the same. Many have said that our critics are often our best friends because they tell us what others are afraid to say. Truth must be faced if long-term health is to be maintained.

The second side of why acknowledging brokenness is important is that it is disarming if Gordon can admit that he doesn't have all the answers. For someone like myself who for years needed to be right, this was a convicting response. I know that it's easy for pastors to think that being right is a part of what they are paid for. But when a spiritual leader can listen without being defensive, members of his congregation don't feel the need to come to the leader's wife with their complaints. No ministry wife enjoys being put in the middle.

Finally, the third side benefit of acknowledging brokenness is that the man in the pulpit will be the same person at home. Not perfect, but open and teachable. I know of nothing as powerful as a man who knows how to be genuinely repentant.

The second gift Gordon gave me came out of a long car ride we took—also in our ninth year of marriage. As we drove along, I read a biography of William and Catherine Booth to him. Because Catherine had breast cancer before they performed mastectomies, she died an awful death while watching her chest being eaten away. The stench was ghastly, the pain unbearable, but William was there for her. As I read this detailed description of the way he would touch her, embrace her, and kiss her in the midst of all this, I began to weep uncontrollably.

Gordon had never seen me like this, and he began to probe. Where was this emotion coming from? I finally was able to articulate why I felt so deeply about what I was reading. I didn't believe any man would ever be able to love me like that. He would dump me long before that happened. In a way, I was still living with some of the fallout of that sudden, devastating broken engagement that had happened more than fifteen years before.

Later Gordon told me that seeing me in the midst of this catharsis caused him to have a whole new love for me because, finally, I was showing weakness and vulnerability. He asked himself, How can I show more love toward my wife? For the next few days, he gave special attention to the question, How has she loved me? And it wasn't long before he realized that week after week, I loved him by pointing to Sunday and his sermon as though they were the peak of *my* week. Whatever was needed to make that sermon God's tool was done.

This insight caused Gordon to ask, "*What is Gail's sermon?*" And he answered, "It's the home she prepares for the children and me." He would later write:

I realized that day that I had become incredibly selfish in matters of our home. . . . Gail preached her sermon when she cooked a meal, arranged an artistic centerpiece, kept the house neat, and planted flowers in the front yard.

When I failed to show interest in cutting the lawn or threw my sport coat over the front doorknob or left my toilet articles on the bathroom sink, I was being selfish, doing the very thing that would have shattered me if she had done it to me. I was disinterested in her "sermon." "O God," I prayed, "forgive me for being so insensitive to the things that are important to my wife; train me to understand the importance of hearing and enjoying the sermons in her life.[4]

From the day this insight hit him until now, twenty-nine years later, Gordon has honored my "home" sermon. What a difference it made in the amount of time it took him to find things. He literally became disciplined overnight but never told me what had happened. He simply lived it.

Need I say that my enjoyment of Gordon's sermon only increased after that? Love has a way of either mushrooming when it is received and responded to, or it slowly diminishes when it senses it is unappreciated or ignored. Whenever I have spoken to men who are pastors, I've challenged them: *Do you know what your wife's sermon is?*

When the children were about eight and eleven, Gordon gave me a third gift. I loved being a stay-at-home mom, but one day the children came running in from school, dropped their books, and said, "See you later, Mom."

Gordon happened to be there that day, and I turned to him and said, "The children don't need me anymore." Hearing that brief comment caused him to ask himself, *What are my wife's spiritual gifts and how can I help her find her way to use them as the children need her less and less?* He told me it was only right that if he were to help others in the congregation to discover and use their spiritual gifts, he should do the same for me.

That was the beginning of another personal growth spurt. He began observing me, nudging me to read and study more and think more deliberately about the themes of spiritual life that were most important to me. Then one day he said, "Gail, you are a teacher-encourager. The next time someone asks you to speak someplace, you are going, and I'll stay home with the children." And so it was. He helped me on my outline, even shared his best illustrations with me (not to be used within five hundred miles of him, of course).

I still remember how terrified I was. My face got blotchy, my knees knocked, and I was generally scared to pieces. But when I came home, I knew that he was right—there was an embryonic gift to be fanned. That was nearly thirty years ago. If you had told me that I could ever speak without every word being manuscripted, I would have told you, "No way." But that day has come. This is a gift.

It seems difficult for most women to stop and ask questions like, "Where do you most supremely experience God's pleasure?" or "What do you dream about doing in the kingdom?" or "What do you do that you can't stop talking about?" Most of our lives are lived asking how can we help others do this. What a relief if people make us think through these questions—especially if they are our husbands, the ones we treasure and whose opinions and affirmations we need most.

Over the years, I have queried dozens of women about their gifts, and most often they say, "I haven't thought much about that. I'd have to think long and hard to come up with any kind of meaningful answer for you, Gail."

Some women feel their husbands are jealous of anything they do well. One told me that her husband refuses to let her do anything in the church. He keeps telling her she's controlling and needs to wait for the church to see her gifts. She has waited three years and is a volcano about to erupt. The despair such a woman feels is hard to describe. Perhaps Eleanor Roosevelt put it best when she asserted, "When you cease to make a contribution, you begin to die."

I often have the opposite experience and need Gordon to assist me in saying no to the many opportunities that become available. His help is important because at first I want to say yes too much. He also draws wisdom from me when he needs help in knowing when to say no. One thing is for sure, people in the congregation watch how the pastor treats his wife and children. Are they flourishing in Christ because of the way he loves them? People weigh this heavily when they think of their spiritual leader's authenticity.

Once I spoke to a group of young church planters about how they might keep their wives from falling through the cracks of ministry. I had mentioned that I would turn cartwheels, as it were, for Gordon because all through our marriage I knew one of his priorities was that his energies were used to be sure I also grew to Christlike maturity. That meant that when the children were small, and Gordon sensed my longing for time with the Lord but found it impossible with small, active children, he would *make the time* for me to get away by myself so that I also might grow in the Spirit. As I said earlier, every Friday morning was mine to do with as I chose. Filling my soul came first, but I also did other things I could not have done if he had not given me this gift of time.

I also told these church planters about Jill Briscoe's tribute to Stuart who made a break with the way he had been brought up—having been taught that women should be seen but not heard. He was aware, he said, that women might be sitting on the outside, but they were standing on the inside, screaming for permission to be used by God. So he decided that part of being Jill's leader meant that he would accept responsibility for seeing that God could use her gifts to the fullest. And so he has. Jill Briscoe's worldwide ministry is the result. If we can thank Biddy Chambers for Oswald's books, I said, perhaps we can thank Stuart for Jill's.

When I finished speaking, there was a line of men who wanted to talk. Most of them wished to confess to me that they had not done these things and that they were going home to stop competing with their wives and start valuing their gifts. I remember returning from that trip and being newly moved by my husband's delight in the ways God graciously used me. More than once I've heard him say, "I get more excitement out of seeing the Lord use Gail than anything I do." I don't understand how he can say this, but I believe him because he has never ceased expressing pleasure every time I've had a chance to serve.

Gordon and I have talked to more than a few crowds of ministry people about the gifts we have tried to bring to each other. We have always concluded our talk with one final gift which Gordon will not permit us to forget, *the gift of mercy*. We've had to give it to each other ... many times.

Our lives are no secret to most people in the evangelical Christian world. Those who care to know are aware that we have tasted the best and worst moments of ministry (more about this in a later chapter). It is easy to talk about a strong marriage and ministry partnership when things are going well. But it's another story when you come to one of those dark moments when someone fails or sins against the other. And sooner or later, we all do this in greater or lesser ways.

No matter the magnitude of the event, the issue always turns toward mercy: Will it be given, and will it be received? Over these many years of marriage we have learned—first in the smaller issues— that if you don't live a life of recurrent mercy-giving, then you'll fall apart should the moment ever call for great mercy. And we've known both the small and the big ones. Always, until this day, our first instinct has been to be merciful, forgiving to one another. This gift, I think, ascends above all the others. And it is why, on the day I write this chapter, I can tell you that the marriage that Gordon and I share is stronger, more vital, more satisfying than ever before.

Where would the world of Christian missions be today if the Judsons had not been able to resolve their differences and play to their complementary strengths? How about the Booths? The Briscoes? And in our tiny world, where would Gordon and Gail MacDonald be if we had not learned from them? Oh, the gifts we've been given by God, and oh, the power when we can give them to each other.

SEVEN

PKS CAN BE OK

Part One

If I could get to the highest place in Athens, I would lift up my voice and say, "What mean ye fellow citizens, that ye turn every stone to scrape wealth together and take so little care of your children to whom ye must one day relinquish all?"   —*Socrates, 450 B.C.*

A few years after our Collinsville days had ended and our children were entering their teenage years, Gordon was asked to consider the leadership of an organization for which we have much affection and respect. It was a difficult decision. Both of us prayed about it, discussed it endlessly, and agonized over it in our private thoughts. Saying yes would have meant leaving the pastoral ministry, which had been our life for almost fifteen years.

"Let's talk to Mark and Kristy," I suggested to Gordon. "Perhaps they can bring some new light to this process."

What would they say about a move to another part of the country? How would they feel about leaving our congregation, their schools, and lots of good friends? So we brought up the subject at an evening meal. Gordon described our dilemma and the possibilities that would come along with such a change. He did his best, so it seemed to me, to sweeten the deal by suggesting a number of things that might become available to the children. A horse for Kristy, perhaps?

Proximity to a part of the country that had always intrigued Mark? What did they think?

"You mean that you wouldn't be a pastor any more, Dad?" Mark asked.

"That's right, son," Gordon replied. "The family would probably get to go to a church where you'd hear someone else preach. Think of it this way, you wouldn't always be known as a PK."

I could read Gordon's mind. He was appealing to the part of the children that might not have always enjoyed the perceived pressure of the congregational spotlight.

"I'm not sure I want to go to a church where Dad's not a pastor," one of them (I don't remember who) said.

"How could you leave here? Look how much we love these people and how much they've done for us?" said the other.

"No way. Dad's a pastor, and we're a pastor's family. Let's not go any other place."

I guess we should have known better than to consult such biased children. We'd taught them to love the life of the pastorate, and now they were handing the teaching back. Why should we have been surprised? Both children had shown tremendous loyalty to the two congregations they'd known in their lifetimes. Leaving Collinsville had been something of a shock for them. It had taken a long time for them to face the fact that the people we left behind could get along without us.

Through their childhoods and youth, they never seemed to be aware that churches could be anything but fun, supportive, united communities. And, frankly, that's the way we wanted it. If Gordon or I had concerns about people in the church or were processing someone's criticism, we kept it between us. We wanted Mark and Kristy to be free to be children whose key friendships could be freely formulated within our local body. They had accepted this and profited from it. Now we were asking them to leave what they'd grown to love, and they weren't buying it. Not for a moment!

That was many years ago. Today, as I've said, our children are grown, married, and parents themselves several times over. Both they, their spouses, and children are integral members of congregations, serving in numbers of ways. They pursue faith-centered lives, and we could not be more grateful. Nothing brings more satisfaction to our hearts than knowing that they each desire to love and obey God—a tribute to his grace and kindness.

Today I'm a grandmother who looks back and once again recounts the principles of parenting that we followed in our pastoral home. Each has stood the test of time, and there are few changes I would make if we had it to do all over again.

℃ Our Family Comes First

"What's more important: my family or the Lord's work?" Gordon had once asked an old pastor when we were just starting our family. "Your family *is* the Lord's work," the old man had said sharply, almost as if the question were impertinent.

Gordon had been rocked by the obviousness of the response, had brought it back to me, and we adopted it as our key operating principle of family life. *Our family would come first in the so-called Lord's work.* Home would be the place where we would sharpen our relational skills. What happened in the congregation would only be an overflow of what was being practiced at home.

The implications? As keeper of the calendar, I made sure that family events got placed there far in advance of all other activities beyond the home. A decided asset to pastoral life is the fluid schedule that allows for participation in afternoon activities *if* they have been placed in the calendar ahead of time. Many men and women in industry don't have such freedoms—something our children learned to value about ministry.

We were able to be at school events where parents were invited, on the sidelines of games, and in the audience at performances. We arranged our days so that one of us was at home when the children arrived from school. We committed to eating dinner together at least four out of seven evenings. And when at the table, we were open to almost any topic of conversation.

Both Gordon and I remember a Friday afternoon when Kristy was playing her first year of organized soccer. Her coach, a somewhat young and immature high school athlete, had shifted Kristy from her normal position as a halfback to the fullback defensive position. A ball bounced down the field through several stumbling players. Kristy moved to her right to kick it. Just as she pulled her leg back, the goalie yelled at her to let it go, but she couldn't quite check her kick. The ball caromed off her foot, past the goalie's hands, and into the net, a goal for the other team.

Kids can be cruel. Gordon and I watched as some of the girls on the team rushed back to where Kristy was standing in shock. "You jerk, you've lost the game for us!" someone shouted. The coach, using the break in the game to change players, unwisely substituted someone else for Kristy, compounding her humiliation. We watched her run dejectedly toward the sidelines. Then suddenly her eye caught her father's, and she veered in his direction. Burying her face in his stomach, she sobbed, "I didn't mean to do it."

Gordon and I looked at each other as if to ask, "To whom would she have run if we had not been here?" Of the twenty-two players on the field, only four or five had parental spectators on the sidelines to witness the good and bad moments of play, to share the ups and downs of their worlds. How grateful we were to have a flexible enough lifestyle that made it possible to be two of the five.

Home: A Place of Fun and Thankfulness

For the family to come first in our ministry meant that we gave heavy attention to prevailing attitudes in our home. An enthusiastic outlook on life is no accident. We work at it relentlessly. Our goal: a home marked with anticipation, with a sense of excitement and fun, and with feelings of genuine accomplishment.

It may seem that I'm stretching a point, but I thought it important to set this priority of enthusiasm in motion when our children were still in their cribs. As infants awakening from their sleep, they were greeted with a song and a smile.

And while it didn't always work, I tried to assure that mealtimes would be punctuated with lightness and appreciation. Harsh words or critical attitudes were simply not welcomed at our table, and we made that very plain. We made frequent use of our version of an "instant replay."

If a grouchy or critical Mark or Kristy entered the kitchen and grumbled, "Are we having *that* again for supper?" he or she might be asked to leave the kitchen. "Now what I want you to do is come back in and say (with ultra-dramatic gestures and exaggerated enthusiasm), 'Oh, boy! We get to have that again for supper!'" Negative attitudes and critical spirits usually succumbed to laughter through such instant replays. In game-playing of that sort, our children learned a better way.

It helps if humor plays a significant role in pastoral families because all too often we are dreadfully serious. I used to love preparing suppers I called, "Italy Nights." No offense to Italians, but I wanted the lights dimmed to resemble a romantic table setting. But the reason for low light had nothing to do with romance and everything to do with the fact that I was serving leftovers. That way nobody could see them! It was great comic relief—especially when it was the third night on the same casserole. Shame on me.

We moms need attitude adjustments, too. One young mom who was good at details told me that she had to watch her critical spirit toward her pastor-husband when he forgot to bring in a piece of equipment he had used while playing with their children. Instead of being thankful that he took the time to play with them, she was dwelling on what he didn't do. A misguided response that any of us might have. Attitudes need monitoring all around the family if the children are going to learn the right ones.

We also placed a high premium on the spirit of thankfulness. We wanted Kristy and Mark to see everything good as a gift from God. "Leftovers" for supper, bargain-basement clothing, the gift of a second-hand bike: *all abundance from heaven*, never to be taken for granted.

Such a spirit of thankfulness, it seems to me, is likely to create a corresponding spirit of generosity. A child is given a wristwatch as a gift. The question then emerges: To whom shall he/she give the old watch? Why shouldn't he be encouraged to pray and to ask the Lord to bring the name of a person to mind who would benefit from such a gift? It was very important to Gordon and me that Kristy and Mark not see ministry life as always receiving. We would encourage every possible opportunity for them to experience the joys of giving as well.

I remember those times when I felt that all of us were flagging in our attitude of thankfulness. Concerned that we faced the problem squarely, I set up a "thankfulness jar". Each time someone did some-thing for another, we wrote it on a piece of paper and dropped it into the jar. At the end of the week, we opened the jar and read what had been deposited. We shared a special time while recalling the hidden and quiet things that we'd done for each other. This renewed our spirit of gratitude while having fun.

❖ CONSISTENCY

Not long ago, Eringail, our eldest grandchild, came to visit in our home for the day. As we settled into conversation over milk and cookies, she called me by the name our grandchildren have assigned to me. "Guya, do you have rules in your house? We have rules in my house. I can't say *shut up*, *stupid*, or *hate*. Do you have a rule like that?"

I laughed. "Where do you think your daddy got that rule, sweetheart? That was a rule in our house when he was a little boy." I couldn't help but be pleased that the attitudes we'd taught in our home twenty-five years ago were being passed on to another generation.

Eringail's comment caused me to think of how important the principle of *consistency* had been to us. Our code had been, *Have a few universal rules of behavior and stick to them.* Teach them, model them, and assure constant, not spotty, compliance. The schedule in the home of a pastor can become irregular; children can get uncertain signals about what is expected of them. Consistency, no matter what, is all important.

One of the positive aspects about ministry is that our children get to see both parents at work. Is how they see us at home the same as at church? We often gave our children permission to tell us if there were discrepancies here. After all, who of us doesn't have blind spots that we need others to point out to us?

❖ DISCIPLINE

A pastor's home needs consistency in terms of discipline, also. A friend whose siblings have all followed their parents into ministry once told us what he thought had been the key ingredient to the effectiveness of his mother and father. "We were taught," he said, "that *delayed obedience is disobedience*."

Apparently his folks did not believe in counting to five or ten when children were given instructions. They anticipated an immediate response and were consistent in that expectation. Our friend was emphatic that it had been the consistency and the discipline embedded in his father's expectations which had made it easier for him as an adult to obey his heavenly Father. Furthermore, there is a direct relationship between how we as parents obey God and how our children do. If they see us as authentic in our attempt to live in obedience, they will take courage to do the same.

In the semipublic home of a pastor, children need to learn who is in charge and whose word is final. That knowledge brings security, which in turn makes it easier for each one to grow. When the source of authority becomes uncertain or unclear children become uneasy and insecure.

I remember a soccer game in which our son once played. The referee had failed to appear by game time. Two college boys volunteered to officiate in his place. But soon they were in disagreement about the rules, uncertain as to when to blow the whistle, and quick to change their minds when someone protested a call.

That night I wrote about the game in my journal:

> What a lesson in leadership! Whistles were blown halfheartedly; the substitute "refs" could be talked out of a call; the boys played terribly; arguments broke out; one boy quit and walked off. A disaster! Having no one in charge meant that no one had a good time because anarchy broke out. Whether a game without a ref, a child without limits, or a church without a leader, the result is the same. Like this game, it is a sick reproduction of the real thing.

Because I'd been at the game, Mark and I had a good opportunity to discuss the "event." Subsequently, whenever he was tempted to resist authority in our family, I was able to remind him of that contest during which consistent authority had been nonexistent. It helped him get the point.

❧ OUR CHILDREN NEED TO BE PASTORED

I'm not sure where I first read it, but somehow a brief list of reasons why children in ministry homes may turn from faith came to my desk. Because it rings true with our experience, I include it because it is helpful to ask ourselves if any of these things are true in our homes. They are:

- Being duplistic—one person at home, another in public
- Complaining at home about the ministry
- Lack of unity between parents
- No interest in the child's world
- Church is perceived as more important than family life
- Consistency in discipline isn't necessarily acted upon

It is easy to forget, as we minister to the congregation, that our children also need to be pastored, to be given individual spiritual attention. When our Lord was trying to show his disciples the importance of children, he said:

> And whoever welcomes a little child like this in my name welcomes me. But if anyone causes one of these little ones who believe in me to sin, it would be better for him to have a large millstone hung around his neck and to be drowned in the depths of the sea. (Matt. 18:5–6)

Those are strong words. But within them lies the secret to loving even during times when mothering in a pastor's home might seem mundane or repetitive.

A mother of six children once said to me, "It takes maturity to deal with the obscurity of motherhood." She was right. And it also takes maturity to realize that Christ himself is in our children. It is Christ I am serving when I give my strength and affection to our son and our daughter.

Let's be honest. Sometimes we simply don't make being a Christ-follower appetizing. Ruth Graham writes of a time when her children were quite small:

> I remember one time when Bill was away. We had four children then, all terrible sleepers. I used to get up from three to seven times a night. I awoke one morning looking a wreck—hair a mess, no makeup. I grabbed my bathrobe. Franklin was a baby, and I didn't bother to change him; I just picked him up and plopped him in the high chair. And that morning every time Gigi, the oldest girl, started to say something, Bunny, the youngest girl, interrupted her. Finally Gigi slammed down her fork and said, "Mother, between looking at you, smelling Franklin, and listening to Bunny, I'm just not hungry."[1]

A woman who raised five sons and daughters, all of whom went into Christian ministry, once told me that she believed that *her gift to the world* was to raise children in whose hearts Christ would be Lord. What a powerful sense of mission for any woman to have. Another ministry wife, whose two sons also entered Christian service, saw it this way: "As a mother, I am a discipler of children. My husband is out discipling men and women. I'm discipling our children." Both women contributed to my own sense of mission as to how our children would be pastored.

In the years before Mark and Kristy left home, my mission as a mother was to prepare our children to be all that God intended them to be in their generation and to release them to his guidance at the proper time. While I wanted to serve people in the name of Jesus, the children came first in this effort. They were my primary disciples.

I can still clearly remember how hard those so-called irrational years were when they were small. Like all mothers, I knew the many times of weariness when all the best intentions of parental discipleship were close to being forgotten.

A journal entry reflects one of those disheartening hours:

> I feel as if so much of my time is spent in doing nothing but saying no to the children. I wish I could see myself as Mrs. Brady on the *Brady Bunch* television program. But all too often I find myself looking like an ogre or some sort of Simon Legree. That discourages me. When will the day of response take place? And when will I be able to reason with the children instead of always seeming to say no to them?

All of us lose our capacities to see the finished products from time to time. But I recovered from those dark times. A nudge from *somewhere* would get me up and going again, and soon I would regain my enthusiasm for helping our children pursue a vision of Christlikeness. That, after all, is the goal of any discipleship or pastoring process.

"Hold a crown a few inches above your children's heads, and then watch them grow into it," someone has said. I love that word picture. We produce what we believe in. If our relationships to our children are strong, then when they have to be disciplined, they will try harder the next time—not because of any rule but because being loved, trusted, and believed in brings out the best in each of us.

I often recall the patience with which Jesus treated his disciples when they turned out to be as obstinate as our children could some times be. Over and over I would renew my resolve to be to Mark and Kristy what Jesus was to the twelve. The fact is that he loved them, prayed for them, disciplined them, encouraged them, believed in them, and then released them to service in his kingdom. He believed that they would eventually get it right, and that was the same long view that kept me going in our home. Today I am delighted to be reaping the benefits of those efforts.

EIGHT

PKS CAN BE OK

Part Two

The things revealed belong to us and to our children forever, that
we may follow all the words of this law.   *(Deut. 29:29)*

A few days ago I overheard our now-long-married son Mark on
the phone with a person who was obviously troubled. I couldn't
hear the other end of the conversation, but I was aware of Mark's
responses and his questions. I was impressed with how much his words
emulated both his father's way and mine in similar conversations.

And then it dawned on me: *All those years he'd been in our home
as a growing boy, he'd been formulating these processes of leadership,
perhaps without even being aware that he was doing it.* What he was
doing was the perfect example of the objective of what they call *discipleship*: being present to a learner as a model, as a listener, and as an
encourager. The disciple literally "catches" or imitates the motivations,
convictions, and lifestyle of the discipler—*if* he finds it appealing and
consistent.

Allow me to elaborate on a few more of the themes that
marked our parenting years and in retrospect seemed to make the
most difference.

∾ LISTENING

We all take for granted that listening is a key principle in marital relationships. But let me highlight *that listening to our children is of paramount importance when it comes to raising children in a pastor's home.*

In ministry we have to listen to everybody. But that doesn't mean that all pastors know how to listen to their children. The youngsters see their father stand in the front of a church sanctuary, shake hands, smile, and focus on anyone who seeks him out. Do they feel as if they get the same treatment?

In a home which is often in public view, it is extremely important to be sensitive to those times which my husband calls "open-window moments," when a child snaps up the shade that is over his or her heart and lets you take a peek inside.

"Open-window moments" can come at rather predictable times —during sickness, mounting pressures at school, a time of failure with friends, exhilaration, mealtimes, or bedtimes. If we as parents have open ears, we may hear some wonderful insights or searching questions from our children.

When Kristy was seven, she had long blond hair that easily tangled because of the overly active play life she pursued. One night when she was trying to get to sleep, I sat on the edge of her bed and rubbed her back, a tradition started when she was younger. She observed, "You know, Mom, tangles in your hair are like sin."

"Oh?" I responded. "In what way?"

"Well, both hurt when you try to get rid of them. But if you don't get rid of them quickly, they can really mess things up, and they get harder and harder to comb out."

It was a sermon I'd never have to preach to her. She'd said it all herself, and by sharing it with me, we both knew that she had a sense of the importance of short accounts when it came to dealing with sin in her life.

No baby-sitter would have appreciated the importance of that moment between a mother and daughter. Some would say that there are better things for a woman to be doing with her time. But today I'm twenty-five years past that unforgettable moment, and I still can't think of anything that could have been more significant than being there that night to hear her insight.

When Kristy was a young teenager, she had to make an important decision. It was an open-window moment. We wanted her to know that we trusted her judgment, but we also wanted to be available as sounding boards if she needed us. I watched my husband handle the situation, and I learned from it. There had come a point in the process of decision making when he realized that she did not have the accumulated years of wisdom to make up her own mind. She was feeling peer pressure, and the battle was on between *her* convictions and *their* opinions.

Father and daughter sat talking in the living room. Then Gordon asked, "Honey, do you think of yourself as an oak tree or a tulip?"

"What do you mean?" she asked.

"Well, an oak tree can be fully grown and strong, so big that people are forced to walk around it. No one steps on an oak. But a tulip can also be grown up; nevertheless, it's vulnerable. A tulip is beautiful to look at, of course; but it can be stepped on and destroyed easily. Which do you think you are in this decision: an oak tree or a tulip?"

A minute or two passed. And then, she said, "I'm a tulip, Daddy, and you know it." And there was the beginning of tears.

It was an important moment for Kristy and her father. He and I had always assumed that she saw herself as strong and impervious to any outside pressure. Now she was admitting that she wasn't—at least at that moment.

"Sometimes, tulips need a fence to be built around them to protect them so that they can continue to grow," Gordon suggested. "Perhaps this is one of those times when God has given you a father to be like a fence, and the best way I can protect you is to tell you what I think the wisest decision would be, although in the final analysis you'll have to make it for yourself."

Kristy saw the wisdom of her father's proposal and subsequently embraced it. Once again both he and I saw the importance of our being in a place where we could listen and ask questions that would draw out cries for help.

Some years later this conversation came back to bless Gordon as he stood with Kristy in the lobby of Grace Chapel. He was about to walk her down the aisle where she would meet Tom and exchange wedding vows. Gordon was clearly rattled. He worried about not keeping his emotions in check, anxious that somehow he might botch up that part of the ceremony where he would be presiding.

Kristy, sensitive to her father's discomfort, put her arm through his and said, "Come on, Daddy; you're acting like a tulip, but I'm an oak tree today. And I've got enough strength for both of us."

Because of the busyness of a pastoral lifestyle in which telephones intrude and people yell for attention, it is emphatically important that a husband and a wife committed to ministry also take prime time to listen to what their children are saying and, of course, to *what they're not saying*.

☙ SERVING

What better place to learn to *serve* than at home—especially if your parents lead others to minister? Mark and Kristy are aware of a number of people who have been introduced to Jesus Christ in our home. They understand that changed lives do not come through preaching sterile theology but rather through learning to love people in practical ways.

Gordon and I sought to teach the principle of servanthood first of all in the maintenance of our home. That principle started with simple jobs our children could do at the ages of three and four. We insisted that bedrooms be straightened on a daily basis, clothes folded, the dishwasher emptied, and the dog fed. Certain hallways and rooms of the house were vacuumed; trash from all the wastebaskets was collected. These chores were done equally by both our son and our daughter. It was important, for example, for our Mark to understand—as his father believes—that there is no such thing as "women's work." It is all servants' work, and servants of Christ do it in order to serve one another.

I'd be dishonest if I conveyed the idea that our children always did this gladly. When Mark discovered that he was the only boy in the seventh grade who was doing the sort of things that he did before leaving for school, he suggested the possibility that perhaps his parents were a bit unjust.

As I listened to his protestations, it occurred to me that his opinion was the result not only of what he'd learned about his peers but also because I had not affirmed or thanked him for his work in the past weeks. We sat down together, and I reminded him that because he did his chores, I was free to accomplish certain other things that he enjoyed my doing—such as being in attendance when he played soccer. I shocked him by informing him that I really didn't love ironing, washing, and picking up, either. The fact was, I said, that I did those things because I loved him and enjoyed serving him. Our conversation made a big difference in his attitude.

But servanthood is most exciting when the family enters a serving experience and shares in the fruits of accomplishment. I think something like that happened years ago when we decided to build Peace Ledge, our New Hampshire retreat.

In 1978, Gordon took a summer sabbatical leave. Along with the generous help of a friend who is a contractor, we decided to build a retirement home in New Hampshire.

Whenever possible, the children were alongside us, helping to build. One day a young man drove up from Boston to help us install the kitchen cabinets. So he wouldn't have to make the long return trip the next day for another day's work, we invited him to stay overnight.

Almost immediately we noticed that he was in a very restless state. It wasn't long before he was sharing with us at the table some of the confusion in his life. Later, after supper, as he continued to talk with Gordon, Mark pulled me aside in the kitchen and said, "Mom, he's going to receive Christ if we give him a chance. Let's get out of Dad's way and see what happens."

Kristy, Mark, and I disappeared into the bedroom, knelt, and prayed for Dad and the young man who had come to our country cabin. It wasn't long before Mark cracked the door open a bit and listened. His face lit up. "Hey, God answered our prayers! The guy's asking Christ into his life right now."

And so he was. Later the children found a Bible they thought the cabinetmaker could use and presented it to him with their own note of Christian best wishes inside. The entire experience was a truly meaningful family exercise in servanthood.

You might call the pastor's home a difficult place to raise children, but I wouldn't trade the possibilities it presents since it gives us such varied and effective opportunities to demonstrate to our children what Christian living and ministry are all about. Servanthood is certainly one lesson easily learned if the family members want to teach one another.

❦ COMMUNICATION

I was troubled one day when the son of a preacher we know said to Gordon and me, "The only time I ever really hear my father speak is when he's behind the pulpit. At home he's a virtual recluse." A comment like that makes me realize how important it is to make sure that our homes are a place of warm communication.

"Reach out and touch someone," the phone company once advised. And in no place is that sort of thing more important than in the home of people in Christian leadership.

As in the marital relationship, it's all too easy for parents and children to let our communication with one another fall into a state of disrepair. It is not enough to talk about events and people. Someone has said that most people talk about people, and a few people talk about events. But, the observation went on, healthy and mature people talk about ideas, dreams, and visions and, might I add, matters of faith.

It's hard work, I discovered as a mother and a wife, to keep a family with teenagers together for meals. I'm alarmed that many homes have given up and permit each member to grab food for a meal as he or she can. A mother must often take the initiative when future schedules look destructive to family times. By planning ahead before we get into the middle of such busy periods, we can often avoid the drift or the conflicts which may occur from a lack of communication. If planning does not come naturally to you as a mom, this may be an important area to develop beyond your comfort zone.

I would be kidding myself if I tried to convince anyone that our mealtimes were always successful. Which of us in the MacDonald family did not at some point bring a "down" mood to the table that everyone caught before the meal was over? Like every mother, I know the sickening feeling which comes when I prepared a special meal in anticipation of the joy it would bring my family, only to see the lovely experience collapse due to the uncooperative attitude of a family member.

Since I'm prone to generalize about one bad moment and think it to be a sign of total family disaster, my husband patiently reminded me that every home has an occasional negative encounter. And ours was no exception.

But for all the bad moments, there were certainly many good ones. We tried to end many of our dinners with a time of reflection and devotions. If we had problems during the meal, Gordon might suggest that we meet later after things had cooled off. There were many nights when either the schedule or the situation didn't seem conducive to specific devotional exercises.

When we had periods of worship together, however, they were often rich memories for our family. Bible readings, a passage from a Christian book, and conversational prayer were usually part of our togetherness. Sometimes we would simply have an intense discussion that highlighted a Christian value. Not infrequently, our prayers were interrupted by impromptu laughter due to any number of gaffes or slips of the tongue. We elected never to be overly disturbed by prayers or quiet moments which didn't make it to the "Amen." "Perhaps," we reasoned, "God enjoys laughter just as much as we do."

Now, twenty years later, when Gordon and I talk with our adult children about their fondest memories of childhood, it is impressive to me how often they point back to mealtimes and family conversations.

Family traditions also aid in communication. We've enjoyed reading books together on trips or attacking jigsaw puzzles together during school vacations. By the way, many of our completed jigsaw puzzles have then been pasted to boards, framed, and hung in our home as a reminder of family cooperation and shared memories. Other traditions include: pizza on Saturday nights, ice cream sundaes or popcorn after church on Sunday nights, family basketball games in which Mother was allowed to play dirty, and an automatic stopover at Dunkin' Donuts each time we traveled to our retreat in New Hampshire.

Communication takes work. Who knows when an opportunity for it will occur? One day Mark and one of his friends joined Gordon in the woods for a day of cutting timber for the next winter's firewood. A dull chain saw blade became the center of their attention. As Gordon taught the two boys how to sharpen the chain saw cutters, it became a perfect moment for showing how a dull cutting edge can cause needless work and waste precious time. He observed that a dull inner spirit, impervious to the voice of God, can cause a young man to waste a lot of time making mistakes and reaping consequences he wouldn't have had to face. We called such times "teachable moments," and took advantage of them whenever they arose.

⟳ RESOLVING CONFLICT

Conflicts and misunderstandings are a part of all relationships. They simply cannot be avoided. If they are, it is usually a sign that something is seriously wrong with the communication. The critical question is not whether conflict should exist in a family but rather how it will be resolved. Conflict always creates a delicate situation in relationships; it has to be dealt with wisely.

We have seen the effects on children when a father or a mother leaves home after an unresolved verbal brawl and goes to minister in the congregation. I'm personally convinced that unresolved conflict under those conditions will quickly cause children to develop a cynical attitude about the nature of Christian faith.

When our children were very young, we entertained a family of professional Christian musicians in our home. I was greatly impressed with the quality of their family life: the level of respect that the children had for each other, the affection and regard that passed between the parents and children. When I had the chance, I asked the mother what she thought was the most important principle behind the development of this remarkable family.

The answer? A relentless pursuit of the forgiving spirit. "If any of the children got into a conflict with someone else in the family, I insisted that they stop, look each other in the eye, and quote Ephesians 4:32:

> Be kind and compassionate to one another, forgiving each other,
> just as in Christ God forgave you.

"They were then to hug one another and say, 'I'm sorry; I was wrong.' I would not rest until this had happened," she said.

That family made a tremendous impact upon me. I determined that we also would be a family of peacemakers through forgiveness and reconciliation.

There were those occasions when our family needed peacemaking badly. I recall the day we were on our way to church. We'd had a terrible start to the morning, and none of us was speaking to each other. The question we had to face was obvious: *How can we, the pastor's family, go to church in such a state of heart and mind?*

Gordon pulled over to the side of the road where each of us looked each other in the eye and said, "I'm sorry; I was wrong." And we had a good laugh over it. In so doing, we made our peace as a family before we entered the house of God.

If we want to teach our children to apologize and to forgive, we must do it ourselves. I often found that hard to do since in my younger years I equated an admission of being wrong with imperfection. But little by little, thanks to the modeling of my husband, I learned the importance of being broken before the Lord and before my family. When I made a mistake, my children needed to hear me admit that I had been wrong and needed their forgiveness. When I acknowledged my weakness before them in that tender moment, I was able to show them that I also am in the process of maturing as a Christian—just as they are. I wanted them to know that I am a real person, not a plastic one. Real people make many mistakes. And godly people forgive those mistakes.

ᕫ One More Bonus of Pastoral Life

One of the great bonuses of being in a pastor's home is the opportunity to meet unusual people. Since our parsonages lacked guest rooms, it was often necessary for one of our children to vacate his or her room and temporarily move to the basement.

I am not aware that this ever caused resentment, since most of our visitors went out of their way to express gratitude to our children. There were special times when persons of great repute in the Christian world joined our table for dinner, and our children had the chance to get to know them. Such times gave Mark and Kristy the opportunity to see godliness up close and not simply behind the pulpit.

Perhaps no one person made more of an impression upon our children than Dr. John Stott. He made it a point to greet our children by name and with an embrace. Once, when Mark was a boy, Dr. Stott stayed with us for several nights. As was the custom, Mark turned over his room to Dr. Stott and moved to the basement.

Some weeks later, Mark received a letter postmarked from London. The first paragraph read:

Dear Mark,

Many thanks for the use of your room as a place to both sleep and study. I shall remember you as my good friend and keep you in my prayers.

Yours,
Uncle John

That letter remained on our son's bulletin board for a long time. When Mark heard others speak of John Stott, he enjoyed the quiet satisfaction that the great English preacher was his friend. We grow under such circumstances, and a pastor's home makes that kind of opportunity possible.

In studying the Gospel of John, I was once struck with the phrase "the disciples remembered." Such remembering occurs only when information has been both taught and heard during earlier teachable moments. Years later when the disciples faced unprecedented challenges, they were able to look back and remember the things the Lord Jesus had taught them through his words and his own example. They knew exactly how to act as a result. There were very few surprises.

That is exactly what we were trying to do as we raised a couple of young PKs in our home. We wanted them to store away memories so that they could draw upon them when they were on their own and had to face the moral and spiritual decisions from which no one is forever protected. We were hoping that they would remember moments in our home when they saw us serving hurting people. We were trusting that they would remember how we stayed close to them when they were defeated or felt rejected by someone in their own world.

We were anxious for them to remember particular patterns of response, insights, answers, affirmations, and convictions discovered and applicable to their own future. In short, we could only pray that our children had seen Christ in our home and that they, too, would remember when the time came for them to accept responsibility for all their actions.

When John wrote to Gaius, he said:

> I have no greater joy than to hear that my children are walking in the truth. (3 John 1:4)

He, of course, referred to spiritual children, but I did not hesitate to claim the same words for Mark and Kristy whom the Lord gave to Gordon and me. They were our number one ministry, and our lives before them were definitely the Lord's work.

NINE

THE JOURNEY CONTINUES

Becoming Yankees

There was a day when I died, utterly died—died to George
Mueller, his opinions, preferences, tastes and will!—died to the
world, its approval or censure—died to the approval or blame
even of my brethren or friends—and since then I have studied
only to show myself approved unto God.   —*George Mueller*

In the summer of 1972, we visited Grace Chapel in the town of
Lexington, Massachusetts. It was the third time in our lives that
we'd entered the candidating process.

The weekend had been relatively pressure free, probably due to
the fact that neither Gordon nor I had felt constrained to impress
anyone. A quiet inner confidence had come, I believe, from the Holy
Spirit so that we were able to leave the results of the weekend to the
Lord. Three days later the outcome became evident. The call was
enthusiastic, and so was our acceptance.

The next day we immediately embarked upon the bittersweet
experience of disengaging from one congregation which we greatly
loved while entering a new relationship with people we looked forward to serving.

When you are happy where you are, a pastoral resignation is an
emotional experience. As I've said before, good-byes are difficult. We

had to leave people who remain our friends to this day. And we knew it was important that we make it clear that once we were gone, the people of First Baptist Church in Collinsville would have to look to other spiritual leaders and give them the love and the loyalty that they had once given us. For some people, especially those for whom we had become spiritual parents, that was a hard thing to do.

When we left Collinsville, we purposely reserved several weeks to ourselves in order to "drop out." Friends made a cottage available to us by the shore of Lake Erie in Ohio, and we used their generous gift as a place to read, to talk, to pray, and to enjoy an extended and rare privacy with our children. We could feel the hand of God upon our lives, filling us more and more each day with new energy and expectation about the future.

Gordon and I immersed ourselves in the Scriptures and the writings of Elton Trueblood, A. W. Tozer, Paul Tournier, Dietrich Bonhoeffer, and E. Stanley Jones. Each of them had much to give us, especially since our anticipation and excitement had become slightly tempered with an awareness that New England was not the easiest place in which to launch a pastoral ministry.

We looked backwards to appraise the Collinsville ministry. It was good for me to confess to Gordon and the Lord that I knew I was one of the reasons we'd left Collinsville. I had become exhausted from allowing the expectations of others to control me. I needed to become a quieter person, living at a slower pace. And I needed to enhance my spiritual disciplines by becoming a deeper student of the Scriptures and great Christian thinkers.

I came to feel a bond with Sarah Edwards, wife of Jonathan Edwards, who had known similar struggles. Her biographer, Elizabeth Dodds, writes: "One hurdle Sarah still had to surmount was her need to be liked by everyone." Sarah and I could have had some good talks about a common weakness.[1]

Looking ahead, we'd heard frightening stories about New England. Some called it the "graveyard of ministers". One famous preacher had written that New England churches were so cold that one could ice-skate down the center aisle on a Sunday morning. The coldness he referred to had nothing to do with physical temperature. The liberal, secular attitudes in the public school system tempted us to be anxious about the influences our children would face when they entered school in the fall.

Had we made a mistake? Collinsville, after all, had been a comfortable place for our family. Would New England indeed be our graveyard, the place of failure for our family? Would we be accepted, or would people scorn our Midwestern background?

After the respite on Lake Erie, we drove eastward with a mixture of hope and apprehension. Gordon and I knew we were entering a congregation that had deeply loved its former pastor. He had been there for ten years and had, along with his wife, served the people well. When they'd left, more than one person had asked whether the church could actually survive. Now, in our wistful moments, we were tempted to ask whether that former pastor's shoes could be filled. Would the church accept new leadership? Would we come out on the short end of constant comparisons?

This was a new state of affairs for us since in the previous two congregations the preceding pastors had left under duress and friction. It had thus been relatively easy for the people to respond to us out of a desire to forget their past. Things were different now.

But love comes in unlimited quantities, I concluded. If the Grace Chapel congregation had loved its former pastor, it probably had enough love left over for us. Moreover, if we set out to pursue the same approach we had at Collinsville—loving people unconditionally and affirming their past and present—perhaps the new people would begin to respond to us and love us, too.

By the time we spotted the Entering Lexington sign signaling the end of our long trip, the Lord had graciously put our minds at rest and had convinced us that he had everything under control. Our children would be safe as long as we maintained our family disciplines. New England would not become our "graveyard" provided we maintained our spiritual disciplines. And, yes, the congregation would receive us if we concentrated on being true to the biblical disciplines of ministry. As for myself? I need not turn out to be like the snapshot that Howard Hendricks once described as "overexposed and underdeveloped." I would keep determined to say healthy no's when tempted to get involved in too much, and I would continue to develop my quieter, more reflective side.

Charles H. MacKintosh understood something of these anxieties when he wrote:

Happy the man who ministers (Christ), whatever be the success or reception of his ministry. For should the ministry fail to attract attention, to command influence, or to produce apparent results, he has his sweet retreat and his unfailing portion in Christ, of which nothing can deprive him. Whereas, the man who is merely feeding upon the fruit of his ministry, who delights in the gratification which it affords, or the attention and interest which it commands, is like a mere pipe, conveying water to others, and retaining only rust in itself. There is a most deplorable condition of every servant who is more occupied with his work and its results, than with the Master and His glory.[2]

God responded to our prayers in several ways and gently addressed those fears which we, or anyone, might bring into a new situation.

Take our concern for our children and their experience in public school. Two days after we were settled in our new home, the principal at Mark and Kristy's school invited them to visit their schoolrooms before classes began in a few weeks. Gordon looked at me in amazement. "Think of it!" he said, putting down the phone. "We thought this was going to be a depersonalized school system, and the principal calls and issues a personal invitation to come down to the school."

The following day Gordon and the children visited the school and discovered that the principal was a Christian layman. He had been eager to make our children's entrance into the new school as trouble free as possible. That evening we were moved to great thanksgiving as we realized that God had spoken directly to our fears about Mark and Kristy's education. They went on to have the finest public school experience we could have asked for. In effect, the Lord was saying, "See, your times are in my hands; trust me."

If New England was a cold region, especially in the churches, we certainly didn't see it. Right away Grace Chapel began moving along with Gordon's approach and his emphasis upon celebrative worship, relationships and Christian character building. Services were marked with silence and reverence, laughter and holy joy. Attendance at the various services began to increase almost immediately. Sundays were times of great jubilation.

On one of the very first Sundays, Gordon was greeted at the back of the sanctuary by a young man with a solemn face. The wrinkled clothes, shaggy beard, and long hair frightened Gordon a bit, he later confessed. So bracing himself, he stuck out his hand and asked, "What can I do for you?"

"Did you mean what you said this morning?" the young man asked.

"What do you mean?" Gordon responded.

"About forgiveness . . . that we can come to God and find complete forgiveness and get right with him?"

"Absolutely," Gordon said.

"Then that's exactly what I want. How do I get it?"

Gordon could hardly believe what this representative of the counterculture was saying. Thirty minutes later the two of them were kneeling and praying about forgiveness—Gordon in a three-piece suit and this young, long-haired man whose name was Anthony.

A few weeks later Gordon married Anthony and his girlfriend, Chris. Today they are still active members of the Grace Chapel family. We watched them grow spiritually and raise a beautiful family of their own. Recently, we took them out to dinner to celebrate their twenty-fifth wedding anniversary. Such experiences make long-term pastorates a delight.

When we pursue the goal of God's approval as leaders, we begin to learn that there is a high cost to pay. Women who want to enjoy the privileges of leadership must simply face that fact. Leadership is never cheap. We mustn't deceive ourselves about this.

When David, king of Israel, wanted to establish a place of worship and dedicate it to God for the benefit of his people, he was offered a free plot of land. The Bible says that he refused to accept it as a gift because he knew that he couldn't offer the Lord something that had cost him nothing. Thus he made sure that the land was paid for properly.

Jesus highlighted the principle of costs when he pointed out the gift of the widow at the temple offering box. He also made note of the boy who'd brought a small lunch to a large gathering and offered it for everyone to eat. Of Mary's sacrificial gift, he said, "She has done a beautiful thing to me" (Mark 14:6).

In each case, Christ was not concerned about the exact value of the gift. What impressed him was what it had cost the person who gave it.

The privilege of being leaders in a congregation like Grace Chapel means counting the cost. Dale Evans Rogers once wrote:

It is my conviction that when one chooses to live a public life in any profession, one should first count the cost of living such a life and not whimper at its pressures.[3]

During the thirty-eight years I have been in ministry, I have had frequent conversations with women who hadn't counted the cost before they faced these realities. Among those have been women whose husbands decided to enter the ministry after a number of years in the business world. For such wives the rules of the game seemed to change abruptly, and they often followed their husbands unaware of the real cost. I also know some women who refuse to pay the price, and they go through each day kicking and screaming. Some pursue their own careers while others become increasingly embittered about a lifestyle that they never bargained for. One such woman wrote:

> I resent the people who need my husband. I used to be the consummate people person. Now I'm "peopled" out, and I resent that my personality has changed. I often long to be part of a "normal" family.

I have also known those who have struggled with the cost and have chosen to pay it. This is not to say that everything became tranquil for them, only that in the midst of the situation they began to grow. I don't minimize the fact that pain is involved in answering the call to leadership. The fact is, we follow a Savior who knew suffering intimately and warned his followers to prepare themselves for it.

Although in Collinsville I had made a major error by not sharing the ministry with others, in Lexington, all of that changed. Before, I had failed to trust others adequately. Why? Because my standards had been so high that I'd felt compelled to do most things all by myself. That was wrong! At Grace Chapel I was surrounded by highly competent people. It was important that I free them to use their gifts and capabilities. Often I only had to step out of the way.

Sharing the load meant ceasing to be a lone wolf and becoming a team person. We saw its delights and stresses first in the area of our pastoral staff. As the congregation began to enjoy fast growth, the pastoral staff had to expand with more men and women who could pick up the load. One of Gordon's heaviest responsibilities came in choosing people to be part of that team. A wrong choice could cause enormous challenges.

Soon my husband had a growing number of pastors and specialists for whom he felt responsible. Just being a spiritual and administrative leader to this group, including spouses and children, was a full time job. It changed his entire view of what the pastoral ministry was all about.

Both Gordon and I had to make many adjustments over this period. Some of them frankly were uncomfortable. There was always the Corinthian hazard. That's when members of the congregation pick their favorites among the staff (some are of Paul, some are of Apollos . . .). There was the potential of disagreement as temperaments, convictions, and work styles came into confluence in the daily work. And there was always the challenge of continual communication of vision, direction, and priority.

Gordon often found that the extra responsibility caused him to withdraw from contact with some in the congregation. Finding an appropriate balance was a challenge, and neither he nor I was sure that we achieved it. If we tilted our attention toward the congregation, the staff felt neglected. But if we inclined toward the staff, parts of the congregation soon protested.

For me the challenge came in learning how and if to become a friend to each staff member's spouse. Some of them wanted to be part of the ministry; others did not. Some were responsive to my offer of friendship and spiritual leadership; others preferred their distance. I could fill a chapter describing both the joys and the disappointments of this effort. No one had trained either Gordon or me for this kind of shepherding, and we had to feel our way through the process. We still are.

Because all of us lack complete insight into one another, we quickly learned that conflicts and misunderstandings could arise among us. Something said in a casual moment could be misinterpreted. An administrative decision which might be contrary to the desires of a staff pastor could easily alter the relationship between me and the wife of the man involved. It was hard for me to learn how to relate, knowing all the time that Gordon had to be involved in sound administration and accountability.

Whenever I am asked to speak to young women whose husbands are headed toward staff ministries, I urge them not to influence their husbands in directions that cause disloyalty to the pastoral team or its leader. I know something about the kind of support the leader of a pastoral staff desperately needs. When there is a difficult moment, a staff wife usually hears only one side of any problem, and she can easily be tempted to take a resistant or even resentful attitude toward a team leader. If she does this, her husband is likely to pick it up. The results will soon be felt on the team.

The time and affection we have put into these relationships has mattered, and we don't regret the priority we have placed on it. No situation is ever perfect, but for the most part, we have found the staff has worked hard to come to unity within diversity.

Because I finally learned the joy of sharing the load with others, the work I did with women at Grace Chapel was pure delight. Choosing them, training them to facilitate small groups, being their teaching leader, encouraging and praying for them became a full-time job. Since our children were in school all day, I now had the freedom again to be involved in a major way. There are few things as exciting as helping others discover and use their spiritual gifts—giving themselves away and being blessed in return.

As the teaching ministry moved toward maturity, there came a moment, nine years later, when I chose to step aside and put everything in the hands of others. It wouldn't be honest to say it was an easy decision. But one of my operating principles for life helped me release it to those who could carry it to places I could not. And they did. The principle is: *Hold on to everything loosely; it's on loan. Nothing (including ministry) is owned.* "A man can receive only what is given him from heaven" (John 3:27).

Yes, there was loneliness, a sense of loss as I gave away this "ministry-child." Knowing that the women were moving ahead on their own each Tuesday morning and that I wasn't there had much the same feeling that I had when our children left home for college. There was grief. But the timing was right.

Another part of what the Lord taught us when we became Yankees was what I'll call the *shepherd's instinct.* A shepherd knows when his flock needs to be led to better feeding grounds, when the sheep must be protected from danger, and when it is time for changes to be made. We've learned the importance of sensing the moods that seem to permeate the congregation at different times of the year.

Gordon's journals have shown that our congregations have periods of emotional fluctuation just as individuals do. We noted, for instance, that February and March were particularly stressful months in New England. During the winter the temperatures are cold, and people have to work harder to keep themselves going in the routine of daily life. Harsh weather makes cars undependable; getting to work becomes a daily challenge. Older people are often on edge due to the risk of falling on ice or problems engendered by snow shoveling or colder temperatures. All of this raises stress levels.

According to his biographer, the great New England pastor of the eighteenth century, Jonathan Edwards, hit terrible personal "lows" in the month of March. We understand his struggle 250 years later. That's why it is important to remind the congregation of what is ahead so that people can understand why the spiritual, emotional, and relational struggles of winter take their toll. Shepherds watch out for things like that.

Shepherds also have to *lead people through experiences of change*—especially those which are challenging or painful. Change is a part of life. And that is certainly true for churches. But for New Englanders, change is a struggle. We often find ourselves serving the "people who never left." Folks who embraced change went West, pioneering new worlds. Those who stayed, refusing to move away from the familiar, have also often embraced status quo—in and out of the congregation.

So doesn't a growing church delight everyone? No! More than one young pastor has resigned from a church because his leadership has drawn people into the fellowship, but he was not allowed to shepherd the "old timers" to cope with the continuing changes of a growing congregation. It's an enormous and often complex challenge to keep the two groups together.

Gordon and I tried to let the people at Grace Chapel know that change through growth was painful for us, too. I suspect that many felt that we naturally rejoiced in the growing numbers of people coming through the doors. To some extent we did, since it meant that the world around us was being reached in a small way. But Gordon and I were also frustrated trying to know so many people. Because of the limits on our time and our capacity, we often went away from worship with the feeling that we let somebody down.

At one point, we invited everyone who had been at the chapel before 1972 (when we first arrived) to come for an evening of fellowship. We had a wonderful time of reminiscence while reminding the "old-timers" that we missed them and the years when everyone knew each other's names. It was an important night for all.

During our years at Grace, I also learned that the shepherding instinct includes the development of a *calming influence among people*. When sheep are frightened by something unknown or mysterious, the shepherd has to move among them, restoring their sense of stability and serenity. A pastor and his wife can do that if they are sensitive.

For instance, when death or resignations within the leadership occur, people become insecure and questioning. The wise pastor and spouse move among the congregation to bring hope and reassurance to troubled hearts. I ask questions about how someone is feeling about the changes and listen to his/her apprehensions. Many times all that is needed is simply being heard, expressing fears, and praying together. Other times, I might write a note with a Scripture reminding this person that "our times are in his hands." In some cases, I might make a cassette tape with soothing music that makes a statement of how much I care about a person's confusion or anxiety.

We once watched a high school basketball game where the coach of the opposing team lost his temper with the referee and the team was charged with a technical foul. His team soon absorbed the anxiety from the bench and before long the captain of the team had another technical foul. Slowly the squad disintegrated and the team ended up losing the game by a lopsided score. As we left the gym, Gordon and I commented on the graphic illustration of how a leader's mood can poison the demeanor of an entire group.

Conversely, I am impressed as I read of the time when Jesus stood among a crowd of Pharisees who had brought him an adulterous woman. The prevailing mood was hostile and revengeful, but Christ remained above the mood and slowed everything down by his silence. Stooping to write in the sand and remaining in total control of himself, he broke the momentum. When he was finished, the confrontation was diffused by a simple statement. The woman was restored rather than destroyed.

Jesus acted in a similar way in the Garden of Gethsemane when faced with his captors. While they were frenzied, his demeanor was calm and forthright. Even Peter forgot everything he'd been taught as he lashed out with his sword. He could serve as a negative model of the way many of us often act under relational stress. How important it is that a leader learn to develop a cool and determined manner in the midst of crisis. One or two calm persons in a crowd of frightened people can usually restore confidence and stability.

That principle came into play one evening when in the middle of a mother-daughter banquet, a friend came to tell me I had an emergency phone call from my parents. My brother's wife had just taken her life. I immediately thought of Jesus' response to Lazarus' death. No panic; no needless rush. I finished the evening with our daughter and then attended to plane arrangements. I remember being aware both of the power of sustaining grace and the eyes that were watching me as the evening progressed. Why ruin Kristy's moment with her mom? Was Christ in control or not?

After arriving at my brother's home where he and his large family were in deep shock, I realized that they didn't want me to be rattled and rushed, rather they needed the calmness of the Lord, and a spirit of trust in God's grace.

Gordon and I had already found out in Kristy's turpentine emergency that God was present in the midst of trouble. Some days later as Gordon presided at the funeral, I saw how important it was that he and I, even in the midst of our own grief, maintain strong right arms on which others could lean. Because this death was such a meaningless tragedy and there was no pastor in my brother's world, it was necessary that someone bring a calming influence. It is not unusual that leaders have to bracket their own grief for another day in order to help others.

Our desire to serve people in the midst of terrifying moments had not come cheaply. It was in part the product of the anguish of our own lives. In our extended families, both Gordon and I had tasted divorce, death, wife swapping, and other tragedies.

We knew firsthand what happens when people get crushed or make choices no one seems to forgive. We were deeply sensitive to single parents, to homosexuals, and to mothers and fathers who have given their very best only to feel total failures. Each time God has permitted us to face family pressures, we have asked, "What can we learn from all of this? How can God use it to comfort others?"

From these crises emerged a ministry to singles, to the formerly married, and to addicts. We were living in a broken world. Should not the church be a place where the broken could find safety? Little did we realize that one day we would need such a place ourselves.

We have numerous birch trees at Peace Ledge in New Hampshire. I'm always impressed with their resiliency. One winter when we had a lot of snow, a storm changed to sleet and coated the branches with so much ice that they finally bent all the way to the ground. They became frozen in that position. Then another layer of ice trapped them. All of the birches stayed that way for a couple of months. Will they survive? Will they ever stand tall again? I wondered.

They did! In the spring when the birches again stood straight, I wrote in my journal:

> What a beautiful lesson the harsh winter and the resilient birches have given us. These trees can experience hardship, accept it, bend, but not break. They are flexible, not brittle. When relief comes, they are able to bounce back and experience the warmth and growth of spring. To resist is to break. O Lord, make me like a birch.

Susanna Spurgeon, the wife of the great English preacher, became an invalid at thirty-three. She was, therefore, always at home when her husband returned from the great tabernacle where thousands had come to hear him preach. Invariably, he would be exhausted and depressed, partially the result of a condition which plagued him. As Charles Haddon Spurgeon attempted to recover from his sense of emotional emptiness, his wife would often read to him from Richard Baxter's book, *The Reformed Pastor.*

"He would weep," she said, "and I would weep, too." She was always sensitive and receptive to Charles' pain because she knew suffering in her own life. Watching an oak log burning in her fireplace, she observed, "We are like this old log; we should give forth no melodious sounds were it not for the fire."[4]

During the time that we were "Yankees," Gordon and I learned one other thing about the shepherding instinct: In accepting the role of a model for others, the leader risks the *loss of some privacy.*

In leadership, our personal lives and our marital relationships serve as models. And to an extent so do our families. Gordon and I knew that people would look to see how we treated our children and how, in turn, our children responded to us.

When we came to Grace Chapel, our children were still quite young. During Sunday morning worship services, they sat with Gordon and me on the front row. Gordon would leave the family only when it was time for him to preach or to lead various portions of the service. He thought it important for all of the team to sit with their families and go to the pulpit only when they would be exercising their particular spiritual gifts. This made it possible for families to be together for worship.

There were various by-products of that discipline. The children loved getting as close to their dad as they could. People couldn't help but observe his obvious enjoyment of and affection for Mark and Kristy, and that, I believe, helped authenticate his ministry.

For others, it was a modeling experience. One young man, a seminarian, shared with us that he and his fiancée had deliberately sat behind our seats at Grace for many months. The young lady he wished to marry had been deeply hurt by the breakup of the marriage of her pastor years ago; she found it impossible to believe that a marriage in the pastoral ministry could actually be healthy. Her fiancé, realizing that she needed to believe in that possibility again, encouraged her to be part of the congregation at Grace Chapel and watch Gordon and me. After several months, her heart was settled. Today two decades later, that lovely couple serve Christ as a team in western Canada.

It was during our Grace Chapel years that I first stressed the importance, through modeling it myself, of developing spiritual gifts, not just my talent. Since my training had been as a singer, it was easy for me to pour my few hours of service into singing in the choir. But I began to observe that with the passage of years, voices grow old. What do you do with a talent that is fading, especially if that's the key to your serving? If my usefulness to God and others had been seen only in terms of singing, I might be a troubled woman today.

Talents most likely diminish with age, while spiritual gifts seem to improve and deepen with the passing of years. As I came to enjoy the gift of teaching more and more, the less interested I became in developing the talent of singing. Being sensitive to this matter, I have been aware again and again of singers who are growing old and losing the edge to their once beautiful voices. Rather than becoming sweeter with age, they have grown more and more miserable in their attempts to serve the Lord with a talent which fewer and fewer people desire to see them perpetuate. If only they could have had a point at which they might have been open to receiving gifts and see how God could multiply them to build his kingdom.

Finally, we pursued the concept of teaching-by-modeling one year when we offered hospitality to eight seminary couples on six different nights. One of those evenings in the midst of dinner, the doorbell rang, and we were all confronted with a hysterical young woman who had a serious problem. The couples had a chance to observe how we handled the situation. While Gordon continued to serve the seminarians, I took the unexpected visitor to another room, where she and I discussed and prayed about the problem she faced.

If a leader resents the loss of privacy and the fact that someone is always watching, the pastoral life can quickly become miserable. Yet which one of us doesn't yearn for some obscurity? Isn't it tempting to think about how nice it might be to go to worship one Sunday and not have a single conversation centered on a problem or a decision? When I begin to think those thoughts, I know I need time to reflect on my audience of One—he who had nowhere to lay his head. He was without a home where he could shutout the needs and be himself. It is he who still calls us to "come and follow."

There came a day in our twelfth year as "Yankees" when I began to hear my husband make noises that sounded like change and a move might be forthcoming. I felt rooted and didn't look forward to leaving, yet I wanted to be prepared when the day came. As a result I began writing a "move journal." I reasoned that it could be a place where I could deal with my feelings. I would record insights from Scripture and other sources with the expectation that it would prepare me for the trauma of any impending move.

During the same period, I had been writing a Bible study for the women of our church concerning women in the Scriptures. As always, what we do for others comes back to bless us.

My reflection disclosed a significant lesson for my world. I saw that the first six women of the Bible who were major players in God's dealings with people—Eve, Sarah, Leah, Rebecca, Lot's wife, and Hannah—all faced one of two challenges: either they were asked to leave their homes, or they passed through a period of infertility. It was as if early in God's relationship with women, he wanted them to understand that he was both *Lord of the move* and *Lord of the womb*.

Few things have been more important to most women than the opportunity to be mothers and to create homes. So to permit us to face insecurity in one or both of these areas is to challenge us at the very core of our beings. Yet this is what God permitted.

I picked up these same themes in the lives of some of my favorite people in Christian history. After five years of marriage and three children, Catherine Booth, wife of the founder of the Salvation Army, wrote to her parents:

> It appears that God may have something very glorious in store for us, and when He has tried us, He will bring us forth as gold. *My difficulty is in leaving home.*[5] (italics mine)

When Amy Carmichael prepared to leave England for Japan, where she had her first missionary experience, people thought her a hero. Only she seemed to know that she was in deep personal pain. She wrote:

> They think I want to go. If they only knew how torn in two I feel today, and how precious the home ties are, they would understand.[6]

I was comforted to know that God was not silent or unfeeling about these women or those in Scripture—nor is he unfeeling about us. But this comfort only comes when God is given the title deed to our lives and is permitted to take our pain and turn it into a growing experience. (I have written at greater length about this in *A Step Farther and Higher*.)

For us, the twelfth year at Grace Chapel was a time of confusing messages. Sometimes hearing God's will is not easy. He will teach us at all costs to trust him—no matter what. Gordon was very tired. Looking back, we've often wondered: if we had taken a much-needed sabbatical, would we ever have left? But if not, think of all the lessons we would have missed.

The love expressed when we left Grace was both surprising to us and deeply touching. We had no idea how deep the affection was until we decided to leave. New Englanders tend to keep their feelings to themselves. It was especially heartening to me when we reread the hundreds and hundreds of letters they gave us when we left, that it was our family relationships that touched them the most. They had known our children for most of their growing-up years, and now they were both following Christ at different colleges. Saying good-bye was tough for all of us.

But we left New England for other places. The next few years would be more difficult than either of us could ever have imagined. If it seems that God's guidance was vague as you read, that's because we were not as sure about this leading as we had been in past years. It would be our time to descend into the darkness that we'd seen in the lives of many others. And there would be moments when one false step would have destroyed everything God had graciously built into us. But that's for another chapter.

When we drove past the Leaving Lexington sign for the last time, we had no way of knowing that one day we would return. We would be invited to do something that almost no one ever gets to do.

But that's for another chapter, too.

TEN

THE JOURNEY CONTINUES

Forgiving and Being Forgiven

It is a fatal mistake to suppose that we cannot be holy except on the condition of a situation and circumstances in life such as shall suit us. It is one of the first principles of holiness to leave our times and our places, our going out and our coming in, our wasted and our goodly heritage entirely with the Lord. Here, O Lord you have placed us, and we will glorify you here! —*T. C. Upham, 1799–1872*

The worst and best year for Gordon and me was 1987, three years after we moved. It seemed as if our lives fell apart. For almost three years Gordon had been president of InterVarsity, a dynamic ministry to university students across the United States. Having said good-bye to a congregation-based ministry, we had followed what we thought was the guidance of God into work with students and their spiritual directors. We had become convinced that the further we moved past midlife, the more we should be eager to spend time pouring back into the young all that God had invested in us.

There are many things my husband and I would do differently if we had those three years to live over. And this might be the appropriate place to say something that too few people seem to think about. There is a tendency to believe that if one tries to do everything right (and you understand that I am exaggerating), then nothing in life will go awry. That simply is *not* the case.

A rigorous spiritual discipline, working hard at healthy relationships, and trying to pursue the life of a biblical servant are unquestionably the only way to live. But they are not guarantees against pain or failure. When I have made this point at various places, I have seen anxiety cross the faces of many women. Their response tells me they hoped the opposite were true, that there must be a fail-safe, consequence-proof way to live. I can't deceive you.

Scan the Bible from one end to the other, and you will see that some of the finest men and women knew personal failure or the consequences of the failures of those around them. Job was apparently a remarkable man, and yet he entered into some of the greatest pain known in all of literature. Could anyone question the faithfulness of Jesus to his disciples? Yet one of them, in fact all of them from time to time, failed him terribly. Chambers puts it well:

> The Bible indicates that a man falls on his strongest point. Abraham, the man of faith, fell through unbelief. Moses, the meek man, fell through losing his temper; Elijah, the courageous man, fell through losing heart; and Solomon, the most colossally wise, wealthy, luxurious, superb king, fell through groveling, sensual idolatry.[1]

Relationships, our marriage in particular, was our greatest strength. But *an unguarded strength is a double weakness*. The battle for the soul is real. Battles mean casualties. It stands to reason that an enemy would try to conquer the one out in front—as well as those who support that one.

The bottom line: While we've tasted much ministry gratification, we also know a lot about failure. About shame. About humiliation and loss. We are well acquainted with what it's like when people talk about you . . . and not always truthfully. But most importantly, we know what it is like to call out to God for a touch of hope and see him give it.

In 1986 Gordon and I celebrated our twenty-fifth wedding anniversary. On my birthday that year, Gordon gave me a special present. At the time, I wrote about his gift in a monthly letter we used to send to the leadership of InterVarsity:

> Gordon gave me a gift that was a picture of such love, presented in truth, given in mercy, and resulting in hope. He had found our love letters written during our courtship between February 1961 and August 1961. Because we were poor, we couldn't afford to call from

Boulder, Colorado, to Denver, so we wrote daily letters instead. Am I thankful we were poor! Tenderly, Gordon wove the story around those letters, matching my diary entries and other family letters. He filled four volumes—100 pages in each! To keep what he was doing a surprise, he devoted "sleep hours" to it. (Easily done because I sleep so soundly.) A gift of a lifetime!

What the staff did not know was that those letters were Gordon's way of telling me that he believed in our marriage and our future together. But the two of us were living with a terrible secret concerning the fact that Gordon had broken the covenant of our marriage and was living with the agonizing sorrow of grieving his Lord, me, our children, and the many who had trusted him. Looking back, we both feel it would have been wiser to have withdrawn from public ministry long before we did. But we didn't. Those to whom we were accountable and under discipline encouraged us to continue under certain stipulations.

Each morning during that difficult time, we had arisen, gone to our knees, and asked God for protective mercy and strength. We told him (perhaps naïvely) that if he would protect us, we would continue to give him everything we had, one day at a time. And we did that—terribly aware of our utter dependence on his kindness. In our brokenness, I am not sure that we always made wise decisions. But seeking wisdom was among our most frequent prayers.

In those days of private anguish, certain verses of Scripture almost flew off the page like arrows and imbedded themselves in my heart. Psalm 57:1–3 is a good example:

> I will take refuge in the shadow of your wings until the disaster has passed. I cry out to God Most High, to God, who fulfills his purpose for me. He sends from heaven and saves me, rebuking those who hotly pursue me; God sends his love and his faithfulness.

When I wasn't sure I could make it for another day, I would turn to lines like, "When my spirit grows faint within me, it is you who know my way" (Ps. 142:3).

Our readings from the church fathers and mothers became a rich resource of direction and hope. For years I carried in my notebook a quote attributed to Amy Carmichael:

Do the commonest and smallest things as beneath his eye.... If you have made a great mistake in your life, do not let it becloud all of it; but locking the secret in your heart, compel it to yield strength and sweetness.

During that period, we traveled the country, meeting with students and student workers. Despite our own personal sadness which we held closely to ourselves, it was often a wonderful time. We were refreshed by the questions and curiosities of university students seeking relationships with God, and even more by campus staff workers who, while often living under incredibly difficult financial circumstances, gave themselves unreservedly to the development of younger Christ-followers.

Many times we would sit with young men and women into the early hours of the morning talking about spiritual things. With increasing frequency, we found ourselves raising the issues of repentance, the horror of sin, the importance of grace, and the freedom forgiveness gives. Perhaps we were talking to ourselves as much as anyone, but it was clear that people were listening. We knew we were connecting with the hearts of others.

Many times people would come up to one or both of us and say, "You speak with a tenderness" or "You have a perspective on grace that is rare." We would quietly thank them. But we knew, rather sadly, what they didn't know—we were not speaking out of cold academic, theological knowledge. We were speaking out of present experience. As we spoke into their hurts, so we were hurting. In a small sense, we both felt like the boxer who is "out on his feet," but who keeps on going because that's the only thing he can do. Knowing we had grieved the heart of God and abused the trust of being his representatives brought a sorrow we cannot to this day describe. We worked harder and harder—perhaps feeling the need to pay penance.

That was also the time when some well-known Christian television personalities were facing public disgrace because of sin in their lives. More than once we sat in groups where confessing Christians talked about those people. We heard their sarcasm, their ungracious expressions of judgment. We knew they felt betrayed and embarrassed by what was being said by the media. What was alarming was how little we heard from anyone about the need to forgive, the terrible effects of sin and its temptations, or the hope that these people who had so utterly disgraced themselves and their Lord would find some solace in Christ who never forsook anyone.

As we listened to people talk, Gordon and I often exchanged knowing looks with each other. We wanted to, but couldn't, dodge the reality that repentance and forgiveness, both given and received, are difficult issues for many Christians to handle when they move beyond doctrinal formulation into real-life situations. Sadly, we knew in our hearts that the things said about certain prominent leaders who had failed, would also be said about us should our secret reach the public.

That moment did come. How it happened is not important. The why is also not important. What was important was our response. Long before that moment, we had met with godly men (whom we came to call our Angels). In those conversations, we decided that we would never try to explain or defend ourselves. If our secret should ever reach the public, we would immediately and totally withdraw from the ministry. And we did. Gordon, with me at his side, gave his resignation to the board of directors, repenting in deep sorrow and accepting full responsibility.

That morning before going to stand before those people, I read this in Chambers' *My Utmost for His Highest*:

> God says— "I will never leave thee," then I can with good courage say, "The LORD is my helper, I will not fear"—I will not be haunted by apprehension. . . . I will be full of courage like a child "bucking himself up" to reach the standard his father wants. . . . It does not matter what evil or wrong may be in the way, He has said, "I will never leave thee."[2]

Once again the habit of coming to Christ's fire had helped to prepare me and given me a sense that I was armed for battle. It was not a time to turn back. Painful? You have no idea! But God in his kindness cushioned the blows by allowing our son to join us as a loving support for the weekend to follow. Mark's steadiness, even rock-like demeanor, was an immense help as we took phone calls from all over the world and had to assure "visitors" who came from the media that there was no salacious story to be unearthed.

Within a few days, we (with the help of some caring friends) packed a U-Haul truck and began to make our way across the country from Wisconsin to our beloved Peace Ledge, our safe place where we could become quiet, assess our situation, and try to hear God speak in the midst of all the mess we'd created for people.

The next eighteen months of our lives were a mixture of some of the deepest personal sorrow you can face and yet some of the most beautiful experiences you could ever hope to have. Gordon has written about our perspective of those months in *Rebuilding Your Broken World*.

I don't mean to minimize how long those months were. We talked endlessly and then talked some more. Together we found that forgiveness is not a once and for all choice but a process. Just when you think you have the hurt licked, it comes over you like a tidal wave ready to engulf.

We came to realize as never before that the human being is much like a tall skyscraper which has a diversity of activities going on from floor to floor. At level twenty-five, there is excitement, while at level thirty-three there is despair. On level fifty-two, there is sloth; on level seventy-seven, there is renovation. We found that we were much like that: at one level of life hopeful, on another despairing, on a third struggling with anger, on a fourth finding new depths of love and affection.

The choice to give each floor over to Christ when it consciously surfaced was the key. To acknowledge the "garbage" was important, but if we lingered on that floor, surrounded by it, we would risk coming out smelling like it. A deadly risk.

Please understand that under such conditions there is much grief. A dream has died. And almost like a mother gives over a dead child to Jesus, I had to give a dream of mine back to him. Those were days in which the dynamic of forgiveness was tested and found to be absolutely reliable.

I have tried to outline the ways forgiveness worked for me in *A Step Farther and Higher*. I knew I had to embrace it as fervently as I could. The life of the cross demanded that I not get stuck here. I was convicted by Corrie ten Boom's words concerning people whom she met who had refused to forgive:

Since the end of the war I had had a home in Holland for victims of Nazi brutality. Those who were able to forgive their former enemies were able also to return to the outside world and rebuild their lives, no matter what the physical scars. Those who nursed bitterness remained invalids. It was as simple and as horrible as that.[3]

It became clearer than ever that we can't hold onto both Christ and resentments. The call of the cross demands that we renounce any attitude which cripples our ability and willingness to love—without condition. Over the past ten years, we have spoken with and tried to encourage scores of couples who have also gone through a period of failure and/or betrayal. It has been clear that if the enemy of our souls can't get the marriage through the original act of betrayal, he will be content to win the battle through the anger of a mate who is unwilling to forgive.

We had a great resource at our disposal during those months at Peace Ledge. It came out of a habit that we had both worked hard at over the many years of our marriage. Gordon calls it the repentant life-style: the effort to make forgiveness and mercy-giving a way of life between us. Please be assured that I am not trivializing anything when I say that this was a time when we drew upon the habits that had been growing in both of us for twenty-five years. It meant that our personal commitment to each other in the worst of moments was never, never in jeopardy.

The most difficult aspect of our sorrow was the public humiliation. But I had to come to peace with the knowledge that some things have to be left to mystery and trust. I had to keep reminding myself that I served a Savior, who though sinless, gave himself over to being humiliated and spit upon by people he had made. And Gordon and I were sinners—deserving of hell.

On Sundays we would sneak into various New Hampshire churches where we felt we would not be known (sometimes we were successful). We often left greatly disappointed because we had the feeling that the people in charge of worship had absolutely no sense that there were those in the congregation (anonymous, of course) who were in terrible personal struggles. We became highly sensitized to the contents of prayers, the thrust of sermons, the demeanor of spiritual leaders. We often left church with the sense that the people up front were "doing a program" more than trying to discern the broken hearts of more than one worshipper.

It caused Gordon to think carefully about the way he had led worship over the years. He wondered how many times people had left the services he had led lacking hope and feeling there was nothing to cling to. Many times Gordon would say to me, "Not that I ever expect to—or feel I deserve to lead a service again, but if I were asked to, I would make absolutely sure that every broken heart present heard a word of hope before the worship was ended."

During those months, we learned the power of a letter because we received literally thousands of them from people who were kind enough to send words of love, of encouragement, and of hope. Though we had no assistance, we answered every one of those letters personally. If Gordon wrote a letter, I would write a brief handwritten postscript on the bottom as a reminder to the recipient that we were in this together—sinners level at the cross. *We were focusing on the years, not the months*, and we wanted to make that clear. Keeping our minds on those letters and giving thanks for those who wrote them was an important part of our healing.

We also learned about the value of friendship. Gordon and I received an amazing amount of calls from men. Several times Christian men of renown traveled long distances to spend entire days with us. They brought encouragement, words of grace, and remarkable love.

A pastor with whom we had only had a casual relationship became one of our closest friends as he called each week for months. One night, unable to sleep, I had passed through the deepest anguish I had known. I felt utterly alone and cast down. Hour after hour I sat in the darkness. Then suddenly relief came as if a wind had blown away a dense cloud. I returned to our bed and found the blessedness of sleep. I remember being confused as to how this moment of release had come.

Then a few days later I received a letter from this pastor/friend saying that he had arisen from his bed during the night with a sense of concern for me. He had spent the rest of the night praying specifically for God to touch my life. As I worked my way back through the calendar, it became clear that he had commenced his praying at the exact hour I had come to the point of relief. I guess you could say, he was awakened so I could rest.

One couple who had been close friends for years insisted that the four of us meet once a month for fun. They seized the initiative, made the plans, and left us no alternative but to join them. This was an incalculable gift. We looked forward to those moments all month long because, apart from those times, we rarely left our isolated place on the hill called Peace Ledge.

Another friend gave us a scripture from Daniel that became an important watchword:

> Some of the wise will stumble, so that they may be refined, purified and made spotless until the time of the end, for it will still come at the appointed time. (Daniel 11:35 TLB)

At Peace Ledge, we learned in greater depth the lessons of how to love each other without condition, of how to ask hard, ruthless questions about the place of sin in the heart, of how you can get so caught up doing what you think are good things that you end up making a fool of yourself. We confessed that there is a lot of activity in organized Christianity that seems so attractive and significant but which, nevertheless, leaves the soul empty and the mind and body spent.

One morning early into our months on the Ledge during our "fire-time," we read the following from Oswald Chambers' *My Utmost for His Highest*:

> I *cannot* make myself right with God, I *cannot* make my life perfect; I can only be right with God if I accept the Atonement of the Lord Jesus Christ as an absolute gift. Am I humble enough to accept it? I have to resign every kind of claim and cease from every effort, and leave myself entirely alone in His hands, and then begin to pour out in *the priestly work of intercession.* . . . *Enter into the ministry of the interior.* "*The LORD turned the captivity of Job, when he prayed for his friends*" (Job 42:10). . . . *Pray for your friends now.* [4] (emphasis mine)

We were captivated by what we heard from "our book friend," Oswald (OC as we came to call him). He was telling us that, even if you lose the right to every outside ministry activity, you can always be an intercessor . . . for your friends. This privilege no one can deny you. We wept, both of us, as we knelt that morning and offered our lives as intercessors. That ministry began to mark every Peace Ledge morning.

As we wrote letters both to well-wishers and to those who identified themselves as broken-world people, we added names to our prayer list. What we did not appreciate until much later was that this daily intercessory exercise would become a rich gift to our marriage and that it would turn our withdrawal to Peace Ledge into an outer-directed experience which pointed to the Lord and to his people rather than an experience of morbid introspection.

To this day, eleven years later, the freedom we have to intercede together endures. But we know it was bought at a great price and given as a rare gift.

Mood swings are great when one is grieving, and we had them. Often my journal helped me do what I've come to call "pen therapy" on myself. I've written about this extensively in *A Step Farther and Higher*. A review of my journal now reminds me of the many talks I had with our daughter Kristy who, though only twenty at the time, had an amazing facility for challenging me to readjust my perspective during a low moment.

One day, feeling tempted to swim in self-pity, I wrote:

> Today has been a day of more inner-work, this time concerning those who were two-faced toward us and what my responses toward them must be. It has been amazing to read Amy Carmichael because she addressed my soul's need so precisely. She speaks of the myrtle plant being a small but lovely plant. Its fragrance, however, can only be appreciated when its leaves are crushed. And so it is with us. There's no way to deceive. When we are tried (crushed), in that moment what is inside is known! Courage or cowardice, truth or falsehood, kindness or selfishness, strength or weakness, anger or sweetness.

As I said before, certain Scriptures took on a whole new meaning for us. I resonated with St. Paul who talked about hardships he'd suffered:

> ... beyond our ability to endure, so that we despaired even of life. Indeed, in our hearts we felt the sentence of death. But this happened that we might not rely on ourselves but on God, who raises the dead. (2 Cor. 1:8–9)

I remember wondering if Paul ever found himself being reminded of his earlier life when he'd persecuted the church so vigorously. Were there those who found creative ways to let him know they'd not forgotten the dark days of his former life? Did he ever wonder what people were saying behind his back?

What of King David who had to live with the label of adulterer and murderer? How kind of Jesus to refer to him, not as the failure, but with affection as a "man after his own heart." It is highly significant to me that the New Testament writers remembered Solomon, King David's son's admonition that "love *covers* over all wrongs" (Prov. 10:12), for there is no mention of his offenses anywhere.

One of the best decisions Gordon made during our eighteen months at Peace Ledge was for us to go to Europe for an entire month of walking the Alps. We had amassed enough frequent flyer miles to fly to the moon and back; so expense was not a problem. We walked and talked and found new, fresh layers of love as we rediscovered how to have fun together. We talked about the carousel called ministry and how we had been jolted off of it. We framed a new sense of conviction about life and relationships. And we counted our blessings: our loving adult children and incredible friendships. When we returned from that trip, we were new people.

Books we read during those months reminded us that all tunnels are going someplace and that, if we chose to say yes to the pain, God can redeem the experience (no matter how bad) and make it a source of healing for others. The choice—embrace the pain or run from it— was ours. With interest we read how C. S. Lewis was aware that he was making such a choice.

He had found that pain often tempts us to shut down and not risk loving again. For most of his life, he was afraid to love deeply because he feared the suffering that came with loving. But when he gave his love to Joy Davidman, he risked everything without reserve. Their short marriage because of Joy's death from a fast-growing cancer brought untold grief to Lewis, but he would not have traded those years with her for anything.

Lewis taught us that the ancients and those who said yes to suffering can bring great instruction and comfort. One of his students once commented to him, "We read so we know we are not alone." The comfort and teaching of those who have gone before is incalculable when the heart is stricken.

During our Peace Ledge months, we also recommitted ourselves to being careful about who we listened to and leaned on. We learned not to answer our critics. There were those who found it impossible to offer hope for a life of service beyond failure. But we trusted our lives to the counsel of older, wiser, more godly acquaintances, and to our honorable "book friends" who inevitably raised our hopes for a Jonah-like second chance.

We couldn't escape the feeling that Amy Carmichael had us in mind when she wrote of a believer's thoughts in contrast to his heavenly Father's thoughts:

His (own) thoughts said, "There are some things that I cannot forget."

His Father said, "The humbling memory will help you walk softly with Me and tenderly with others. But even so there is relief from all distress. . . . When I spoke to Israel in the visions of the night, I did not use that glorious name; I used the old name which had so sorrowful a meaning. I said, 'Jacob, Jacob,' and he answered, 'Here am I.' Jacob, Jacob, the deceiver, the schemer, that name is a reminder of your fall, but also and far more of *my mercy*. It is to you I am speaking, to you, not to another, worthier one, but to you, My child—Jacob, Jacob."

His thoughts said, "I am not what I meant to be, or what others think I am."

His Father said, "It is written, 'He restores my soul. The Law of the Lord is perfect, restoring the soul.' "Let some word of Mine restore you. Let My love restore you. Did you think you had a Father who did not know that His child would need to be restored?. . . I will heal you of your wounds. I will restore to you the joy of My salvation. I will renew a right spirit within you. I will not cast you away from My Presence. Child of My love, trust your Father. If the Spirit speaks some word in your heart, obey that word. And, before you are aware, you will know yourself restored." [5]

There is no human way to measure what words such as this did to help us rise from the ashes. During those months, we invited a Christian counselor, one of the men known as the Angels, to come and spend a week with us. To be frank, we were at first hesitant to do this. After all, hadn't we always been the people *to whom others came with their questions*? We'd never been on this end of the conversation before.

We wondered if he would unearth some dimension of our lives or our relationship of which we were unaware that would be too painful to face, that would present an obstacle to the future that we'd not foreseen. So when the moment for his arrival came, we sucked in our breaths and waited to see what would happen.

Each day this gifted man visited with Gordon for two hours and then with me for an equal amount of time. Then in the afternoon the three of us would spend several more hours in conversation as he reflected back to us what he'd heard in the morning visits.

In such fashion, he walked both of us across the map of our entire lives and relationship. It became a marvelous experience as we did something few people get to do: take a deep and personal look at the whole of life and see where the patterns of possible failure and poor choices may lie. By the end of the week, Gordon and I looked each other in the eye and answered this question for each other: "What would make you feel most secure in my love?" We each listed five things. It felt like a new start to a twenty-five-year-old marriage.

During those sessions with our friend and counselor, I had to face the fact that I had "elder-brother" tendencies. In the story of the prodigal son, the elder brother was the one who found it hard to rejoice with a younger brother who was being comforted and celebrated by their father.

Gordon received dozens more phone calls than I. The part of me made of God rejoiced with him but the part not made of God took offense. The self-centered part of me reasoned, wasn't I the "offended" one? There's no question in my mind today that if I had not repented of this, a root of bitterness would have grown in me that would have changed our entire future. Self was being denied. Would I dwell on it or on how much I needed mercy? Larry Crabb's words convicted me:

> People are wounded and people are self-centered. We must decide which is the greater problem. We have to start with our subtle, pervasive, stubborn commitment to ourselves—not our sense of identity.... *We believe that if others knew the extent of our pain, they would be less inclined to judge us for our self-concern.... We want to be in charge of the way we experience life, and that's the essence of our commitment to ourselves.... Think how seldom we confess our self-centeredness and how often we request help or guidance or comfort.... There's much rage beneath the surface stemming from self-centeredness. When angry we become less concerned with the welfare of others and more protective of our own.* The greatest obstacle to building truly good relationships is *justified* self-centeredness, a selfishness that deep in our souls, feels entirely reasonable and therefore acceptable in light of how we've been treated."[6] (emphasis mine)

When I was able to frankly face my own selfishness and pride, God was able to begin the necessary work in me to bring about a deep mourning *for my own sinfulness.* "Those whom I love I rebuke and discipline. So be earnest, and repent" (Rev. 3:19).

No one sins alone. We are interdependent, and while my husband assumed full responsibility for our pain, I knew that God hated spiritual pride most of all. It was the repentant tax collector who said, "God have mercy on me, a sinner," that Jesus said we should be like, not the proud Pharisee who felt "above" such people (Luke 18:9-14).

A lot of things came to a head for me during a trip we took to Israel. One night when we were visiting Galilee, I suddenly became captured by the most terrible of moods. I felt engulfed in an anger that felt more like rage. I was amazed to see such hostility within me, and after a few hours, I realized that this must be confessed and dealt a death blow. It was a humbling hour. Only when I put it all into words to my husband and to the Lord did release come.

Now I understood more clearly why Oswald Chambers once said, "I have never met the man I could despair of after discerning what lies in me apart from the grace of God."

That night I discovered repentance for myself. Gordon had faced the issue in another way. This was my time. In a strange sense we were now both aware that we did indeed stand on level ground before the cross, that the *condition* of sinfulness (the ability to fall into any kind of sinful act) is the most important issue that we all must face. Bringing whatever we are and whatever we have done to the cross is the only thing that leads to wholeness.

We both came to cherish that sense of newness that follows genuine repentance. There's a tenderness, a precious feeling of being under the mercy of God that we can ever know until we have poured our hearts out to him in passionate repentance and been assured of his restoration. "How can we retain this experience of new life?" we asked each other, somehow aware that we wouldn't always feel this level of openness to God.

As Gordon wrote in *Rebuilding Your Broken World*, we came to appreciate that this spirit of "being mercied" is easily disrupted when one indulges in any of these three thoughts:

1. My sinful acts are not quite as bad as everyone thinks. There were extenuating circumstances. Let's smooth things over, and get on with it.

2. What I did is not as bad as what someone else did. Compared to him/her, I don't look *that* bad. What's the big deal?

3. Look how people are treating me. I deserve better.

Coming away from Israel and that dramatic moment at Galilee, I knew I was in a period of deepening insight into myself. R. T. Kendall stated it succinctly:

> Every trial is designed to show you something about yourself you didn't know. . . . Job was "perfect and upright" (Job 1:1), but God saw a gross imperfection in Job. . . . He got very self-righteous. God put him through the kind of trial that forced that imperfection to surface.[7]

So it had in me. As more light came to our souls, and we embraced the freedom that truth received with both hands brings, we knew God was doing a new thing in us—most of which no one else would ever know about. No matter. We knew; that was enough.

Paul Modesto, a family therapist/Bible teacher, helped me quantify the good things that were coming out of this season of intense self-discovery. If one allowed it, he said, the following seven things could be the rich harvest when things fall apart:

> We learn to reprioritize.
> We learn how vulnerable we are.
> We are humbled.
> We become more patient—peaceful instead of frenzied.
> We learn to reframe life and its situations.
> We have a chance to get "unstuck" from a victim mind-set.
> We are pulled away from this world toward heaven.

All these things and more were blessings that arose from the pit in which we found ourselves. The psalmist was right, "All things serve you [God]" (119:91). We became proactive about choosing to dwell on the pluses rather than on the downsides of the public humiliation.

I began to repeat a short sentence to myself which Ann Frank once said of her years of grief and loss. "*I don't think of the misery, but of the beauty that remains.*"

As healing came, we were deeply grateful to realize that with God's help, we had beaten evil together. This *enemy* who loves to take marriages captive may have won a battle but not the war. No one sins alone, and each of us must see our part in any broken world experience.

After about one year at Peace Ledge had passed, Gordon's successor at Grace Chapel, Howard Clark, suggested that the elders of the church appoint some men to join our other Angels in working with us toward restoration. We were gratefully humbled by Dr. Clark's kindness and began meeting regularly with capable men who held our feet to the fire concerning how the process of mutual healing was progressing.

Many months later, there was an amazing service held at Grace Chapel. It was called a Service of Restoration to Ministry. It occurred almost two years to the day after Gordon had resigned from InterVarsity and we had made our sad retreat to Peace Ledge.

The church was packed. Ask anyone who was there, and he will tell you that it was a most powerful service because it fleshed out truth, mercy, and grace. Easy? No. But important. A necessary closure for us all. Vernon Grounds, our friend and mentor, brought the service to a thunderous conclusion when, with Gordon standing at his side, he said, "Preach the gospel of the second chance. Tell as many people as you can that there can be a second chance when the worst of failures has occurred."

When that service ended, we began to believe that there could be new life, new kinds of service, and a ministry dedicated to themes of grace, mercy, and a second chance, as dear Vernon had put it.

For months we had been receiving mail from a small, struggling congregation on the upper East Side of Manhattan (New York City), Trinity Baptist Church. They'd been seeking a pastor for three years, but—in those days—it seemed as if no one wanted to accept their invitation. At first Gordon turned away their requests to come and visit. But they persisted. They kept underscoring the fact that they too were a group of broken people who understood sin and forgiveness. We'd be very much at home among them.

We were attracted to their kindness, but for many months we simply thanked them, saying that the timing was not right. We needed to

keep the covenant made with the Lord, our Angels, and each other—
to stay quiet. Besides, there were two obstacles in our mind. Gordon
was not sure that being a pastor was the next right step. And I was sure
that I would never want to live in the middle of a big city.

But God has his ways of changing minds. In the following
months, he rekindled a love for congregational ministry in Gordon's
heart. A visit to a couple of city churches brought back the old love to
be among people, to serve them, to pour our lives into them.

But there was my reluctance toward the city. I'd grown up as a
country girl; I liked open spaces, lawns, safe streets, a predictable and
quiet community. But two thoughts began to grow in my heart. First, if
we were to return to congregational ministry, it should be in a place
where we could get lost, sort of like little fish in a big pond. And second,
that we should give ourselves to something that, in a sense, no one else
wanted to do. One day it became clear that if I could swallow my
antipathy toward the city, a small congregation in Manhattan would be
the best place to go and stick our oars in the water.

And so it happened. I ended up in the middle of one of the largest
cities in the world, and Gordon ended up back in the pulpit preaching
the Bible. When it came time to leave the quiet, protective place called
Peace Ledge and head south for New York City, I was excited yet
apprehensive. How could I have realized that we were about to
experience four of the happiest years of our lives? We were on our way
into the second chance.

Note: This chapter reflects events which happened more than ten years
ago. Since Gordon and I have written about the details of those days in
other places, I chose not to bring them to the page again. If we are to live
enveloped in the restorative grace which is provided through the cross, it
becomes important to practice a kind of proactive "forgetfulness" which
buries sin and holds onto the lessons of value. What I have written is
meant to acknowledge the reality of the awful consequences of sin and
something of the ways in which God restores through his people.

ELEVEN

THE JOURNEY CONTINUES

Getting Lost in New York City

Seeing my intentions before he beholds my failures;
Knowing my desires before he sees my faults;
Cheering me to endeavor greater things, and yet
    accepting the least;
Inviting my poor service, and yet above all,
    content with my poorer love.
      —Cardinal H. E. Manning, 1808–1892

Actually, the trip to New York City began with a strange phone call. The caller identified himself as Bernie Romberg, and he was phoning, he said, from lower Manhattan. Bernie had been a member of Grace Chapel many years before. He had come to faith as he listened to Scripture being preached. Now he and his wife Margot lived in New York City where he was a successful business entrepreneur and leader in his congregation.

"Gordon, I'm inviting you and Gail to come to New York for a weekend. My treat! Let the city wash over you. Perhaps you'll get a burden for New York and find a way to come back here to serve Christ."

Gordon thanked Bernie and told him that we'd keep the invitation in mind. The truth was, however, that neither of us thought it would ever happen. Why would anyone want to go to New York . . . for a visit *or to live*? But he was persistent, and after several follow-up calls, we bowed to pressure and agreed to visit the place known as the Big Apple. But just for a weekend.

The weekend came and went. In a little more than seventy-two hours, we walked (it seemed) miles of city streets, ate in cafes and restaurants, attended the theater, talked to scores of New Yorkers (we found most of them remarkably responsive to our questions), and worshipped. The city "washed over us," and the result was that we were hooked. We saw human need; we met wonderful people; we sensed a place where we could make a contribution. You could say that our love for the city started right then and there. God was in this.

It was Bernie Romberg with his unexpected, almost Macedonian phone call who was responsible for this change of mind. And so it was that when the people at Trinity Baptist Church on the upper East Side of Manhattan called again—as they'd done before—we said, "Let's talk." Three months later we were New Yorkers.

From the very beginning, we felt embraced by the people at Trinity Baptist. The past was not an issue. There were no labels placed on any of us. "We're all broken people here," someone said. I was soon reminded of the comment of a five-year-old child who had become aware of the language of ecology. One day, looking at a representation of Jesus at the Last Supper, she said, "I know who that is. That's Jesus and his *recycles*."

And that's what many of us were at Trinity: *recycles*. Most of the hundred people who came through the door were veterans of the city. Many seemed to have a story that was tinged with intense sadness. On any given day you could hear accounts of abuse, anger, addiction, and AIDS. But just as prevalent were the reports of life-change, answered prayer, and selfless service.

Our home in New York was a twelfth floor, Roosevelt Island apartment overlooking the East River. Our neighbors were international and multicultural. Soon we included among our friends men and women of different races, classes, and experiences. The smells, the foods, the noises: all very different from what we had been used to.

Every day was unique. We began to live an adventure unlike anything we'd ever known before. What a distance we'd come from the days in Sainty where you might see one car in an hour zooming down the dirt section road at eighty miles per hour. Now there were nothing but cars and taxis crawling along in constant traffic jams. Sainty had been a place of quiet; New York was a mass of sirens and hawkers and jackhammers. In Sainty you never locked your doors; in

New York you never opened your door without absolute assurance that all was safe. The journey from Sainty to Manhattan was all the proof you needed to say that you should assume absolutely nothing when you live a call-based life in the ministry.

The first thing we had to do was to make sure that we would seek the glory of God in the city. In New York? Absolutely. It can be found there, which is to say that we must seek the glory of God wherever we are called. So we arose each morning with the mind-set that New York was our home and its people were our people. We learned to praise God as we saw him expressed in the architecture of the great buildings, in the parks, in the cultural experiences, and in the diversity of people. We determined that we were not there to *do* things *to the city* but rather that we were there to be *part of* the city.

Trinity was a young church, predominantly made up of single young adults who were caught in the frantic work culture. It seemed everyone was always on the edge of fatigue and frustration. The workplace was harsh. Burnout was a constant threat. It took a relentless toll on these people who became our sons and daughters in the Lord.

If the city was exciting and energizing, it was also saturated with every sort of evil known to humanity. Lonely young men and women were constantly tested in terms of their moral convictions. I met women who had sold themselves to raise extra money just to survive for another month. One woman called me in hysterics one morning, terrified that she was pregnant. For most women, that would be a great joy, but for her it brought utter terror because she was bulimic and afraid she would destroy the baby's chances to live within her.

I tried to learn from those who were gay what it felt like to lose a partner to AIDS. Others tried to explain to me what it felt like to know their jobs were under siege. There was always someone else willing to come along and work a bit harder and longer than they. Stories of being mugged were not unusual; tales about the difficulties of finding living space, conflict with apartment mates, and sleep deprivation were common. As a pastor's wife, I was in a position to listen, to intercede, and to give spiritual assurance. Hardly a day passed that I was not besieged with requests for conversation as young men and women sought direction for their lives.

It was quickly apparent that in our early fifties, we were among the very oldest people in the church. A small group of mature Christ-followers had sacrificially held the struggling remnant together for the years they were without a pastor. There were those on the church board who could have been our sons and daughters. We welcomed our priority task: to pour ourselves into the lives of the young, to encourage them, challenge them, to raise a standard for them, and to train them. This was sheer privilege.

Over a three-month period, I taught the first of a series of groups about personality gifts and how to care for others in the congregation. The candor and spiritual intimacy those nights afforded were rare. You don't have to spend much time in the city convincing people that we are all sinners. They were well aware of the fact.

Some in these groups were recovering alcoholics; others had come from dysfunctional family backgrounds with stories that strained my credulity. Many were brand-new to faith and needed a solid foundation to change the way they'd learned to think. Again, I was something of a mother figure to them. The respect and affection they gave to me cannot be described.

As long as I live, I will always treasure the hours spent with them. They were living pictures of what the gospel can do in the human experience. As never before, I saw how a community of broken people who care for each other can make a difference. There was no room for individualism or solo players. We all knew we needed each other. City life forces that perspective.

It was not uncommon for a group of us to talk about how we felt when we came together on Sunday. The streets were draining. Often we felt like saying as we came through the door on Sunday morning, "Whew, I made it through another week." For many of us, Trinity was a safe place where we could find care and grace.

The congregation began to grow. The singing of the people became more and more exciting; their enthusiasm to serve in and beyond the church swelled. There was an international, multiethnic dimension to our fellowship, and we had the feeling that it reflected a bit more of what heaven would be like than most suburban churches.

Frequently, Gordon arranged for as many as eight or nine people to lead in portions of the worship. Each employed their mother tongue to read Scripture or pray. One Sunday morning a Nigerian woman from the United Nations entered the sanctuary as a first-time visitor. She was startled to hear the Bible being read in her tribal language. It was a profound spiritual experience. What happened to her was not uncommon.

When the offering plates were passed, the woman at the piano, a professional entertainer, would play old gospel songs in a rhythm-and-blues style. Sometimes a young African-American woman who was a nationally known recording artist and songwriter with Motown records would head for the front, grab a microphone, and sing for us "soul-style." These were absolutely electrifying moments of worship that will remain high-water marks in my life of exaltation.

We never knew what might happen next. A homeless man might enter the sanctuary and snore loudly while Gordon preached. Baseball players from other cities in town to play the Yankees might show up at a service. We sometimes welcomed entertainers from Broadway, United Nations diplomats, and people from the artistic community. No weekend was ever the same at Trinity.

New York is a walking city. We didn't need an automobile. On many evenings Gordon and I would walk ten or twenty blocks, reveling in the energy and diversity of city life. We made friends of all kinds. In our apartment we often entertained: bus drivers we'd met, neighbors in the apartment building, and the unchurched people we'd encountered in the course of daily city life.

Living in the city also afforded us unique contact with the business community. Gordon spoke several times a month at noon meetings for business people in different parts of Manhattan. Each week I went to the headquarters of one of the banks to lead a Bible study for executive women. It forced me to move far beyond my comfort level to engage a world I knew little about.

More than once I was convinced that I was in over my head. As I would take the Number Six subway to 51st Street and Lexington Avenue, I would beg God for that extra ounce of wisdom and understanding that would enable me to keep up with these brilliant, hardworking women who were so hungry to understand how the Scriptures spoke into their marketplace lives. When it was time to return to our apartment, I was often awed at how God had entered that conference room and bound us all together with some insight or perspective that was just what would be needed for a kingdom-building life in the next days.

One of the women in that weekly gathering was a bank vice president. As a young woman, Janet Avery left a housing project in Brooklyn, vowing that she would never go back. After acquiring a postgraduate degree, she had come to the bank and began climbing the career ladder. But there came a moment when she faced up to a sense of emptiness in the pursuit of business success. Janet's real dream, it turned out, became the serving of men and women who wanted to identify, enhance, and develop skills so that they could lead productive lives.

I had the inestimable joy of watching Janet go through the struggle of hearing God's call to embark on a life of faith. The day came when she resigned from the bank and entered what the spiritual masters call a life of "hiddenness, littleness, and powerlessness"—losing herself in the lives of others.

Soon Janet Avery launched a not-for-profit organization that has grown beyond any of our wildest dreams. Today "Vehicles" makes its home in Harlem (are you smiling?), and the woman who chose to get lost in others has been featured on New York television as one of the ten most powerful women in New York. Janet knows and happily tells where her power comes from. Recently, I took the train to New York and sat in the ballroom of the Waldorf Astoria as Janet was honored by a cast of the city's luminaries for her work.

Each week we saw the congregation grow a little more until there were two services. What had been a two-thirds empty sanctuary at one time, in fact a church that many thought should have been put to death, was now very much alive, thanks to God's power and the perseverance of a handful of people.

Following the final service, everyone adjourned to the large basement area where we enjoyed coffee hour. Not a few people stayed well into the afternoon as they refreshed themselves in the ambiance of Christ-centered fellowship. It took a heap of people to make coffee hour happen. But among them all, the most unforgettable was Barbara McCall, an African-American woman who had come within an inch of dying of a massive stroke as a young woman. One day during her prolonged hospital stay, she heard the story of the saving Christ preached by a television evangelist, and she was moved to commit her life to God.

Barbara eventually recovered and returned to work as a nurse. She often arrived at Trinity on Sunday morning after having worked all night. But even if she'd been up for twenty-four hours, we'd see her coming down 61st Street with her shopping cart (all New Yorkers have shopping carts, it seems) full of the pastries and goodies that we'd be serving at coffee hour.

I've often wondered how many lives were changed because of Barbara McCall and her commitment. More than a few men and women met their future spouses at coffee hour. Others came to faith as a result of time spent off in the corners in earnest discussion. It was a remarkable experience of connection for those who sometimes felt strangled by city life and craved a safe place to enjoy the community of Christ-followers.

One day Gordon received a letter from a young man on the Young Life staff in Texas who had read one of his books and was writing to express his appreciation. The two men began to exchange letters about life and ministry in the city, and it wasn't long before Keith Boyd was invited to come to the city for a visit. That visit, not unlike the one that had first brought Gordon and me to New York, changed Keith and his wife DeeAnn. Before long they returned to us when the church called him to be Gordon's assistant.

The two men got along famously, and we delighted as the congregation took Keith and DeeAnn into their hearts. It seemed a miracle that two people with a Texas style could make it so quickly with New Yorkers.

Four years in New York went very, very fast. Up in New England, our son Mark married his sweetheart, Patty. Three years later, to our joy, they presented us with our first grandchild, Eringail. Our daughter Kristy (married to Tom) graduated from Gordon College. Gordon's mother and my father died. Between us we managed to write three books. All of this could have been a mishmash of experience had I not kept returning to the fire each day where the presence of Christ brought meaning and perspective to it all. We'd done a lot of living, and almost every bit of it had been exhilarating.

The day came when we began to think about leaving the city we'd come to love. It was clear that Trinity had the potential of a successor-pastor in Keith Boyd. We were pleased that there was a cadre of young leaders in the church who were prepared to take it to a new level. Our task, we perceived, had been to bring energy to a church trying to regain its legs. That had happened. Another pastor could take it from there.

One day we received a surprising inquiry from Grace Chapel back in Lexington. Gordon's successor, Dr. Howard Clark, had resigned, and the chairman of the pulpit-search committee was calling to ask if Gordon would be open to the idea of returning to the pulpit ministry in Lexington. We couldn't have been more amazed at the question. Could such a move be God's doing?

"You can't go home again," Thomas Wolfe once wrote. Would it be possible to return to a former place of ministry and pick up a work left behind eight years before? Some said no; others said yes.

I recalled the words of the great spiritual master Fenelon who wrote:

> Open your heart wide, unboundedly wide, and let God's love flow in like a torrent. Fear nothing on your way; God will lead you by the hand, if only you trust Him wholly, and are filled rather with love for Him than fear for yourself.[1]

The decision to return to Grace Chapel was among the most difficult we've ever made. It would be untruthful to say that everyone wanted us to return. Only after the board of elders assured Gordon of their unanimous belief that God was in such a move did we give the invitation favorable consideration. Finally, in January of 1993, Gordon sent a message of acceptance to the Grace Chapel leadership.

Once again the good-byes were difficult. The Trinity family presented us with a magnificent scrapbook of letters and pictures of the four years we'd had together. The last days were drenched in tears as we hugged our neighbors, the bus drivers, and the café owners, the business people we'd come to know, and the hundreds of Trinity people who were such a powerful force in our lives.

There was a special sense of contentment as we realized that the congregation was in good hands under the leadership of Keith and DeeAnn Boyd. In fact, Trinity never skipped a heartbeat. The Sunday after Gordon preached his farewell sermon, Keith was in the pulpit guiding the people in worship and in the study of the Bible. A few months later, the congregation made it official. Keith was designated the senior pastor. Today he remains the spiritual leader, and the Trinity congregation flourishes. He has led them in ways we never could have.

In February of 1993, Gordon once again stood in the pulpit of Grace Chapel preaching his first sermon. He preached about repentance and the power of restoration when God's grace is unleashed into the broken places of the sinner's life. I was back in my old front-row seat, taking notes and praying for my husband as he spoke. In a short time, it seemed as if we had never left.

Who could have conceived of such a journey? We were back in New England. Here were people, many of whom we'd known for more than twenty years. The babies Gordon had once held in his arms for infant dedication were now headed off on summer missions and taking leadership positions in ministry programs. Gordon's staff included men and women he'd once discipled. At the end of one of the first services, a man stepped forward and pointed to a place to the side of the pulpit. "That's where I knelt ten years ago," he said to Gordon, "and you led me to Christ."

We could not have been more thankful. The preceding years had been among the most stretching years imaginable. From the years of travel with InterVarsity, through the dark days spent in deep soul-searching at Peace Ledge, through the wild sounds, smells and sights of New York City, and back to the place we knew most as home. We were Yankees again. It had been an amazing trip.

TWELVE

FRIENDS

The Difference They Make

Those are our best friends in whose presence we are able to be our
best selves.   —*Kahler*

In the past few years, I have been given the privilege of speaking to
numerous conferences and retreats for ministry wives. As I have
opened myself to questions on such occasions, one issue quickly
ascends above all others as something of great concern: the longing
for close friends, confidants.

How is it that we can be surrounded by scores of people in a congregation and yet feel lonely and isolated? Ask these women about the quality of their relationships, and what you frequently conclude is that most
have many *acquaintances* in their congregations but not many *friends*.

An exhaustive definition of friendship would fill an entire book.
But in this limited space, may I suggest out of my experience what I
think we're looking for in friends?

Pastor's wives soon realize that we are in the congregational eye.
At best, people are seeking us out as models of Christian grace and
maturity. At worst, people are watching with the intent to critique
anything that is out of alignment with what they think are the

highest standards of Christian behavior. Somewhere in the midst of all that, we need friends who accept us as normal Christian women and not as those playing roles.

We are aware that some will seek us out simply because we are seen as the "first ladies" of our congregations, and that there is a snippet of social value that comes in saying, "I was with the pastor's wife the other day." So we need friends who value us for our strength of Christian character and intellect rather than for titles.

We also learn that some will attempt to use us as conduits to the pastors about their concerns or complaints. Over these four decades, there have been a few times when the wife of a staff member has invited me for a visit. Then sadly, I've discovered that the real purpose was to express feelings about an administrative decision Gordon had made concerning her husband. And certain church members, if permitted, will also begin to use the pastor's wife to communicate with the pastor. For some of us, this can be disillusioning.

Just recently, a young ministry wife I know was approached by a woman in their church who said, "I want you to know that we love you. It's your husband we can't stand." The point is, since we are in the spotlight we need friends who are able to sustain relationships that are entirely independent of the dynamics of church life.

Finally, sometimes we learn to our sorrow that in a moment of weakness, a friend has relayed confidential information to others which has spread through the larger congregation. Most of us get burned once or twice this way, and sadly, we wonder if we can trust anybody with the delicate sides of our lives. But the fact is that we *need* friends who are able to lock things in their hearts and disclose them only to God.

So what is a friend from a ministry-wife perspective? We're talking about a person of extraordinary flexibility and discretion. One who understands that this is a friendship best observed quietly, not talked about. One who appreciates that at a moment's notice a change in plans may be necessary due to the unexpected that so often enters the life of a pastoral family. This is a friend that doesn't expect us to be perfect in every department of life and doesn't hold it against us when those imperfections occasionally show themselves. (And I might add, we have to allow our friends the same grace.)

We're describing a person who knows how to laugh, how to handle tears, how to pray, how to be silent and listen, and how and when to offer counsel and perspective. Finally, we're talking about a woman who knows how to help us to occasionally walk away from the intensity of pastoral life and discover all the fun there is in simply being a woman who loves God and the larger world that he has given to us.

I must add one more quality to this mix. Such special friends must be persons who understand that we may not always be able to respond in kind in the friendship. We cannot be "possessed" by friends because we have to give ourselves to so many people in the body of Christ. I am thinking of my present friends who understand this principle completely. Some of them give and give and give to me, but they never expect the same intensity from me because they know that I have to be present to scores of other women.

🕊 MRS. STRENGTH ON THE GIVING END?

As a younger ministry wife, I enjoyed some rich friendships, though few in number. I'm speaking of women who could keep confidences, didn't flaunt our relationship, and were wise beyond their years. With these few I found it rather easy to be vulnerable. But with those with whom I served as leader on ministry teams, I found it more difficult to be transparent.

I have been privileged to enter the lives of many, many women. But I erred by thinking that I had to always be *Mrs. Strength*. This was the way my generation of Christian women were trained. Be the counselor, the woman with all the answers. Keep your weaknesses and fears to yourself.

But when you are seen *only* as *Mrs. Strength*, who out there imagines that they have anything to give back to you? Therein may lie the core of the reason why ministry wives have so often felt a stifling loneliness. Friendships are based on some sense of reciprocity. If I am all *give* and no *take*, then how can there be friendship?

There came a moment when that changed for me. In our darkest days, Gordon and I both learned the importance of having friends of our own gender who would cause us to broaden the bases of our life experience. We also found it essential to have others who would join us on a more or less equal footing, giving and receiving, challenging and being challenged, weeping and laughing with us.

I began to see the importance of having friends who could help me see life from a woman's perspective. While my husband and I keep no secrets from one another, I realized there are things about men and women that only someone of the same gender can fully understand.

Because I have a nurturing personality that feeds on lifting others up, I find great satisfaction in being the helper. That's good news for anyone seeking help. But I learned something from Rebecca, wife of Isaac, mother of Jacob and Esau. She showed me the bad news behind my nurturing instinct. Her helping turned into manipulation and even destruction. Rebecca wanted to control family affairs, to make sure that everything turned out all right according to her definition. What was probably a good trait in the beginning turned sour. Everyone lost something because of her.

When I insist on being the *giver* in every relationship, I run the risk of becoming a controlling person. I now see the possibility of this as a rather serious shortcoming. I look back and see that there were times when I could have fallen into this trap.

Several years ago Helen Roseveare, a physician and missionary to Central Africa, spoke at the great Urbana Missionary Convention. She described a time she was stricken with cerebral malaria and hepatitis. What compounded her struggle, she said, was the realization that her illness caused her to be a serious burden to her hospital staff.

For years she had been the only physician for approximately a half-million people. As such, she had been the one in demand, always on the giving end. The Africans, on the other hand, had always been on the receiving end—the ones having to say thank you. Now the roles had been reversed; Roseveare was the *receiver* and the Africans were the *givers*.

One day when she protested the attention being given to her, staff members laughed and said, "Oh, no, Doctor, what you don't understand is that this is the *only* time we feel that *you need us.*"

✆ If Given Prime Time, Friendships Renew Us

I must add that friendships are not likely to grow for a very practical reason: time. If I am too busy, too wrapped up in the doing of church and family work, the development of friendships will simply be shoved aside as a nice idea but not a priority. Should each of us have a dollar for every time we said to someone we liked, "We've got to get together sometime," we would be wealthy indeed.

The fact is that friendships take time . . . prime time. They are not developed in the backwater of time left over from other things when we are exhausted, distracted, and disinterested. You've got to desire a friendship so badly that you're willing to set aside other things to develop it and maintain it. In earlier days, Gordon and I did not see the need for this.

Now I know that friendships are an indispensable key to personal renewal in the ministry. Without them, we can expect dryness of life, loss of spiritual perspective, and almost certain discouragement.

The prophet Daniel said that it is part of our enemy's job "to *wear down* the saints . . . " (Dan 7:25 TLB). We rightfully worry about a moment of devastating sin that can terminate ministry. But I would like to suggest that *being worn down* may be the greater, the more universal threat because it comes about so insidiously. We don't think of fatigue, of loss of spirit, or of loneliness as efforts of the enemy. But it may be at this very point that more pastors and spouses are rendered ineffective than any other place.

Ever get a set of pictures developed only to find that the very best picture of your grandchild is out of focus? Daniel's wearing-down-the-saints is not unlike a description of people out of spiritual focus. Things once sharp become increasingly blurred as one tackles all the ministry challenges each day brings. It makes little difference whether one is part of a large or small ministry, whether one is surrounded by staff associates or has to work alone, whether the congregation is urban, suburban, or rural, there will always be the relentless drain of energy, of spirit, and of vitality.

Ministry is ministry: It means that one is *on the give*, or, to use old King James language, "virtue hath gone out of me." This is a kind of depletion we have to accept; it comes with the territory. But it forces us to ask the question, How do we replenish our souls and regain perspective? One of the indispensable answers has to do with our friendships.

My discovery of Daniel's comment was a defining moment for me. There was a time when I was getting out of focus too frequently, and I needed others to help me see how this was happening and why. I needed friends who were close enough to ask, "Gail, are there knots in your life? Are you listening to God's voice? When was the last time you had a good laugh?"

I have found the New Testament instructive on the subject of friendships. Jesus worked hard to develop a sense of community and friendship among his disciples. He was their mentor, their spiritual father figure. He seemed to live well with the tension between comments like, "I came to minister, not to be ministered unto," while at the same time allowing the disciples to minister to him.

Equally significant was how hard Jesus worked to get them to love each other. He knew that after he ascended to heaven, they would have to lean upon and support one another. There had to be a strength of relationship if they were to persevere and fulfill his dream for them.

The tendency of twentieth-century evangelical Christianity has been to emphasize "solo faith," walking through life alone, the rugged individualist. What a lot of us are awakening to now is "community faith"; we need each other. It is we, not I.

I once reasoned that the ideal would be to find one chum that encapsulated everything I thought a friend should be. I realize now that in my lifetime I may find one or two such friends. But it's far more realistic to have several friends who bring differing perspectives.

Today as I assess my friends, I notice that they have several unique traits. For example, I have a *fun* friend who keeps me looking for the bright side no matter what. Just being with her makes me laugh; all of life can become praise when I'm with her.

A new adventure in friendship has been having several *praying friends* who have the gift of intercession, often fasting and praying over significant matters. May I never be without such friends again! I am ever in their debt.

I have a *reality-check* friend, who befriends me by asking hard questions. Not all friends are capable of doing this. Let's face it, some people aren't dealing with reality. And I have a *stretching* friend who challenges my soul and mind to deepen and to think. She reads circles around me, challenging me to grow. And she causes me to encounter hard, sometimes unanswerable questions. I'm grateful she will not let me live the life of a simplistic believer.

Because I don't want to lose touch with what is happening in the working world, I'm glad to have a *marketplace friend* who keeps me current on what women in the world of business are thinking. Where are the struggles in living for Christ out there? Where are the moral and ethical dilemmas? I love to walk into her world and meet her colleagues and hear about their goals and challenges.

Several *former disciples*, now friends, have become such delightful friends. They renew my understanding of the dynamics of a younger generation. They remind me that I must not get stuck in my ways, that I must see the world through fresh eyes and recognize that the younger generation may have better ideas than we ever had.

Finally, I enjoy having a *friend* who shares my lifestyle. She is a fellow ministry wife who also, as in my case, shares a public life with above-average travel. There is a "knowing" between us that doesn't need many words but affords a deep understanding that helps to sustain both of us.

Some of these friendships span thirty-seven years. Some of them are with women who are ministry wives, others are with women who are not. Each of them is strong; they have independent spirits; they are not "leaners." Our conversations do not center on people but on ideas, not on events but learning experiences, and on complaints but opportunities. There is no reluctance to talk about what we hear God whispering into our lives, where we need wisdom, where we face challenge, and where we have blown it.

Several of these women do not live near me. When we cannot see each other face to face, we talk by phone or exchange E-mails. We know how to pray together, if not by voice, then by writing.

When I think of these women, I am reminded of something Elizabeth Mauske wrote about a Latin American Indian woman who used to frequently visit Elizabeth's mother. The visitor knew no Spanish, and Elizabeth's mother knew nothing of her Indian language. Still she came. The two women would drink tea, smile, and gesture, and then the Indian woman would leave. Always upon leaving, she would make an identical comment in her native tongue.

Mauske memorized the sounds of the comment and then repeated them to a linguist who knew the tribal language. When she heard the translation, Elizabeth Mauske wrote, "[The words] have stayed in my mind as the nicest compliment ever uttered: *I shall come again*, the Indian woman was saying, *for I like myself when I'm near you.*"

And this is how I feel when I am with my friends.

Perhaps another way of expressing it comes from the Old Testament where the friendship of Jonathan and David is described:

"Jonathan went to David . . . and helped him find strength in God" (1 Samuel 23:16). I understand this experience well.

Among ministry wives, talk about friends always leads to the question about relationships in a congregation. Is this possible in a small church? May I be candid enough to say that there can be difficulty here. In a larger congregation, friendships with a few women seems easier. But in a small church, it is too easy to offend other women who feel left out, not good enough, neglected. It's not impossible, but it can become a delicate matter.

I have known of a few exceptions. One woman wrote to me:

> Despite the fact that we live in a small town and function in a small church (135 members), it has worked for us to be very open to anyone and everyone in our church. Those who have desired more than a pastor/parishioner relationship with us have had it. We entertain often in our home and are freely invited into the homes of others. People also have become freer to minister to us at times. In our six years here, we have been aware of no difficulties arising from this. If we had made it a practice to distance ourselves from our congregation and develop relationships only with other pastoral families, we would be quite isolated and have missed out on a lot.

What this woman underscores is that each situation differs because people differ. If she were saying that she talks confidentially with these women about church issues, I'd say over the long haul it won't be without bumps. However, if she is saying that they are with people, sharing themselves and their hospitality along with insights from Scripture, then it could be rewarding and mutually sustaining.

But if the pastor's wife in a small congregation repeatedly singles out one person as her special friend, so that others feel left out and know they can't ever hope to be the same to her, it could boomerang. The two questions to ask ourselves are: Am I giving out confidential information, and do I repeatedly choose one friend over everyone else?

By now you are asking, where can I find friends like this? First, ask yourself, *Am I prepared to be the kind of person a friendship requires? Do I want to have a friend more than* be *one?* A greeting card I once received put it this way: *You have the quality I like the most in a person.* Inside: *You like me.* As Lila Troutman, the wife of Dawson Troutman, founder of the Navigators, once underscored, "Never enter a life except to build." If this is our mind-set, others will delight in our friendship.

Secondly, ask, *Do I have the time to pursue common interests which engender deep friendships?* C. S. Lewis once said, "Lovers are normally face-to-face absorbed in each other, friends side-by-side, absorbed in some common interest."

Nineteen years ago a group of twenty ministry wives in New England planned a "coffee" to see if any relationships might "click" long-term. From that group, four of us have met on and off (when we all have lived in New England) for almost two decades. It was an experiment, and the aftermath was that we found each other. Because of our "common interest," as C. S. Lewis put it, we understand what the others are experiencing. Over the years, we have walked through some deep valleys with each other. I cherish these women and am grateful for their consistent lives and unconditional love. "As iron sharpens iron, so one man sharpens another" (Prov. 27:17).

Why not try having a small "coffee" (perhaps five or six women)? Invite ministry wives from the surrounding area. After a time of refreshments, begin a period of nostalgic reminiscence by telling where each of you were during the seventh grade. (Strangely, this is a year most of us remember.) Then perhaps each woman can tell about the time in her life when she felt closest to God.

Having used these two questions dozens of times, I can assure you that fellow ministry wives will get lost in the fun of nostalgia. Connections are often made that can eventuate in future friendships.

A third question you need to ask yourself is the deepest and hardest to answer: *Am I prepared to take human weakness into account— mine and hers, when pursuing a friend?*

Not long ago I did a convicting word study on Jesus' last days. I'd come across the word "troubled" several times in my Bible reading. Jesus described himself as being "troubled," and he expressed concern for his friends: that they were troubled.

What was the significance of this word? In the Greek language *troubled* meant *in angst* and *away from home*. When you're in a troubled state, there's nothing better than a friend.

It's interesting to see how much Jesus wanted to be with his friends when he was troubled. He leaned on them even when he knew they would ultimately fail him in his darkest hour. He never became cynical or bitter but *kept walking toward them—to the end* (John 13:1). And if he could not physically keep moving in their direction because of the hardness of their hearts, as in the case of Judas Iscariot, he still kept open. "Why are you here, friend?" were his final words to Judas in the garden just before the kiss of betrayal.

It is no surprise that it was Jesus' close friend John who used the word *troubled* most in describing Jesus under fire. When seeing Mary and Martha after Lazarus had died, "he was *deeply moved in spirit and troubled*" (John 11:33). These were three of his closest friends. He personally lost someone dear, and he was angry at the pain and separation death caused.

Soon after this happened, Jesus spoke with his disciples about his eventual death. He would be like a seed put into the ground, he said. But the result would be many more seeds. Then, "*Now my heart is troubled....*" Jesus poured out his broken heart to his friends (John 12:27).

Following the washing of the disciples feet, he again opened his heart to them. "Jesus was troubled in spirit," and he said to the twelve, "I tell you the truth, one of you is going to betray me" (John 13:21).

Even later, Jesus had to face Peter with the fact that Peter would betray him. It's a shame that there is a break between chapters thirteen and fourteen of John because the thrust of this event would grip us more if we put the two sentences together. "I tell you the truth, before the rooster crows, you will disown me three times! Do not let *your* hearts be *troubled*" (John 13:38; 14:1).

Was it not magnanimous of our Lord to be most concerned that his friends would not have to experience the same anguish while he was going through this? Even though he knew they would soon betray him, still he stuck with them. He looked beyond the immediate events to what would be possible when they all got together again. "When you have turned back, strengthen your brothers," he said to Simon Peter in Luke 22:32.

Mark's gospel tells us the rest of the story. There are the distressing moments in the Garden of Gethsemane. We learn that he not only took his three closest friends, Peter, James, and John along, but he allowed them to see him in deep anguish. "'My soul is overwhelmed with sorrow to the point of death,' he said to them. 'Stay here and keep watch'" (Mark 14:34).

Think about the last time you told anyone how deep your pain was. Too often when I am struggling, I am worried about my "image." But the Son of God gave himself the freedom to be open and vulnerable with humanity. Something is wrong with how different we are from him. Today, for the most part, we will only find this kind of transparency in the community of the formerly addicted, who maintain no airs since they have no image to protect.

The invitation to his friends to stick with him in the garden seems to be Jesus' last appeal to humanity. Three times he went from his place of prayer to arouse the sleeping disciples. It is instructive that he never rejects them in their weakness. Finally there came the point where he seemed to move ahead on his own, his only comfort coming from the heavenly Father until even that was broken off at the cross.

Do you want friends like Jesus had? Could you begin to get close to his loving responses in the wake of friends failing you like this? This takes the supernatural love of Christ within. Nothing short of it will do.

A friend and I were once talking about how easy it is to judge friends harshly when they fail us. She wisely pointed out that at such times, the key is where our eyes are. If we look at our friends without gazing first at Christ, we will fail—giving them a graceless response. But if we observe our friends *after* first looking at Christ and asking for his mind, then our thoughts of them will be entirely different, gracious and humble.

Let me tell you about the events of one week with my treasury of friendships. Very recently, I spent an hour on the phone with one of my friends who lives in the Midwest. (For the last several years on a monthly basis we have *met on the phone* for sixty minutes on the evening when Gordon meets with the elders of our church.) We talked about our families, books we're reading, challenges we or our husbands are facing in our ministries, and prayer concerns for the coming weeks.

The next day another friend dropped by with five grandma scrapbooks. She'd been to a book sale, she said, and knew I'd love to have these for our five grandchildren. So she bought them and put them in my hands. That afternoon I called another friend to ask if she would be willing to care for two of our grandchildren while we took their mom and dad out to dinner. She was delighted to do so.

Another friend, a ministry wife, called. "I need to tell you what's going on in our house this morning and how I'm feeling about it. You've got to tell me whether or not I'm being reasonable in my reactions." I was able to be her reality check with my words. Another friend is coming over this afternoon to pray with me. We do this regularly. Before we begin, I'll tell her that I'm tired, that finishing this book by deadline is hanging over me, that I'm concerned about a couple of people in our world whose marriages aren't doing well, and that I need extra wisdom as I make an important decision. She'll understand, keep these things in her heart, and pray.

It would be hard to find better friends than my daughter and my daughter-in-law who are on the phone with me almost every morning. "Mom, do you have a recipe for . . . ?" "Mom, you'll never believe what Lucas said . . ." "Mom, Eringail and I made some brownies and thought you and dad might like some." "Mom, I thought I'd call and pray for you before you and Dad make this trip."

Then there's my fun friend who loves to do card stores with me. One Sunday after worship, she slipped a card into my hand as she went by. It read, "At Christmas time, remember: No two flakes are alike . . ." Inside: ". . . *but you and I sure come awfully close.*"

You'd easily be willing to die for friends like these.

THIRTEEN

PROTECTING THE PERMANENCY
OF YOUR MARRIAGE

Love is an unconditional commitment to an imperfect person.
—*Unknown*

For many years Gordon and I enjoyed a friendship with Paul and Edith Rees. Paul had been one of America's great preachers, first in Minneapolis and then as minister-at-large for World Vision. He was ninety-one when he died, Edith, just a few years younger, was ninety when she died.

Even though there was almost a forty-year difference in our ages, Gordon and I used to love to spend time with the Reeses because their faith was so dynamic, their thinking so forward-looking, and their marriage so vital. Before Paul and Edith entered Christ's presence, they celebrated their sixty-fifth wedding anniversary.

Years ago, Paul wrote to me about his relationship to Edith:

After two years of engagement and fifty-five years of marriage, we are still very much in love. If anyone says, "Pardon me, but your love is showing," we don't mind a bit.

This comment about his marriage was typical of him. And true! The love between Paul and Edith did indeed show, and we used to tell them that when we grew up, we wanted to be like them. The line was always good for a laugh.

In Paul's eighty-eighth year, the four of us were driving in a car together. "You'll never guess what happened to Paul the other day," Edith said from the backseat. "He got an invitation to speak in Japan *five years* from now."

She paused for a moment so that we could gather the significance of the thought. Then she said, "I told him, 'Paul, go for it!'" The implications and the enthusiasm of Edith's comment hit us both at once, and we roared.

Gordon and I have a long way to go to reach sixty-five years of life together. But we do have nearly thirty-eight of those years behind us now. We often observe that thirty-seven of those years have been very good ones. Thirty-seven out of thirty-eight isn't bad. We've had some regrets but many delights.

Who can say whether a marriage in the context of pastoral ministry is harder to maintain or easier than other lifestyles? The fact is that for every pitfall that congregational ministry might present to a marriage, there is a parallel advantage.

Yes, life is lived as if in a fishbowl. But time is much more flexible.

Yes, one does move from one home to another more frequently, but we have the privilege of a marvelous mixture of experiences and relationships.

Yes, there can be criticism that hurts and humbles, but there is also the challenge of living to a higher standard and a sense of satisfaction when God has given the grace to do it.

Yes, we don't get rich doing what we do, but we learn something about faith and living life linked directly with God's purposes and promises.

What have the years taught us about marriage in the ministry context? *That you have to work hard to preserve what you have and to keep on the growing edge, lest things go stale and begin to unravel.* Scripture says, "Your enemy the devil prowls around like a roaring lion looking for someone to devour" (1 Pet. 5:8). Let's assume right from the start that Satan loves to devour or destroy marriages of pastors and spouses. Neutralize or even kill such a marriage, and a substantial number of people are affected in the wrong way.

When Gordon and I sit with ministry couples who want to discuss their relationships, we often ask a simple question: "On a scale of one to ten, how would you assess the quality of your relationship?" We hear more fours, fives, and sixes than we like.

This is not a chapter with an exhaustive list of principles about marriage, but it is a brief attempt to acknowledge several important themes which have gone a long way to preserve our marriage. After nearly four decades, I'm prepared to call these principles nonnegotiable. That is: You probably can't have a healthy marriage in a congregational setting without them. They won't guarantee a fail-safe marriage, but they can serve to diminish the possibility of a relationship headed for mortal damage.

❧ Mutual Time at the Fire

In the earliest pages of this book, I spoke of time at the fire. It was a way for me to point to how important it is to pursue a life of intimate connection with God. But I want to add something to that thought at this point by suggesting the importance of *fire-time with my husband*.

Time together at the fire did not come all that easily for us. Gordon has often talked to men about the struggle that more than a few men (including pastors) have in feeling at ease about praying and worshipping with their wives.

"I am confused," many ministry wives have said to me. "My husband prays eloquently and sincerely when he is before the congregation. He can pray with people who come to visit him with personal needs. But praying with me seems almost an impossibility."

From the start Gordon and I practiced the disciplines of prayer and thanksgiving when it came to all the appropriate occasions. But the free and easy ability to address the Lord on a daily basis about our concerns and our thanksgivings seemed hard to acquire. We'd promise one another that we were going to find time for prayer and worship each day, we'd stick to the discipline for a few days, and then let it drop. I suppose we must have started and stopped a dozen times.

Why this was such a struggle still alludes me. Like many others, we probably didn't believe deeply enough in the efficacy of prayer and spiritual discipline. It was too easy to be convinced that hard work and people skills were enough to do the job. Gordon believes that most men have a difficult time feeling at ease about praying with their wives because there is an admission of weakness that goes along with it. It's no secret that most men struggle to identify with any weakness at all., especially men who feel they are paid to have all the answers.

Again, he says, men worry about expressing themselves too intimately with their wives about spiritual matters because they know it's just a matter of time before they'll fail to live up to their own words. They don't want to hear a wife parroting back words that were said in a prayer a few days before. So prayer and spiritual reflection become a problem for many of them.

And so it was with us in the beginning . . . until, many years ago, when Gordon experienced a series of migraine headaches. It was the unbearable pain that caused him to lose his inhibitions about asking if we could pray together. I was glad to respond to his request that I lay my hands on him and pray for him. That's where it began: our growing freedom to come before the Lord and pray for one another and to pray about issues of common concern.

That moment happened about ten years into our marriage. From what I can discern, it often takes that long for many couples to begin to find their depth in spiritual matters. Obviously, we were no exception.

I've mentioned earlier how, many years later, our mutual life of prayer expanded again as we came to appreciate the significance of intercession. As a result, we have achieved a fairly regular discipline of beginning our day together before the Lord. First of all, we pray for our children and our grandchildren and the future they will face in a world that is not friendly toward the things of God. Next come our friends and congregation who depend on our intercession.

We have become accustomed to praying each time one of us faces a ministry challenge. For example, unless I'm teaching a class, I'm committed to being at Gordon's side on the front pew at all of our four worship services when he is preaching.

When it comes time for him to go to the pulpit to preach, I often grab his arm and whisper, "Preach for change!" It's our code phrase of encouragement, a reminder that preaching must be a life-change event. Then as he opens the Scriptures and begins his sermon, I enjoy praying for him. In so doing, I am his partner as he exercises his spiritual gift of preaching.

Gordon is quick to do the same for me. If I've been somewhere in the country speaking at a conference, it's not been unusual to receive a fax early in the morning in which Gordon has written a special prayer or poem for the day.

We both enjoy sharing clippings or quotes for the spiritual encouragement of the other from things we are reading. Occasionally, we read to one another out of our journals when we've come to some new insight.

In such ways, we have learned how to come to the fire together. It has made a forceful difference on those occasions when one or both of us were under unusual stress. But I hasten to remind my younger friends, what we have in terms of mutual fire-time experiences took years to develop. I'm not sure that anything can be done to rush this process. Learning to trust, sharing pain, and becoming mutually aware of our sinful state all aid in making this type of deepening possible.

❧ TIME TO LIVE

Perhaps *one of the greatest dangers any couple can face is that of allowing their life together to become defined by the ministry itself.* When this happens we call the result a ministry-marriage.

A ministry-marriage is a relationship defined by church work, one so completely centered on the life of the church that it has little room for anything else. Simply put, a woman has married a minister, not a man. And a man has married a pastor's wife, not a woman. It looks admirable at first, but in the long term, it's not healthy.

In a ministry-marriage, most conversation revolves around what's happening at church, all activities are based upon the life of the church, and all decisions in the marriage are driven by what the church might think.

You know it's a ministry-marriage when you ask yourself, Would these two people want to be together if they weren't doing ministry? Would they know how to live in any other way?

"I realized that something was really wrong when I found myself talking church business to my husband while we were making love," a ministry wife once told me. "I can't think of much else that we even talk about except what's going on at church," another wife said. And still another, "Everything we do of a social nature is pegged to the church calendar. We're never free of it."

We were in danger of drifting toward a ministry-marriage some years ago. Our children had left home for their college years. We had been so accustomed to scheduling all of our fun and recreation around their activities that we weren't sure what to do with one another after they left. So we filled the time vacancies with more ministry. Gordon traveled more, wrote more, and spoke more. I became increasingly involved in the life of the congregation and spent more and more time visiting with women who had personal needs. When we were together, our conversation centered on all the things we were doing . . . for the purposes of ministry. It looked good, sounded good, and resulted in some good things. But it was not good for our love relationship.

In short: We were in danger of forgetting how to have fun together and how to be a man and women who simply loved each other with or without all the other stuff. There were times when my husband simply needed me to be a playmate—someone to remind him that life has a light side to it.

We awoke to this drift toward ministry-marriage only because a close friend pointed out that our lives were becoming far too serious, far too laden with ministry responsibilities. It was fortunate, in a way, that our life of ministry came to a screeching halt for a while because it gave us a chance to do a total reappraisal of these tendencies and make some drastic changes.

We took a hard look at ourselves and made some major adjustments. I must add that it was not all that easy. But we determined to learn how to relax, to do new things, to laugh more, to enjoy each other. And we are. What we have today we call *solidarity.* That's our definition of a love that takes you all the way to the end of life.

When Gordon returns home, I want to make sure that it is a *home* he is coming to, not an extension of his office. I am his wife, his partner in life, not an associate pastor. All of our conversation does not have to revolve around church. And so I've worked hard to make our home a place that is separate from church life, a place of peace and order, a place where there is real rest of mind and heart.

We began dating again. We started having "surprise nights." Our married children gave us this wonderful idea. It meant taking turns planning surprise occasions for each other. Even as I write this, we are about to go on one of those surprise nights. The excitement is in the anticipation that something unusual is going to happen. The one who plans simply tells the "surprised" one what to wear, when we will leave and return. The rest is left to the element of surprise. Thankfully, it doesn't need to cost much money.

One day, for instance, I planned a long walk in an arboretum, bringing Gordon's binoculars, bottled water, some cheese, an apple, and his camera. We had a ball discovering God's gift of nature in fresh ways. There was a time when such spontaneity would not have been so easy when the children were at home. But even a little is better than nothing.

I need to emphasize that these thoughts are especially important during midlife. Gordon reminds me this is a season when things can get heavy for our men. The word "trapped" appears more frequently in conversation and thought. Men in ministry begin to feel that everyone has a piece of them, that they can never do enough for the people around them. They (as we) are living with financial pressures, the realities of growing children (and aging parents?), issues in ministry that seem to grow into greater complexity. The pressure is relentless, and the temptation grows to run from it all. There is never a more important time for a husband and wife to be closer, more open, or more active in their personal lives together. We should never be ashamed to play.

☙ TIME TO TALK

Another principle that is key has to do with *our desire and ability to talk to each other*. Communicating isn't learned at church. It must first be practiced between married partners at home. A ministry wife writes:

My husband is an unhappy man. For years he preached about the sanctity of Christian marriage and family and the importance of staying connected. But when he was home, he hardly ever talked to any of us. Now he's a bit older, feeling very lonely and isolated. He wants the family's attention, but it's too late for the children. They got out of the habit of seeing him around and have found other things to do. And he and I are out of the habit of talking. So there's a lot of pain for us both.

Many years ago the late Walter Trobisch, a writer and speaker on the subject of marriage and family, visited in our home for dinner. He told Gordon and me that wherever he went in the world to speak to missionaries and pastors, he found that the number one problem in marriages had to do with talking.

"I was in West Africa last month," he said. "A couple came up to me at the end of the first lecture and said, 'We drove 250 miles to get here and never spoke a word to one another during the entire trip.'" That, Trobisch claimed, was not an uncommon story.

We have always talked about almost everything. It was only when the talk in our lives waned that we faced trouble. We have learned how to talk about our dreams, our fears, our anxieties, our plans. We watch the news and talk about current events, watch sports and talk about our favorite athletes and their teams. We talk about the children and grandchildren; we make plans for travel; we talk openly about God and our walk with him. Now that I think about it, we rarely run out of things to talk about!

In case you haven't figured it out, I am a fixer by nature. My instinct is to find an answer to every question, a solution to every problem. Through the years I have had to remind myself that some things we talk about don't need fixing; they simply need to be heard.

I have this dreadful habit of listening to Gordon describe a difficulty or a question and immediately swinging into motion with solutions. "I don't need you to repair the problem," Gordon will say. "I just want to tell you about it." Slowly, I'm learning. By the time we reach Paul and Edith Rees's age, I may have this one beaten.

On the other hand, sometimes talk has to turn to concerns and critique. When does a wife let her busy, tired, preoccupied husband know that she's disquieted about something, maybe even a little bit angry about things he's let fall through the cracks? How does she tell him that he's let her down, made her feel insignificant? How does she inform him that she gets real tired, too, that he's not the only one living with stress? How can she tell him that sometimes she feels like his mistress, because he's really married to the church?

Answer (learned the hard way): when there's a period of high trust and openness between them. I have found that Gordon will listen to virtually anything I have to say (even if it is a painful matter) if I have prepared the way and waited for a timely moment. But if I say the hard thing impulsively in anger with an intent to hurt or humiliate, the chances are that I'm going to find myself locked into an argument. I don't want a quarrel. I just want to be heard and understood.

Gordon has helped me to understand that from their earliest days after birth, men have learned to trust a woman's voice—it *soothes*. Is it possible, he queries, that a man is in search of that earliest soothing voice all of his life? But, sadly, there can come a time when the voice *scolds* instead. I've had to ask myself which my husband hears.

When I am operating out of wisdom and sensitivity, I have waited until I'm sure Gordon has all of his attention focused on us and our lives together. Then he is more apt to be in a mood to listen, have a desire to learn or grow, and is anxious to know my heart.

We've both learned to preface our comments with words like, "I have a thought for you ...," or "I need for you to know that ...," or "Is this a good time to tell you something that's been troubling me?" Occasionally, it's been useful to write a hard thought in a letter (not to be mailed but personally given and read together) so that expressions are well thought out, not excessive nor understated.

A friend I highly admire for her godliness and intelligence tells me that when she has a tough thing to say to her husband, she disciplines herself to wait a week before talking about it. Each day she chooses to do something that pleases him the most, a deed that isn't natural or easy for her. While doing these acts of love, she reminds herself that God has given her husband to her as a gift, and he has much to teach her. By the time she does talk to him, hers is not a scolding voice but a grateful one that soothes. The spirit of the confrontation is totally different. Admirable!

Talk can be constructive and satisfying, or it can be destructive and dividing. We've had our share of both kinds. But as the years have gone by, we've acquired an ability to enjoy more of the former and less of the latter. It takes lots of practice.

What happens when talk in a marriage is insufficient or unnourishing? One of the greatest minds of the nineteenth century, Thomas Carlyle, lost his wife in death. In his grief, he combed her diaries to find out if she realized how much he had loved her, whether or not she knew of his appreciation. To his consternation and great sadness, he found nothing, no indication at all that she had ever heard his language of love or his appreciation.

What happens when talk is squelched? A seminary wife admitted to me that she was fearful of any significant conversation with her husband because he was so brilliant that anything she said sounded infantile next to his accelerated verbal skills. Result: Talk becomes hollow. Both of them lose.

Sometimes talking is hampered by a hidden agenda. We bring the "excess baggage" of earlier life wounds into our marriages. Past memory plays an important role. There are times when we only seem to be dealing with our spouses, but in fact, we are dredging up things for which our partners have no memory.

Jim and the late Sally Conway once wrote of such an experience. "What's happened today?" was Sally's usual question each evening when Jim came through the door from work. For her, it was a simple way to show interest or curiosity in his day. But for Jim, the question, asked every day, seemed more like an intrusion. One day he blurted, "Why do I have to always tell you what I've been doing?"

Because the Conways had worked hard to master the art of communication, they knew this response was out of character. They began to do some digging. Jim recalled that during his childhood days that his mother always suspected that, when her children were out of her sight, they were up to no good. Her questions became accusative: "Well, what trouble have you been into now?" or "You're five minutes late getting home from school. What have you been doing?"

Many years later when as an adult Jim walked through the door and heard a simple question: "How was your day?" he overreacted. Why? *Because he heard his mother's voice from years ago.* Sally didn't know this and was mystified as he snapped back. Words which hurt like this need to be demystified.[1]

I had a similar experience when we were quite young. In our Illinois congregation, there was an automobile dealer who, out of a generous heart, provided Gordon with a brand new car to drive every six months. Loving new cars as he did, you can imagine Gordon's excitement each time the moment came to drive down to the dealership and exchange cars.

But for me the moment was a downer. For the two weeks before and after, I would find myself surly and contemptuous of the car Gordon was now driving. "It's the wrong color," I'd say. "It's too pretentious. The congregation will wonder where we're getting our money. People will be jealous." With such comments I managed to effectively rain on Gordon's parade.

After this happened three or four times, Gordon asked if we could talk about my feelings. He wanted to give me the *charitable assumption,* one of his favorite phrases. He assumed that I was not out to make him miserable but that there was something deeper, something hidden that might explain my reactions.

As we looked backwards through my life under the category of cars, we both learned something about me that I'd not faced before. I'd grown up in a small town in a family that, while not rich by modern standards, certainly was more comfortable in lifestyle than most in our community. Each year my father had purchased a new car—usually the best available.

On many mornings he would drive me to school. As I would get out of one of these flashy cars, there were often some mean-spirited kids who, jealous of my family's good fortune, would tease me, calling me a "rich bitch." Each new car increased the fervor of that taunting. As a teen, I became hostile to all new cars. They seemed to separate me from people. Put me in a new car, and I heard "rich bitch" all over again.

What Gordon and I learned was that I had never been released from those hurting words. Each time Gordon drove up in a new car, even one that was a gift (really a loan), I heard the taunting all over again. *But this time I imagined it to be the voice of the entire congregation.* And the only way I could express my unresolved pain was to make snide comments about Gordon's car.

Today I'm fine with new cars. We certainly do not get a new one every six months. But when new-car time comes, I have the ability to enjoy the experience as much as my husband does. But if Gordon and I had not acquired the ability to talk openly and frankly so as to get into each other's hearts, I'm not sure we would have ever resolved that problem or many others similar to it.

🌀 MARITAL QUIET TIME

When our last child turned four (it doesn't work if they are younger than this), we began something else we learned from Walter Trobisch, which became a nonnegotiable. Walter had told Gordon,

"Gail has earned the right to hear about your day by staying home with the children so that you are free to pursue your ministry. The least you can do is tell her what her stay-at-home decision has meant to you. Think of it as a *marital quiet time*."

So about twenty minutes before Gordon would leave the office (he was only five minutes from home), he learned to call me and to tell me he was on his way out. This gave me time to prepare the children, brew a cup of something, and clear a path for him to walk through the house without stumbling. If he was feeling especially frazzled, he would tell me so I could adjust my expectations and let him "veg" for a time after coming home.

On most occasions, when he arrived, the children would get their hugs and then back off because they knew that it was time for Mom and Dad to talk. This did several things: All conversation about church was out of the way so that dinner time could revolve around the children's worlds. It also acted as an accountability tool for how *I* was spending my days. It became a mutual marital quiet time.

All day long I found myself anticipating those just-between-us moments. Looking back, I know our marital quiet times helped me over the humps of those years when talking preschool gibberish drove me to distraction. It was a habit well worth putting on our calendars.

⤫ TIME UNDER CONTROL

Marriages are also greatly affected when *time is out of control*. How many conflicts do a husband and wife in ministry have because no one is watching the calendar?

During a seminar at which I spoke to ministry wives, I asked them to brainstorm about defective motivations that tempt us to overwork in ministry. Their list may give you and your spouse or staff a good conversation:

Nothing is ever finished.
Unrealistic expectations
God is our boss (our view of God is faulty).
Must please people to feel good
Church is where the strokes are.
Husband can't admit frailty—covers by working harder

Husband still trying to please Daddy
As a child, my husband was given a sense of destiny to fulfill.
We have forgotten how to laugh.
Husband thinks he is indestructible
Both of us feel too responsible for everybody.
Don't have any margins or realistic boundaries in our calendar
Can't seem to take time off until the work is done—but the work
   is never done
Hard to stop because of too much sensation in life

Most items on this list can be traced to the time-out-of-control problem. In his book *Ordering Your Private World*, Gordon wrote of four things that cause time to get out of control: bowing to the demands of dominating people, playing to one's own weaknesses instead of strengths, being persuaded by the applause (and the flattery) of people, and perceived or contrived emergencies.

We've all known life when time was undisciplined. The demands of people, of programs, of deadlines, they manipulate life. And what was once joy becomes sour. Sometimes we dream of escaping from it all. Life becomes a treadmill of events and conversations, none of which is fun.

The first thing to go in such a situation is the vitality of the marriage. We deny one another in order to meet the demands of everyone else. Love life, talk time, fun moments, they all disappear. More and more we become strangers to one another, respect is lost, and it can even come to the place where we want out.

An entry in my journal describes the problem:

> The speed with which I lived this day is scandalous. I started the morning in North Carolina where Kristy and I finished leading a retreat together. By 11:00 I was in NYC sitting next to my husband for a morning worship service. In the afternoon, we flew to Boston where Gordon preached at Grace Chapel, and after a late night time of fellowship with friends, we drove to New Hampshire to spend the night. Four states where meaningful experiences happened—all in one day. Whew! Makes me weary just thinking about it. Forgive me, Lord. This is not the way to live!

Just as we had once learned to budget our money and discipline our spending, Gordon and I had to learn to budget our time and discipline our efforts. We had to learn how to say no to good things in order to pursue the best things. Not an easy task, especially for those of us in the ministry who are driven to please people and fear ever letting anyone down.

We learned to bring time under control by determining our priorities. Five things were most important: maintaining our inner fire, living together and with family and friends, serving people in the name of Jesus, the business side of our lives (the care of our home, our finances, our health, etc.), and recreation that renewed us.

Within the scope of these priorities, there had to be a balance. That meant we would have to plan our allocations of time weeks in advance, if necessary, so that the less-than-best demands of people and programs would not encroach upon what was best for a healthy life and marriage. Again, we hone our relational skills at home, not at church.

We became more selective in responding to invitations to speak. Attractive as it might be to crisscross the country speaking at conferences and seminars, the fact is that too much of it can diminish the core of our vitality. The stimulation and opportunity can become meaningless if it comes at the expense of neglecting the most important human relationship we will have in our lifetimes.

I determined that I would rarely, if ever, be away from Gordon on a Sunday when he was preaching. His sermon is *our* main event. We will be there together: him preaching, me praying and cheering him on. I've disappointed more than one conference planner when I've accepted an invitation to speak on the condition that I can be home by Saturday evening.

We began to make sure that each month included enough evenings for our own private moments of fun and play. You hear me mentioning these words, fun and play, fairly frequently. It's not without purpose. So we began to write our family and friends into the calendar far in advance of anything else. I assumed responsibility for our social calendar, which is far easier for me as the resident extravert/detail person. Often I need to coordinate with Gordon's secretary to be sure I don't double-date. Friday, our Sabbath, is automatically unscheduled, as is Saturday, Gordon's study day.

Because both of us rise early in the morning, we find it easier to maintain quiet hours each week for personal devotions and study.

When this is all in place, *then* we permit the ministry to flow in all around the edges. In this way, the calendar becomes reasonably balanced and budgeted. To be sure, there are times when things seem to pile up, and I have to stop and go back to the trenches to see where we got off track. Together, we work it out.

⟶ Time to Deal with Your Weaknesses

Finally, when you live a life that is defined by leadership realities, there is the challenge of *facing up to weaknesses, character flaws, and failures.*

How do you live with a man who's generally expected to be right and holy every minute he is "out there?" How do you relate to a husband who comes home either with the fantasy that he can do no wrong or that he can do no right, depending on how things have gone that day? How do you walk through life with a person who spends most of his time telling others how to live but doesn't know how to master some essentials of life himself?

The man who preaches the gospel of Christ is the same man who may leave his dirty clothes strewn across the bedroom floor. The man who leads the charge on a new building program is the same man who may not keep his garage clean. The man who is the ideal for a flock of other women is the same man you often see in an unkempt, unshaven, unbathed condition.

There is a powerful challenge to a marriage involved in ministry: how to project reasonable and honest spiritual leadership in the congregation, yet be humble enough to acknowledge your limits and faults in personal life. The man who cannot make this adjustment will be hard to live with. The woman who makes the adjustment impossible by making unreasonable demands will pave the way toward disaster.

The late Swiss psychiatrist Paul Tournier honestly addressed his inability to lead with weakness before his wife in this way:

> Over ten years ago, a friend challenged me to put into practice the Christian faith I professed. The first step that came clearly to my mind was to unburden myself completely to my wife of many thoughts, memories, fears, and failures, which I had never mentioned

to her. Such a step seemed impossible to me. I felt I would lose her confidence. We had been very close, and loved each other deeply. We used to discuss everything, even religion. I used to develop for her my pet theories, and she would express admiration and approval. But it is one thing to speak on the level of ideas, and it is an altogether different thing to speak of one's own soul. When I took this step, my wife answered me, "Then I *can* be of some help to you!" And she opened up to me in return. In my zeal to help her in her life, my professional vocation had come to hide the person of her husband. It humiliated her by making her into a "case" rather than a wife, and it hindered her personality from coming into full bloom. [2]

Tournier describes the challenge well. How do we juggle the demands of public and private life and be the same persons in both worlds?

There is no simple answer to this question. With God's help, Gordon and I have worked hard not to pretend *out there* that we are something which we are not *in here* (that is, in our home). We do not treat each other differently in public than we do in private. And we do not make claims about ourselves that we cannot live with in private.

On the other hand, we have made every possible attempt to live up to the things we preach. If we are going to challenge people to a disciplined lifestyle, then we must be living it first. If we are going to call people to a life of grace and forgiveness, then we must be first forgivers and grace-givers. And if we are going to call people to lives of simplicity and generosity, then they must see it in us first.

Having said that, we appreciate each other's imperfections. The fact is that Gordon and I both married sinners. We have given up trying to change each other to become something that fits our personal con-venience. As Gordon sometimes says, "Each of us is about 80 percent of what the other person wants. The other 20 percent makes up a very acceptable difference of personality and temperament. And it's our task to accept the differences, not demand unreasonable change."

We've worked hard to give each other room for down moments, bad moments, and failing moments. We are both quick to forgive and quick to challenge each other to continuous growth. Each of us is aware of how much we need each other to help in the process of identifying and living with our weaknesses. This understanding has helped us in our best and worst hours. Permanency or, as we like to think of it, solidarity can't be a reality without weaving these non-negotiables into our marriages.

Not long ago Gordon and I were with a group of people who were discussing depth of marital commitment and how we make marriages survive in this age.

In preparation for our time together, we each read a letter that the German nobleman James von Moltke wrote to his wife Fre'ya the day before he was to be executed for treason against Hitler.

The permanence of their relationship is powerfully seen as you read his expression of love to her:

> You are not a means God employed to make me who I am, rather you are myself. You are my 13th Chapter of the First Letter to the Corinthians. Without this chapter no human being is human . . . only together do we constitute a human being. We are, as I wrote a few days ago, symbolically created as one. Therefore, my love, I am certain you will not lose me on this earth, not for a moment. All the texts of love are in my heart and in your heart. [3]

Imagine what it must feel like as Fre'ya lives out her days in Vermont to have a gift like this to carry her through the lonely moments. None of us knows today how choices we are making to love deeply might affect us years from now. Today is the day to work on tomorrow's lasting love. I think back to Paul Rees' words about the permanence of his marriage to Edith, his delight in their fifty plus years of love:

> After two years of engagement and fifty-five years of marriage, we are still very much in love. If anyone says, "Pardon me, but your love is showing," we don't mind a bit.

As I said earlier, that's where Gordon and I want to be when we grow up.

FOURTEEN

IN RETROSPECT

What Matters Most

Seven times a day I praise you for your righteous laws.
(Ps. 119:164)

It's an old story, but it's worth recycling. A hiker falls off the edge of a cliff. As he hurtles through the air, he grabs a small branch growing out of the rock. There he hangs, unable to climb up or down. In desperation he cries out, "Is there anybody up there?"

A voice comes back, "Yes, this is the Lord speaking. *Simply let go of the branch*, and I will catch you and lower you to solid ground."

The hiker ponders this instruction for a while. Then he cries out, "Is there anybody else up there?"

You can't expect to live a life in ministry and not find yourself hanging, on several occasions, from a branch: nowhere to go, up or down. More than once in such moments you will be tempted to ask the question, "Is there anybody up there?"

These cliff-hanging moments usually come as a result of failure, spiritual warfare, steps of faith, or the ordinary faults and bumps of life together in community with other people. You'll know a cliff-hanger because it seems as if there is no solution, no way out.

In our thirty-eight years of ministry, we have known a number of cliff-hanging moments. Decisions about organizational change, about hiring or dismissing ministry associates, conflicts with people in leadership, terrible tragedies and sins in peoples' lives, and how to take an unpopular stand on some issue. But lest I be misunderstood, let me rush to say that many cliff-hangers have been of our own making.

The cliff-hangers are where I've learned what it means to have utter dependence upon God. As a ministry wife, you have a particular challenge that few will understand. You have to know how to be a reality-check when your husband is receiving undeserved praise. Then again, you have to know how to be an encourager when he is receiving undeserved criticism. You don't always have a public forum to express yourself as he does. You will not be at the board meetings when decisions are made. And you will not be in a position to defend him when others take hard shots at his reputation. Your leadership must be of a different kind.

In cliff-hanging moments, what you have going for you is a life of prayer. I have had the growing conviction that if I am to lead, I must learn to walk in and out of the Lord's presence all day long, like a revolving door, so that prayer, conversation with God, becomes an attitude and instinct of the heart.

On the subject of prayer, E. Stanley Jones wrote:

> Prayer is "co-operation" with God. In prayer you align your desires, your will and your life to God. You and God become agreed on life desires, life purposes, life plans and you work them out together. Prayer, then, is not trying to get God to do our will. It is the getting of our will into line with God's will. So prayer aligns the whole self to the whole Self of God. Prayer is therefore attunement. Just as when a note on a well tuned piano is struck, the corresponding note on a well-tuned violin will vibrate in unison, so when God strikes certain notes in His nature, we find our heartstrings vibrating in unison, provided prayer has attuned us. . . . Prayer cleanses, it chastens our desires, realigns them so that you cannot tell where your desires end and God's desires begin. They are one. The desires are one, the decisions are one, and the power is one. . . . When you learn how to pray, you learn how to live—vitally, vibrantly, victoriously.[1]

Three themes have become foundational to my life of prayer and have played a key role when the cliff-hanging moments have appeared. The first two came to me out of St. Paul's Roman letter. I offer them to you because they have often reoriented my perspective and my ability to cope with cliff-hangers. In one of the gloomiest portions of his writings, where Paul talks about the depravity of humanity, he mentions two things that people resist doing in their natural state. The first is: *They do not honor God.* And the second is: *They do not thank him.*

ᕯ Theme One: Honoring God

As part of my prayer disciplines, I have pursued the discipline of honoring God on a regular basis. St. Paul wrote of the spiritual lostness of civilization and said that the first step downward in the act of spiritual rebellion was the choice not to honor God. To honor (or glorify, as the older translations state it) the Father is to acknowledge his rightful place as the God above all "gods." It means to acknowledge his majesty, his supremacy, and his sovereignty. It carries with it the sense of looking into all of reality and delighting to find God's thumbprint on everything.

These are truths that the natural mind resists. Rather, it is more normal to put ourselves first; indeed this is the great encouragement of our postmodern culture. Thus, when you walk through life *honoring* God, you will have to do it by discipline, by choice, because it will not come naturally or easily, and few will be modeling it for you.

The interesting thing about a heart which concentrates on honoring and thanking God is that it becomes a naturally joyful heart. It becomes resistant to discouragement, negative thinking, and cynicism. Nothing is dull or routine to such a heart; everything has value.

Honoring God begins by heightening our awareness of the genius of creation. This sample comes to mind. Joseph Priestley was an English clergyman and scientist who lived 250 years ago. He was the first person to discover that plants are "chemical factories" which inhale the carbon dioxide in the atmosphere and exhale it as an oxygen which human beings can then breathe. A rather neat arrangement. As I read about Mr. Priestley and his discoveries, it was a natural and special moment for me to pause and honor our God for the genius of his creation, then thank him for its beautiful complexity and balance.

Preparing a meal, a routine exercise for many women, can be a time for exalting God. In the mixing of flavors, aromas, and colors to produce new tastes and eye-appealing combinations, we have a chance to point heavenward to the Lord who has offered such diversities of sense for our enjoyment. Since we need to eat three times a day, isn't it wonderful that we get to relish it?

Some years ago, a man in our present congregation was the president of a camera club that sponsored an annual international competition for amateur photographers. One year he gave our family a special showing of the best slides submitted. We sat alternately laughing and gasping at the incredibly beautiful and odd insects, birds, and animals in nature. Over and over again we were compelled to remark about our Creator God who has combined colors and shapes in ways that defy the imagination.

Do my comments sound "super spiritual?" They're not meant to be. Rather, they're designed to hint at the possibilities of life even in the routine or tough moments, when one acquires the habit of honoring or praising God in all circumstances.

The root of Moses' greatness was his awareness of the glory of God. He had a continuing objective to honor him. His song on the shore of the Red Sea in Exodus 15 is full of themes that describe and honor Jehovah: strength, salvation, power, majesty, holiness, wonder-working might, leadership, love, everlasting rule. Moses knew God and was never hesitant to recite the mighty acts and attributes of the God he'd first met at the burning bush. And that is why Moses was bold, fresh, and authoritative.

Many years ago, it became necessary to drill a well at Peace Ledge in New Hampshire. As we watched the workmen who run the machinery, I thought of the proverb:

> It is the glory of God to conceal a matter; to search out a matter is the glory of kings. (Prov. 25:2)

For those men, drilling for water was a job. For me, however, a "deeper" lesson was being uncovered as I watched. As they drilled, so I saw all of life as a drilling project: seeking God's revelation of his character and purpose in all things.

Many of King David's psalms have an interesting rhythm. Most often he begins by giving praise—looking first at God rather than his problems. Then the praise is followed by honesty concerning his present inner condition. If he is discouraged by his enemies, he says so. It seems as though he is owning his mood until he is able to make a deliberate choice to get his eyes back on honoring God. And when he does this, the psalm abruptly shifts, ending in triumph.

Having observed some women who have sunk into unhappiness or boredom makes me wonder whether their state of mind wasn't formed when they lost the ability to honor the God of their ministry. Worship is slowly replaced by moods of self-pity, regret, and bitterness. The result is a loss of perspective on what God is doing in people and in the world.

I have known these moods firsthand. And I've been aware that a life of color can turn gray. Conversations with others become shallow, insipid. I have nothing to offer others that would lead to encouragement or discernment. My own desire to grow, to learn, to take on challenges diminishes.

A reality check causes me to take a hard look at these symptoms. If I am wise, I will stop everything and rearrange my perspectives. Reminding myself of the grandeur of the living God and his purposes will draw me back toward rightful praise. Immediately, a sluggish spirit begins to come alive again.

Singing great hymns helps make this happen. Reading the poetry and spiritual reflections of the spiritual masters who have had cliff-hanging moments in abundance is a great assistance. Rereading my journal and being reminded of God's past faithfulness also makes a big difference.

☙ THEME TWO: THANKING GOD

St. Paul said that the other mark of a people hostile to God was their lack of thankfulness. The second element of my prayer disciplines has to do with the development of a thankful heart. Remember the old aftershave commercial which ended with, "Thanks, I needed that"? This is what thanking God is all about. It's the habit of looking at life with the recognition that I am dependent upon the Lord for *everything.* Saying thanks makes that clear. And in the saying of thanks, my inner spirit is once again disciplined so that it will not give way to the lie that I'm an island unto myself.

A moment of thanksgiving may be just a brief pause in a day. It need not even be audible. Strangely and wonderfully, the more I *thank* the Author of all giving, the more I find myself able to thank the people he has placed in my life.

Paul was fond of reminding young Christians about the importance of constantly giving thanks both to God and to one another. It took Gordon and me years to discover why. We found part of the answer among older people in our circle of relationships.

Older people who are thankful are a delight to know. From talking with them, we learn that thankfulness, like honoring, didn't simply happen. It was a part of a spiritual discipline which, for most of these elderly people, had begun early in their experience with Christ at the fire.

We learned from them that a consistent daily exercise of thankfulness to the Lord was an aspect of healthy Christian growth. For each individual we spoke with, it was deliberate and lifelong.

Jesus constantly expressed thanks to the Father. At the grave of Lazarus, for example, Jesus prayed: "Father, I thank you that you have heard me" (John 11:41).

Again at the breaking of the bread and during his Gethsemane prayer, thanks was a major theme. Both times Jesus was reaffirming that he could do nothing without his heavenly Father.

If thankfulness is a habit we need to acquire, then how do we go about obtaining it? One day in my Sunday school class, someone suggested that if the Israelites needed to annually remember their deliverance from Egypt, then perhaps we need to have a facility for remembering also. A major aspect of the feasts and the festivals which the Israelites maintained year after year centered on appreciation and thanksgiving to God. Perhaps we ought to celebrate a personal thanksgiving day each year, taking an inventory of newly gained insights, graces, gifts, relationships, and opportunities.

December 31, *each year,* is my personal Thanksgiving Day. I try to spend the day rereading my journal entries of the past 365 days. I look forward to this exercise all year because I am inevitably overwhelmed by how much God has done over the past twelve months. As I uncover the almost daily displays of his goodness, I list them in categories such as: highlights, things to be thankful for, Scriptures that moved me, answers to prayer, quotes worth remembering, sad and regrettable experiences, events which offer lessons to be learned, fun times with our married children and grandchildren, etc. This daylong task creates a reservoir of data for thanksgiving. As the next year unfolds, I find myself returning to these lists as a source of encouragement and praise. There are now eight years of these "rememberings," memorials to the work of God, if you please, which only heighten my sense of gratitude as the years progress.

The apostle Paul reminds us that it is the will of God for us to be thankful in all things. In the MacDonald home of earlier years, you might frequently have heard us ask these questions: "Are you thankful?" or "Did you thank the Lord for what happened?" We tried to get our children to appreciate the priority of such questions. When they became teenagers, they often turned the tables on us and asked us during difficult situations, "Are you thankful?" That's a case of the discipled edifying and encouraging the disciplers.

When I wear my gardening clothes at Peace Ledge, I often find myself doing a good deal of soil testing because the rocky New England soil is so poor. The first thing I test for is acidity—is there too much of it or too little? If the soil is too acidic, or sour, then nothing grows well; if it is too alkaline, or bitter, then nothing grows well either. Both extremes are bad for most of the vegetables I might choose to grow. I have to sweeten the soil when the acid is high.

If I were doing a soil test on my spirit, thankfulness and honoring would be the two tests I'd do first. They are basic to a healthy spirit for they make growth possible.

No wonder the prophet Jeremiah wrote:

Listen, O foolish, senseless people—you with the eyes that do not see and the ears that do not listen—have you no respect at all for me? the LORD God asks. How can it be that you don't even tremble in my presence? I set the shorelines of the world by perpetual decrees, so that the oceans, though they toss and roar, can never pass those bounds. Isn't such a God to be feared and worshipped?

But my people have rebellious hearts; they have turned against me and gone off into idolatry. Though I am the one who gives them rain each year in spring and fall and sends the harvest times, yet they have no respect or fear for me. And so I have taken away these wondrous blessings from them. This sin has robbed them of all these good things. (Jer. 5:21–25 TLB)

That kind of rebellion did not happen overnight. A destructive cycle is represented here. The heart that chooses to neither honor nor thank God becomes rebellious, and the rebellion engenders a further lack of honoring and of thanking. Like the plant that is in soil which is too bitter or too sour, rebellion may *not* be apparent to the naked eye for some time. However, when it is revealed, treatment must be immediate and consistent if health is to be restored.

One evening I stood applauding along with a large audience at the end of a Ken Medema concert. Medema, who is a gifted Christian singer, pianist, and composer without eyesight, stood slowly, raised his hands toward heaven, and began to applaud God. In so doing, he forced the focus of the audience back to where it should be.

Ironically, Ken Medema "saw" what we could not see at first: that behind the beauty of the music was the God of gifts and sounds and that he was the one who should be receiving our worship and thanksgiving.

Brigid Herman, the wife of a European pastor at the turn of the century, wrote:

When we read the lives of the saints, we are struck by a certain large leisure which went hand in hand with a remarkable effectiveness. They were never hurried; they did comparatively few things, and these not necessarily striking or important; and they troubled very little about their influence. Yet they always seemed to hit the mark; every bit of their life told; their simplest actions had a distinction, an exquisiteness which suggested the artist. The reason is not far to seek. Their sainthood lay in their habit of referring the smallest actions to God. They lived in God; they acted from a pure motive of love toward God. They were as free from self-regard as from slavery to the good opinion of others. God saw and God rewarded; what else needed they? They possessed God and themselves in God. Hence the inalienable dignity of these meek, quiet figures that seem to produce such marvelous effects with such humble materials.[2]

The qualities of honoring and thanking God must be part of us who choose life in the fishbowl, who commit to pointing people to

Christ, who seek God's approval above all other approvals. As I look into our culture and, more specifically, into my Christian community, too often I see that whatever honor is being bestowed, is being bestowed upon personalities rather than being conferred upon God. As far as thankfulness is concerned, too rare is the spirit behind these words: "Thanks—I needed that; I couldn't have done it without you, Lord." A woman in a position to lead must be constantly bringing people back to these most important truths.

Acquire the spiritual habit of honoring God and thanking him so that it becomes as natural as breathing (no small challenge), and you will never wonder in a cliff-hanging moment whether or not anyone is really up there. I promise you! I guarantee it!

❧ THEME THREE: REPENTANCE

As Gordon and I inventory our cliff-hanging moments through ministry, we are aware that there was often the temptation to blame or get angry with God when we disapproved of the course of events. Today it seems to be a natural reflex in the human experience. Get mad at God, blame him, assume he made a mistake, that he's unfair, that he didn't have all the facts, that he's out to make life miserable.

The Bible gives us ample evidence of ancient people who thought these ways in their tough times. Adam did it. So did Cain. Moses got a bit testy with Israel's God. The psalmists lashed out at heaven more than once. And there were certain of the prophets like Jonah who grew intensely irritated when things did not go their way.

I've already suggested that honoring and thanking God are not natural events for us, and neither is this third theme I've tried to incorporate in my discipline of prayer. *I'm thinking of the necessity of a repentant and submissive spirit.* I'm not thinking of an occasional repentant spirit, but a constant heart-attitude of spiritual brokenness before the Lord.

Isaiah, a prophet who fully understood the repentant spirit, caught the mind of God:

> This is the one I esteem: he who is humble and contrite in spirit,
> and trembles at my word. (Is. 66:2)

As I said before, throughout the earlier years of my life and into my marriage to Gordon, the hardest thing for me to do was to say, "I'm sorry." I found it easier to pursue the perception of perfection in everything rather than ever face the possibility that I might have to apologize because I wasn't good enough or hadn't done something well enough.

I even found it hard to admit I was wrong to my husband for fear that if he saw I had imperfections, he might abandon me in a way similar to what had happened in my first engagement. If you recall my story, you may remember that no one ever told me *why* the engagement was terminated. I never found out. I was left to figure it out for myself, and so I allowed my imagination to take over. I came to believe I must not have been good enough.

I carried that burden for many years, and one of the side effects was a drive to be as perfect as possible. The result was an increasing reluctance to acknowledge wrong, fault, or culpability to God or, for that matter, anyone else. Such a reluctance can be very damaging to relationships.

But the life in Christ demands a primary acknowledgment that I am a needy human being, that I am not self-sufficient but dependent, not pure but sinful, not perfect but capable of error along with the best of them. God had to teach me a humility I would never have acquired in any other way, a humility which says, "I have no control; I am clay, he is the potter and can be trusted with my life."

One evening our son-in-law Tom gave his young son Lucas his nightly bath. The bath went well until hair-washing time. Then there was resistance. "No, Daddy, eyes," Lucas protested. For all of us when we are young, shampoo in the eyes is a nasty experience.

Reflecting on this, Tom said, "I had the hardest time explaining to him that his daddy had to wash his hair. And then I wondered if this is how God sees my resistance to his washings."

I'm a long way from those days when it was impossible to say, "I'm wrong," or "I'm very sorry," or "Bless me, O Lord, for I have sinned." The years have drained the resistance out of me. Now I know too much about myself. Now I know that coming to the Father with an open, broken heart of repentance, naming those attitudes and actions which have been alien to his way, is the only thing that restores the heart to his favor.

These three themes—honoring God, thanking him, and repentance—have been the foundation of my inner disciplines. What they've done is lay the tracks to the main event: intercessory prayer.

⟪ THEME FOUR: INTERCESSORY PRAYER, THE MAIN EVENT

As a form of prayer, intercession centers more on others than self, more on God's interests than my own. In the past ten years, I have developed a growing number of friendships with people who are intercessors. Their perseverance in prayer and their commitment to the accompanying discipline of fasting has awed me. I see things differently now.

My husband and I have felt the effects of their prayer efforts because these intercessors have committed to be a prayer covering for us. Some of them are keenly aware of the intensity of our lives (pastoring, writing, traveling, correspondence with broken-world people), and they have appreciated the spiritual warfare involved in it all. Their contribution to our lives has been a prayer effort that humbles Gordon and me. We have often marveled at their unselfish commitment to time before the Lord on our behalf. It is a gracious gift that only the Lord can adequately repay.

I wouldn't want to go anywhere or do anything without these people praying. Every ministry family or single person needs to ask God to raise up a team of praying people who see this as their *main* gift to the church. Once in place, you will never want to be without it again. (I've listed books on prayer in the back of this book).

Intercession tends to focus on great, long-term issues. That raises the theme of what some call prevailing prayer, prayer that is offered day after day even when there seems to be no indication that answers are on the way. It is prayer that stands against great odds. It is prayer that will not falter even when others would slip into doubt. It is prayer that continues when God seems to offer no immediate response.

Oswald Chambers refers to these times as the *grace of silence*. It's a sign of his intimacy. The devil calls it unanswered prayer.

> God's silences are His answers. If we only take as answers those that are visible to our senses, we are in a very elementary condition of grace. . . . God has trusted you in the most intimate way He could

trust you, with an absolute silence, not of despair but of pleasure, because He saw you could stand a much bigger revelation than you had at the time.

Again in another place he writes:

Lust in prayer is wanting our answers *now*. Whenever the insistence is on the point that God answers prayer we are off the track. *The meaning of prayer is that we get hold of God*, not the answer.[3] (emphasis mine)

In a culture and time that insists on answers at our fingertips, waiting for anything is at the bottom of our lists. What characterizes the intercessors I've come to know is that they know how to wait, how to prevail, and how to pray against the odds. They don't quit until the Spirit of God releases them from the burden of their prayers. To have a discipline of prayer in your life is to master this kind of patience.

Moses is my biblical model for intercession. Remember when the people disappointed him in the making of a golden calf? You could say that even God was disgusted. In fact, there is this strange reference to God's desire to wipe out the nation and start over. It sounds like Moses could have had a new start with new people. More than a few pastors have pondered that possibility.

If Moses had been a convenience-seeking, power-grabbing, unforgiving person, he might have applauded that idea, but in affect he said in intercessory form, "Let's stick with plan A, Lord." In a cliff-hanging moment, Moses stayed angry and frustrated for only a short time, and then he turned to leadership through intercession. His prayer caused him to plead for lives, not to malign them; to stay, not to run; to love, not to hate.

Where did Moses acquire this grace? You will recall that forty years earlier, Moses had resorted to violence in order to carry out God's purposes. He'd murdered an Egyptian thinking that he could curry the favor of the Hebrews and get on with God's mission. He'd missed God's way completely and ended up doing "desert time" for four decades until he was eighty.

The Bible is not specific about methods, but it's clear that Moses learned something during those forty years. No longer the violent reactionary, he is now the man of intercession who pleads for the lives of his people. What a privilege to be the one who "stands in the gap" for those who are straying, slandering, or in pain. Long ago, William Law wrote:

> By considering yourself as an advocate with God for your neighbors and acquaintances, you would never find it hard to be at peace with them yourself.... Intercession is the best arbitrator of all differences, the best promoter of friendship, the best cure and preservative against all unkind tempers, all angry and haughty passions ... You cannot possibly have any ill-temper or show any unkind behavior to a man for whose welfare you are so much concerned, as to be his advocate with God in private. For you cannot possibly despise and ridicule that man whom your private prayers recommend to the love and favor of God. [4]

Moses lived this well. I'm slowly learning. Very slowly. But I can attest to the great joy of praying the will of God into people and seeing dozens of lives and marriages healed over the past ten years. Not just healed, but deepened. As we have seen broken lives restored, I have come to realize that prayer was the main event in the process. There was, in many cases, no human way and no human explanation to account for why these dead-end situations came back to wholeness. We knew it was God and God alone.

I am a woman nearing my sixtieth year of life. I know how long it has taken for me to come to an appreciation of the power of intercession: the prevailing, time-intensive conversation with God on behalf of others. This is why I caution those who read these lines to be patient and not easily discouraged as they pursue a life of prayer.

There is no excuse to neglect this most difficult ministry. As I grow older I can only pray that intercession will become my major ministry. Long after we have left the center of church life, long after the invitations to speak have stopped coming, and long after the phone stops ringing, I'll be praying for those who are hanging from the cliff.

Most of us learn these things in the cliff-hanging moments. And if that is what it takes, then I will not back away from the cliffs. For when I know that the Lord is "up there," I am prepared to release myself to his assurance, his direction, and his purposes.

FIFTEEN

THE JOURNEY CONTINUES

Going Home

It is great wisdom to keep silent when damaging words are spoken to you. Turn your attention to me and don't worry about rumor or slander. Don't look for support from the mouths of others. You are who you are regardless of what they say. And you shall know much peace if you neither try to please them or care if you displease them.   —*Thomas á Kempis (Bangley translation)*

How many pastors do you know who have returned to a congregation for the second time? Probably not many because it is not normally recommended. And we wouldn't have done it had it not been for the unanimous conviction of Grace Chapel's elders that it was the correct thing to do.

I reread my journal to recall those anxious days over five years ago and marvel at the process that made us Yankees again. The elders had called the Grace Chapel congregation to a day of prayer and fasting. Then they convened, made their decision to ask Gordon to accept the congregation's call, and phoned us. It was a tough decision . . . for them and us. Many of those in the decision process talked of how they wrestled with God in prayer, seeking wisdom. Gordon and I were just as needy, and we spent more than a little time on our knees. We were thankful for the perspective of Lloyd Ogilvie:

Prayer is to get us into the position of willingness to receive what God wants. . . . In the quiet, we begin to see things from His perspective and are given the power to wait for the unfolding plan of God.

We received an avalanche of mail and phone calls from Grace Chapel people asking us to respond positively. But there were also some who felt differently. And you tend to hear those far more quickly than the others.

We would be going back to a part of our past. The core of the Grace Chapel congregation knew us all too well. There was no mystery. Everyone knew Gordon's and my faults and flaws. And of course there were no secrets. Everyone knew that we had emerged just five years before from a very dark hour.

Did we really want to return to this kind of world, especially when we'd had four wonderful years in New York City where there tended to be a much greater appreciation for what it means to bury the past in grace and get on with the future?

I confess to a lot of ambivalence during those decision-days. Frankly, I wondered if moving back meant we would have to live with many tears. Not for a moment did Gordon or I question the right of people to ask hard questions, express opposition, or even say that they simply didn't like my husband or me. That comes with the territory, and some of it is reasonable, if not deserved. Again, the only questions we had the right to ask were: Is this what God wanted? Did we want to face those people? Was there ministry still left for us to do in New England at Grace Chapel?

Then one day, Gordon's publisher, Victor Oliver, who has played a pivotal role in our lives for many years, called to see how we were doing. I described for him the torturous process we were passing through. I shared my dread of living with the criticisms and comments of some people who wanted to keep the past alive.

Victor listened and then challenged me: "Learn to live with the past. Your life experiences are a sacred trust. What you do with them matters to God. You must embrace them. Don't run from being a broken-world person. People feel understood by you and Gordon because you know firsthand both the breaking and the healing."

That conversation was a turning point for me. I remember telling the chairman of the Grace Chapel board of elders the next time we talked that if the board was united in their conviction that God was in this, then they could count on me to give it all I had. I would be more than willing to live with the discontented few and not whine about their responses. My spiritual flag became "Consider him who endured (Heb. 12:3).

One long time friend and staff member at Grace sent a card with some loving comments and then reminded us of these two Scriptures:

> Do not fear the reproach of men or be terrified by their insults. (Isa. 51:7)

> For look, the wicked bend their bows; they set their arrows against the strings to shoot from the shadows at the upright in heart. (Ps. 11:2)

Knowing that friends who had worked with us in our earlier years at Grace wanted us to return was a great comfort. We knew it took time and affection for them to find such verses for us. Then Amy Carmichael once again challenged me to think higher thoughts when she wrote:

> Then, like the scent of flower blown by a passing wind, came the memory of a day in the train some years ago. I was traveling to Puri, a thousand miles north of Dohnavur, on the Father's business, when a silly feather-flutter of local gossip, retold by a guest before she could be stopped, tried to disturb me. And it did disturb till these six words were repeated over and over beaten out, as it were in my ear by the sound of the wheels of the train: "*Let it be; think of me.*" These words spoke to me again now. It was then that the thought of the many to whom unrecorded little pangs must be daily commonplaces came with a new compassion, born of a new understanding. And I wanted to share my crumb of comfort at once, and tell them not to weigh flying words, or let *their peace be in the mouths of men*. For no man can tell what in combat hurts us but he that has been in the battle himself; so how can they, the unwounded, know anything about the matter? But the Lord our Creator knows ... If He remembers, what does it matter that others forget? Thus, being comforted and filled with inward sweetness, we can thank Him for all who trample on us unawares, *talking smooth nothings*. For we know just because they can do it so unconsciously, so easily, and with so airy a grace, that they at least, were never laid in iron (Ps. 105:18); and is that not good to know? [1] (emphasis mine)

Still another colleague found other Scriptures to bolster our courage:

> If you will repent, I will restore you that you may serve me; if you utter worthy, not worthless words, you will be my spokesman. Let this people turn to you, but you must not turn to them. I will make you a wall to this people, a fortified wall of bronze; they will fight against you but will not overcome you, for I am with you to rescue and save you. (Jer. 15:19–20)

For years I had been challenged by the story of the apostle Paul's willingness to return to Lystra where he had once been terribly beaten and left for dead. If he had not forgiven those who had done such evil things to him and been willing to return to that place of stoning, he would have missed meeting Timothy who became like a son to him (Acts 14:19–20; 16:1–2). Compared to what Paul had in his memory bank, what we were experiencing seemed minuscule by comparison. Karen Mains calls such trials *mini crosses.* That certainly provides perspective.

Again, the challenge and comfort of fire-time was life altering. As we entered times of quiet, the Scriptures and our "book friends" were often the refocusing tools which kept us in the battle. The biographies we'd been reading once again offered courage and precedent. The spiritual masters exhorted us to perseverance, integrity, faithfulness, and quiet godliness. Henri Nouwen's simple phrase, "littleness, hiddenness, powerlessness" made more and more sense as an objective of spiritual maturing. These qualities would mark life for me if we were to return to Lexington.

As we thought about what going home to New England might look like, we had to be realistic. Would we expect it to be like it used to be? No, we could not recreate the past. Nor should we. I have carried in my files a wonderful quote by C. S. Lewis, who put it well:

> If all of Heaven and earth can barely contain God expressing Himself once, why should we ask Him to repeat Himself? How much more our joy to allow God to grant new blessings and so experience a new aspect of His expression.

No, we would not seek an "encore." Instead, we would expect God to do something entirely new—an original new masterpiece.

I began to think of the new realities that would be in place if we returned to Lexington and Grace Chapel. What was different about me now? What would I give myself to in this second round of ministry? What would be important? My journal discloses:

- I had picked up eight more years of relationships—another church and the many InterVarsity friends. There were the untold numbers of broken-world people with whom I was corresponding. I was giving at least one full day each week to writing letters to struggling women across the country.

- At this point in our lives, there would be a greater separation between church and home. I had learned my lesson—Gordon would not find me to be an extension of Grace Chapel. We were older, and we would need more privacy in our lives, especially now that we had a larger family of grandchildren.

- As a grandma, I was now going to give substantial amounts of time to our five grandchildren. To whatever extent they and their parents would permit, I was going to give my soul to them.

- I would be increasingly proactive with friendships. Long after ministry at Grace Chapel was ended the second time, we would want to have friends who would be our lifelong community, with whom we could grow old and die.

- We would give ourselves to the development of young leaders who would one day take the ministry from us and extend it far beyond our capacities.

When the day of decision came, Gordon said yes to the Grace Chapel congregation and the elders. Yes, we would come back to Lexington, Massachusetts, to the church that had always owned our hearts. We would try one more time to sink ourselves into pastoral ministry and the vision of New England in spiritual renewal. At some point during those days, Amy Carmichael once again challenged me: "The only thing that can hinder a life from telling for Him is the mind that puts self in the center and the mind that refuses suffering."

More than five years have come and gone since we became Yankees again. Five incredible years. We have had the thrill of working with people with whom, as Gordon says, we have history. Today men and women sit in leadership positions whom we saw come to faith in Christ many years ago. Young people who were born in our first years at Grace Chapel and dedicated in Gordon's pastoral arms are now heading out on mission teams and off to college.

Often Gordon presides over the funerals of some of the original Grace Chapel leaders. These were the men and women who had called us to New England twenty-five years ago. Today they have taken the quieter seats and handed over the ministry responsibilities to new generations. One by one they have gone home to be with Jesus, and Gordon has had the immense privilege of honoring them appropriately because we were there when they were giving themselves so sacrificially to God.

There was another sense of going home at the end of 1996. Gordon was once again invited to give the daily pastoral lectures at InterVarsity's great Urbana missionary convention. For the first time in many years, we encountered one IVCF staff member after another and recounted many lovely moments when we had shared ministry together.

We came back to Grace Chapel thinking we might weep a lot. Not so! Rather, we shed tears of joy and awe as we stand with the congregation to sing the mighty hymns and praise choruses of the church. Once again we kneel with those who come to receive Christ and begin their spiritual journeys. We sit with delightful people listening to their stories and, when asked, offer the kind of mentoring guidance that you're asked for as you get older.

We came to Grace Chapel in the early 1970s so young and full of energy. Our heads are gray now and, we hope, filled with wisdom. We came then full of visions for the future. Today our desire is to finish the course with strength and godliness, to ensure that a new generation is in place serving the Lord with new ideas and dreams fit for our King.

On many Sunday evenings after we have been part of Grace Chapel's fourth weekend worship service, Gordon and I come home to our condo and change our clothes. If it's winter, we grab warm parkas, put on our boots, and walk hand in hand toward Lexington Center. If summer, it's walking shorts and Nikes. Our route takes us a mile-and-a-half up Grant Street past the original home where we raised our two children. As we pass, we often recall some little incident that is part of the memories of those days.

When we reach Lexington's beautiful center (a New England term), we never fail to comment on how lovely it looks in all of its colonial motif. We always go to Bertucci's restaurant where we share a salad and a bowl of soup (we're still frugal). That finished, we continue our walk past the Battle Green where the famous minutemen took their courageous stand against the British redcoats who were on their way to Concord. Just past the Battle Green, we turn down Hancock Street until we are finally back at the home we love so much.

There is a wonderful sense of decompression during these walks. The intensity of preaching four sermons (and listening to them), being with a few thousand people, responding (so it seems) to a million questions or remarks, and praying for those who've come forward to kneel at the altar—it all falls away as we make our way in the darkness. Inevitably, we find ourselves talking about how blessed we are to be surrounded by loving people, by a tremendous pastoral team, by good friends, and a loving family.

We talk about how much we love what we do. We often talk about our marriage and how much we enjoy being together. Slowly we talk ourselves into forgetting the problems that are always hovering out there. We ignore the fact that most working days of the week are thirteen to fifteen hours long. We stop thinking about that tiny knot of people who, unfortunately, always seem like critics. Sooner or later, Gordon says to me, "You know, it really doesn't get any better than this." And I agree, because ministry and being a ministry wife really is a high call and a high privilege.

ENDNOTES

CHAPTER ONE

1. Walter Hilton, quoted in D. M. McIntyre, *Hidden Life of Prayer* (Minneapolis: Bethany House Publishers, 1993), p. 29
2. Henri Nouwen, *Clowning in Rome* (Garden City, N.Y.: Image Books, 1979), p. 41.

CHAPTER TWO

1. Ralph Turnbull, *A Minister's Obstacles* (Westwood, N.J.: Fleming H. Revell), p.58.

CHAPTER THREE

1. Brigette Herman, *Creative Prayer.* (Cincinnati: Forward Movement Publications), pp. 38–39.

CHAPTER FOUR

1. Oswald Chambers, *My Utmost for His Highest* (Fort Washington, Pa.: Christian Literature Crusade, 1979), p. 171.
2. Ibid., p. 45
3. Frederick Buechner, *Wishful Thinking: A Theological ABC* (New York: Harper and Row, 1973), p. 2.

Chapter Five

1. Francois Fenelon, *Spiritual Letters to Women* (Grand Rapids: Zondervan, 1902), p. 16.
2. Amy Carmichael, *Candles in the Dark* (Fort Washington, Pa.: Christian Literature Crusade, 1982), p. 111

Chapter Six

1. Courtney Anderson, *To the Golden Shore: The Life of Adoniram Judson* (Grand Rapids: Zondervan, 1956), p. 146.
2. Harold Begbie, *The Life of General Booth,* Vol. 1 (New York: MacMillan, 1920), pp. 305–306.
3. Ibid., p.164.
4. Gordon MacDonald, *Magnificent Marriage* (Wheaton, Ill: Tyndale Publishing House, 1976, p.73.

Chapter Seven

1. Ruth Graham, quoted in Evelyn and J. Allan Petersen, *For Women Only* (Wheaton, Ill: Tyndale Publishing House, 1975), p. 191.

Chapter Nine

1. Elisabeth Dodds, *Marriage to a Difficult Man: The Uncommon Union of Jonathan and Sarah Edwards* (Philadelphia: Westminster Press, 1971), p.78.
2. C. H. MacKintosh, "*Notes on Exodus*," in *Genesis to Deuteronomy: Notes on the Pentateuch* (Neptune, N.J.: Loizeaux Brothers, 1880, 1972), p. 155.
3. Dale E. Rogers, *Tears, Trials and Tribulations* (Old Tappan, N.J.: Fleming H. Revell, 1977), p.124.
4. Elizabeth Skoglund, *Coping* (Glendale, Calif.: Regal, 1979), p. 37.
5. Harold Begbie, *The Life of General Booth,* Vol. 1 (New York: Macmillan, 1920), p. 289.
6. Frank Houghton, *Amy Carmichael of Dohnavur.* (Fort Washington, Pa: Christian Literature Crusade, 1979), p. 49.

Chapter Ten

1. Oswald Chambers, *The Shade of His Hand* (London: Marshall, Morgan and Scott, 1962), p. 8.

2. Oswald Chambers, *My Utmost For His Highest* (New York: Dodd, Mead, 1935), p. 157.
3. Corrie Ten Boom, *Clippings from My Notebook* (Minneapolis: Grason, 1982), pp. 93–94.
4. Oswald Chambers, *My Utmost for His Highest* (New York: Dodd, Mead, 1935), p. 172.
5. Amy Carmichael, *His Thoughts Said . . . His Father Said* (Fort Washington, Pa: Christian Literature Crusade, 1941), pp. 22–23.
6. Larry Crabb, *Men and Women, Enjoying the Difference* (Grand Rapids: Zondervan, 1991), pp. 65–66.
7. R. T. Kendall, *God Meant it For Good* (Eastbourne: Kingsway Publications, 1986), p. 69.

CHAPTER ELEVEN

1. Francois Fenelon, *Spiritual Letters to Women* (Grand Rapids: Zondervan, 1902), p. 267.

CHAPTER THIRTEEN

1. Jim Conway and Sally Conway, *When a Mate Wants Out* (Downers Grove, Ill.: InterVarsity, 1992), p. 5.
2. Paul Tournier, *Escape from Loneliness* (Philadelphia: Westminster Press, 1976), p. 46.
3. Helmuth von Moltke, *Letters to Fre'ya* (New York: Alfred A. Knopf, 1990).

CHAPTER FOURTEEN

1. E. Stanley Jones, *The Way* (Nashville: Abingdon, 1946), p. 197.
2. Brigid Herman, *Creative Prayer* (Cincinnati: Forward Movement Publications), p. 16.
3. Oswald Chambers, *If You Will Ask* (Grand Rapids: Discovery House, 1985), pp. 43–44.
4. Aldous Huxley, *The Perennial Philosophy* (New York: Harper, 1945), pp. 222–223.

CHAPTER FIFTEEN

1. Amy Carmichael, *Rose from Brier* (Fort Washington, Pa: Christian Literature Crusade, 1933), pp. 19–20.

BIBLIOGRAPHY

NOTE: Titles having asterisks are out of print as far as I know. Many of them can be located at seminary libraries or rare and used bookstores. We found all of ours at used bookstores in New England. Kregels at 616-459-9444 and Book Look at 1-800-223-0540 both are good resources for out of print books.

The serious reader of biography will no doubt prefer two-volume works as opposed to single volumes that only give high spots. For instance, the Judson volumes compiled by Wayland have all of Judson's letters and journal entries, whereas the biography done by Courtney Anderson is far less detailed but well worth the reading.

Where to start? If I could find Begbie, Dodds, Hall, Hopkins, Houghton, Jones, Magnusson, Pollock, and Thompson, I would have found enough insight and stimulation to last for months.

BIOGRAPHY AND AUTOBIOGRAPHY

Anderson, Courtney. *To the Golden Shore: The Life of Adoniram Judson.* Valley Forge, Pa.: Judson, 1987.

Buechner, Frederick. *Telling Secrets: A Memoir.* San Francisco: Harper, 1991.

Begbie, Harold. *The Life of General Booth.* 2 vols. New York: Macmillan, 1920.*

Bentley-Taylor, David. *My Love Must Wait: The Story of Henry Martyn.* Downers Grove, Ill.: InterVarsity, 1976.

Bertrand, Louis. *Saint Augustine.* New York: Appleton, 1914.*

Buchan, James. *The Expendable Mary Slessor.* New York: Seabury, 1981.*

Bunyan, John. *Grace Abounding to the Chief of Sinners.* New York: Penguin, 1987.

Chambers, Oswald. *Leagues of Light.* Diary, 1915–1917. Louisville: Operation Appreciation Ministries, 1984.

Choy, Leona. *Andrew Murray: Apostle of Abiding Love*. Fort Washington, Pa: Christian Literature Crusade, 1978.

Cowman, Lettie (Mrs. Charles). *Missionary Warrior*. Greenwood, Ind.: OMS International, 1928. Biography of Charles Cowman.

Crago, T. Howard. *The Story of F. W. Boreham*. London: Marshall, Morgan, & Scott, 1961.*

Dodds, Elisabeth. *Marriage to a Difficult Man: Jonathan and Sarah Edwards*. Philadelphia: Westminster, 1971.*

Elliot, Elisabeth. *A Chance to Die: The Life and Legacy of Amy Carmichael*. Old Tappan, N.J.: Revell, 1987.

———. *Shadow of the Almighty: The Life and Testament of Jim Elliot*. New York: Harper and Row, 1979.

Hefley, James, and Marti Hefley. *By Their Blood: Christian Martyrs of the 20th Century*. Milford: Mott Media, 1978.

Goforth, Rosalind. *Jonathan Goforth*. Minneapolis: Bethany, 1986.

Green, Roger J. *Catherine Booth*. Grand Rapids: Baker, 1996.

Hall, C. W. *Samuel Logan Brengle: Portrait of a Prophet*. Chicago: Salvation Army, 1933.*

Hopkins, Hugh. *Charles Simeon of Cambridge*. Grand Rapids: Eerdmans, 1977.*

Houghton, Frank. *Amy Carmichael of Dohnavar*. Fort Washington, Pa.: Christian Literature Crusade, 1979.

Jeffrey, David Lyle, ed. *A Burning and a Shining Light: English Spirituality in the Age of Wesley*. Grand Rapids: Eerdmans, 1987.

Jones, E. Stanley. *A Song of Ascents: A Spiritual Autobiography*. Nashville: Abingdon, 1979.*

———. *The Divine Yes*. Nashville: Abingdon, 1976.*

Kerr, Hugh T., and John T. Mulder. *Conversions*. Grand Rapids: Eerdmans, 1983.

Lean, Garth. *God's Politician: William Wilberforce's Struggle*. Colorado Springs: Helmers Howard, 1988.

Magnusson, Sally. *The Flying Scotsman*. Boston: Charles River Books, 1982. Biography of Eric Liddell.*

Muggeridge, Malcolm. *Something Beautiful for God*. New York: Harper and Row, 1971. Biography of Mother Teresa.

Murray, Ian H. *Jonathan Edwards: A New Biography*. Carlisle: Banner of Truth, 1987.

Newton, John. *Out of the Depths*. New Canaan, Conn.: Keats, 1981.

Petersen, William J. *Martin Luther Had a Wife.* Wheaton: Tyndale, 1983.

————. *C. S. Lewis Had a Wife.* Wheaton: Tyndale, 1985.

Pollock, John. *Hudson Taylor and Maria.* Robesonia, Pa.: OMF Books, 1967.

Roseveare, Helen. *He Gave Us a Valley.* Downers Grove, Ill.: InterVarsity, 1976.*

Sangster, Paul. *Doctor Sangster.* London: Epworth Press, 1962.*

Sargent, John. *Life and Letters of Henry Martyn.* Carlisle: Banner of Truth, 1985.

Skoglund, Elizabeth R. *Wounded Heroes.* Grand Rapids: Baker, 1992.

Smith, Goldwin. *William Cowper: English Men of Letters*, 1880. Reprint. Philadelphia: Richard West, 1980.*

Taylor, Geraldine. *Pastor Hsi.* London: Morgan and Scott, 1900.*

Thompson, Phyllis. *Climbing on Track.* London: C.I.M. Publications, 1954.*

————. *D. E. Hoste.* London: C.I.M. Publications, 1947.*

Trueblood, Elton. *While It Is Day.* Richmond, Va.: Yokefellow, 1983.*

Wayland, Francis. *Memoir of the Life and Labors of Adoniram Judson.* 2 vols. Phillips, Sampson, and Company, 1854.*

∾ Snatch Books

For Solitude (When Time Is Limited)

Baillie, John. *A Diary of Private Prayer.* New York: Scribner, 1979.

Bangley, Bernard. *Growing in His Image.* Wheaton: Shaw, 1983. A reinterpretation of Thomas á Kempis's *Imitation of Christ.*

Carmichael, Amy. *Edges of His Ways.* Fort Washington, Pa.: Christian Literature Crusade, 1955.

————. *If.* Fort Washington, Pa.: Christian Literature Crusade, 1966.

————. *Whispers of His Power.* Old Tappan: Revell, 1985.

Chambers, Oswald. *A Place of Help.* Fort Washington, Pa.: Christian Literature Crusade, 1973.

————. *My Utmost for His Highest.* Fort Washington, Pa: Christian Literature Crusade, 1979.

Cowman, Mrs. Charles E. *Springs in the Valley.* Grand Rapids: Zondervan, 1988.

————. *Streams in the Desert.* Vol. 1. Grand Rapids: Zondervan, 1986.

Elliot, Elisabeth. *Keep a Quiet Heart.* Ann Arbor, Mi.: Servant, 1995.

Fenelon, Francois. *Talking With God.* Brewster, Mass.: Paraclete Press, 1997.

———. *The Royal Way of the Cross.* Brewster, Mass.: Paraclete Press, 1997.

Keller, Phillip. *A Shepherd's Look at Psalm 23.* Grand Rapids: Zondervan, 1976.

Lucado, Max. *No Wonder They Call Him Savior.* Portland: Multnomah, 1986.

Sanders, J. Oswald. *Spiritual Leadership.* Chicago: Moody, 1974.

Wesley, Susanna. *Prayers of Susanna Wesley.* Grand Rapids: Zondervan, 1984.*

For Solitude (When Time Isn't Limited)

Blackaby, Henry and Claude King. *Experiencing God.* Nashville: Broadman & Holman, 1994.

Bonhoeffer, Dietrich. *The Cost of Discipleship.* Riverside, N.Y.: Macmillan, 1967.

Carmichael, Amy. *Candles in the Dark.* Fort Washington, Pa.: Christian Literature Crusade, 1986.

———. *Learning of God.* Fort Washington, Pa.: Christian Literature Crusade, 1986.

Chambers, Oswald. *A Place of Help.* Fort Washington, Pa.: Christian Literature Crusade, 1972.

Colson, Charles. *Loving God.* Grand Rapids: Zondervan, 1983.

Gire, Ken. *Windows of the Soul.* Grand Rapids: Zondervan, 1996.

Kelly, Thomas. *Testament of Devotion.* New York: Harper and Row, 1941.

Nouwen, Henri. *The Gennesee Diary.* Garden City, N.Y.: Doubleday, 1976.

Packer, J. I. *Knowing God.* Downers Grove, Ill.: InterVarsity, 1973.

Peterson, Eugene. *Run with the Horses.* Downers Grove, Ill.: InterVarsity, 1983.

Rubietta, Jane. *Quiet Places.* Minneapolis: Bethany, 1997.

Sanders, J. Oswald. *Spiritual Leadership.* Chicago: Moody Press, 1974.

Tozer, A. W. *The Knowledge of the Holy.* New York: Harper and Row, 1961.

———. *The Pursuit of God.* New York: Harper and Row, 1962.

Yancey, Philip. *The Jesus I Never Knew.* Grand Rapids: Zondervan, 1995.

❧ On Prayer

Avila, St. Teresa. *A Life of Prayer.* Sisters, Ore.: Multnomah, 1983.

Blaiklock, E. M. *The Practice of the Presence of God: Brother Lawrence.* Nashville: Nelson, 1981.

Baillie, John. *A Dairy of Private Prayer.* New York: Scribners, 1953.

Chambers, Oswald. *Prayer: A Holy Occupation.* Grand Rapids: Discovery House, 1992.

———. *If You Ask.* Grand Rapids: Discovery House, 1958.

Gordon, S. D. *Quiet Talks on Prayer.* Old Tappan, N.J.: Fleming H. Revell, 1941.

Foster, Richard J. *Prayer, Finding the Heart's True Home.* New York: Harper Collins, 1982.

———. *Prayers from the Heart.* New York: Harper Collins, 1994.

———. *The Celebration of Discipline.* New York: Harper Row, 1978.

Hallesby, O. *Prayer.* Minneapolis: Augsburg, 1959.

Heald, Cynthia. *Becoming a Woman of Prayer.* Colorado Springs: NavPress, 1996.

Herman, Brigid E. *Creative Prayer.* Cincinnati: Forward Movement Publications.*

Huggett, Joyce. *Praying the Parables.* Downers Grove, Ill.. InterVarsity, 1996.

Hunter, Bingham. *The God Who Hears.* Downers Grove, Ill.: InterVarsity, 1986.

Job, Rueben P. and Norman Shawchuck. *A Guide to Prayer for Ministers and Other Servants.* Nashville: The Upper Room, 1983.

Lewis, C. S. *Letters to Malcolm: Chiefly on Prayer.* San Diego, Calif.: Harcourt Brace Jovanovich, 1964.

M'Intyre, D. M. *The Hidden Life of Prayer.* Minneapolis: Bethany, 1993.

Murray, Andrew. *With Christ in the School of Prayer.* Spire, 1953.

Myers, Ruth. *Thirty-One Days of Praise.* Sisters, Ore: Questar, 1994.

Ogilvie, John. *You Can Pray With Power.* Ventura, Calif.: Regal, 1988.

Peterson, Eugene. *Reversed Thunder.* New York: Harper Collins, 1988.

Simpson, A. B. *The Life of Prayer.* Camp Hill, Pa.: Christian Publications, 1989.

Spurgeon, Charles. *The Power of Prayer in the Believer's Life.* Emerald Books, 1993.

Steindl-Rast, David. *Gratefulness, the Heart of Prayer.* Ramsey, N.J.: Paulist Press, 1984.

Torrey, R. A. *How to Pray.* Chicago: Moody Press, 1960.

Wagner, Peter. *Prayer Shield.* Ventura, Calif.: Regal, 1992.

White, John. *Daring to Draw Near.* Downers Grove, Ill.: InterVarsity, 1977.

℞ FAMILY AND OTHER RELATIONSHIPS

Arp, Dave and Claudia Arp. *Ten Dates for Mates.* Nashville: Thomas Nelson, 1983.

Augsburger, David. *The Freedom of Forgiveness.* Chicago: Moody Press, 1973.

———. *Caring Enough to Confront.* Glendale, Calif: Regal, 1973.

Bonhoeffer, Dietrich. *Life Together.* New York: Harper, 1976.

Campbell, Ross, MD. *How to Really Love Your Child.* Wheaton, Ill.: Scripture Press, 1977.

———. *How to Really Love Your Teenager.* Wheaton, Ill.: Victor Books, 1982.

Chapman, Gary. *The Five Love Languages.* Chicago: Northfield Publishing, 1992.

Chapman, Gary and Ross Campbell, MD. *The Five Love Languages of Children.* Chicago: Moody Press, 1997.

Crabb, Larry. *Men and Women, Enjoying the Difference.* Grand Rapids: Zondervan, 1991.

Curran, Dolores. *Traits of a Healthy Family.* New York: Ballantine, 1984.

Dobson, James. *Dare to Discipline.* Wheaton, Ill.: Tyndale. 1970.

Elkind, David, *The Hurried Child: Growing Up Too Fast Too Soon.* Reading, Mass.: Addison-Wesley, 1981.

———. *All Grown Up and No Place to Go.* Reading, Mass.: Addison Wesley, 1984.

Endicott, Irene M. *Grandparenting by Grace.* Nashville: Broadman and Holman, 1994.

Faber, Adele and Elaine Mazlish. *How to Talk So Your Kids Will Listen and Listen So Your Kids Will Talk.* New York: Avon Books, 1982.

Graham, Ruth. *Prodigals and Those Who Love Them.* Colorado Springs: Focus on the Family, 1991.

Hendrix, Harville. *Getting the Love You Want.* New York: Harper, 1990.

Hybels, Bill and Lynne Hybels. *Fit To Be Tied.* Grand Rapids: Zondervan, 1991.

Mason, Mike. *The Mystery of Marriage.* Portland: Multnomah, 1985.

Pipher, Mary. *Reviving Ophelia: Saving the Selves of Adolescent Girls.* New York: Ballantine, 1994.

Powell, John. *Why Am I Afraid to Love?* Niles: Argus Communications, 1972.

Smalley, Gary and John Trent. *The Blessing.* Nashville: Thomas Nelson, 1986.

Tieger, Paul D. and Barbara Barron-Tieger. *Nurture by Nature.* Boston: Little, Brown 1997. Help in understanding our children's temperaments, using Myers Briggs Temperament Indicator.

Wangerin, Walter. *As for Me and My House.* Nashville: Thomas Nelson, 1988.

⟋ Stretching Mind and Spirit

Bourke, Dale Hanson, *Turn Toward the Wind, Embracing Change in Your Life.* Grand Rapids, Zondervan, 1995.

Carlson, Dwight L. *Overcoming Hurts and Angers.* Eugene, Ore.: Harvest House, 1981.

Crabb, Larry. *Inside Out.* Colorado Springs: NavPress, 1988.

————. *Men and Women, Understanding the Differences.* Colorado Springs: NavPress, 1989.

Frankl, Viktor E. *Man's Search for Meaning.* New York: Simon and Schuster, 1959.

Gilkey, Langdon. *Shantung Compound.* New York: Harper & Row, 1975.

Goleman, Daniel. *Emotional Intelligence: Why It Can Matter More than IQ.* New York: Bantam, 1995.

Inrig, Gary. *Quality Friendship.* Chicago: Moody, 1981.

Kendall, R. T. *God Meant It for Good.* Wheaton, Ill.: Tyndale, 1988.

Lewis, C. S. *Letters to an American Lady.* Grand Rapids: Eerdmans, 1967.

Lindbergh, Anne Morrow. *Gift from the Sea.* New York: Pantheon, 1955.

Manning, Brennan. *The Lion and the Lamb: The Relentless Tenderness of Jesus*. Old Tappan, N.J.: Revell, 1984.
——. *Abba Father: The Cry of the Heart for Intimate Belonging*. Colorado Springs: Navigators, 1994.
McDowell, Lucinda Secrest. *Amazed By Grace*. Nashville: Broadman and Holman, 1996.
Muggeridge, Malcolm. *Christ and the Media*. Grand Rapids: Eerdmans, 1978.
Mulholland, M. Robert, Jr. *Invitation to a Journey*. Downers Grove, Ill.: InterVarsity, 1993.
Pippert, Rebecca. *A Heart Like His*. Wheaton: Crossway, 1996.
Sider, Ronald J. *Rich Christians in an Age of Hunger: A Biblical Study*. Ramsey, N.J.: Paulist Press, 1977.
Ten Boom, Corrie. *Clippings from My Notebook*. Minneapolis: Grason, 1982.
Thielicke, Helmut. *The Waiting Father*. New York: Harper and Row, 1981.
Yancey, Philip. *What's So Amazing About Grace?* Grand Rapids: Zondervan, 1997.

☪ STRENGTHENERS FOR TIMES OF SUFFERING

Archer, Norman. *David: When Only the Grace of God Will Do*. Burlington, Ontario, Canada: Welch, 1984.
Bridges, Jerry. *Trusting God, Even When It Hurts*. Colorado Springs: Nav Press, 1988.
Carmichael, Amy. *Gold by Moonlight*. Fort Washington, Pa.: Christian Literature Crusade, 1960.
——. *Rose from Brier*. Fort Washington, Pa.: Christian Literature Crusade, 1972.
Chambers, Oswald. *Baffled to Fight Better: On Job*. Grand Rapids: Discovery House, 1931.
Davis, Verdell. *Riches Stored in Secret Places*. Dallas: Word, 1994.
Kreeft, Peter. *Making Sense Out of Suffering*. Ann Arbor, Mi.: Servant Books, 1986.
Sittser, Gerald L. *A Grace Disguised: How the Soul Grows through Loss*. Grand Rapids: Zondervan, 1996.
Skoglund, Elizabeth. *Coping*. Glendale, Calif.: Regal Books, 1980.

Vanauken, Sheldon. *A Severe Mercy*. New York: Harper and Row, 1977.
Yancey, Philip. *Disappointment with God*. Grand Rapids: Zondervan, 1988.
———. *Where Is God When It Hurts?* Grand Rapids: Zondervan 1977.
Wangerin, Walter. *Mourning into Dancing*. Grand Rapids: Zondervan, 1992.
Wolterstorff, Nicholas. *Lament for a Son*. Grand Rapids: Eerdmans, 1987.

〰 Resource Books for Those Who Minister

Anderson, Bill. *When Child Abuse Comes to Church*. Minneapolis: Bethany, 1992.
Beattie, Melody. *Codependent No More: How to Stop Controlling Others and Start Caring for Yourself*. Center City, Minn: Hazelden Foundation, 1987.
Black, Claudia. *It Will Never Happen to Me*. New York: Ballantine, 1987. For children of alcoholics.
Briscoe, Jill. *Renewal on the Run, Encouragement for Wives Who are Partners in Ministry*. Wheaton, Ill.: Shaw, 1992.
Dugan, Lynn. *Heart to Heart with Pastor's Wives*. Ventura, Calif.:Regal, 1994.
Fortune, Don and Katie Fortune. *Discover Your God-given Gifts*. Grand Rapids: Fleming H. Revell, 1987.
Hancock, Maxine and Karen Burton Mains. *Child Sexual Abuse, Hope for Healing*. Wheaton, Ill.: Shaw, 1997.
Huggett, Joyce. *Marriage on the Mend: The Power of God's Healing Love*. Downers Grove, Ill.: InterVarsity, 1988.
Johnson, Reginald. *Your Personality and the Spiritual Life*. Wheaton, Ill: Victor Books, 1995. Based on Myers Briggs Personality Indicator.
Keirsey, David and Marilyn Bates. *Please Understand Me*. Delmar, Calif.: Prometheus Nemesis, 1978. On temperaments.
Koons, Carolyn. *Beyond Betrayal*. New York: Harper and Row, 1987. For those who have had traumatic childhoods.
Langberg, Diane. *Counsel for Pastors' Wives*. Grand Rapids: Zondervan, 1988.

London, H. B., Jr. *Refresh, Renew, Revive—How to Reenergize Your Ministry.* Colorado Springs: Focus on the Family, 1996.

London, H. B., Jr. and Neil B. Wiseman. *Pastors At Risk.* Wheaton, Ill.: Victor Books, 1993.

Mains, Karen. *Comforting One Another in Life's Sorrows.* Nashville: Thomas Nelson, 1997.

————. *Open Heart, Open Home: Your Gift of Hospitality.* Wheaton: Mainstay Church Resources, 1997.

Merrill, Dean. *Clergy Couples in Crisis.* Carol Stream, Ill.: CTI Leadership Library, 1985.

O'Brien, Bev. *"Mom . . . I'm Pregnant."* Wheaton, Ill.: Tyndale House, 1982. On premarital pregnancy.

Olson, Esther L. and Kenneth Petersen. *No Place to Hide.* Wheaton, Ill.: Tyndale, 1982. On wife abuse.

Oswald, Roy M., and Otto Kroeger. *Personality Types and Religious Leadership.* Washington, D.C.: Alban Institute, 1988. On temperaments.

Ricks, Chip. *Carol's Story.* Wheaton, Ill.: Tyndale, 1981. Anonymous true story about incest.

Seamands, David A. *Healing for Damaged Emotions.* Wheaton, Ill.: Victor, 1981.

————. *If Only: Moving Beyond Blame to Belief.* Wheaton, Ill.: Victor, 1995.

————. *Putting Away Childish Things.* Wheaton, Ill.: Victor, 1982.

Robertson, Nan. *Getting Better.* New York: Morrow, 1988. Why AA helps so many people.

Swenson, Richard. *Margin, Restoring Emotional, Physical, Financial and Time Reserves to Overloaded Lives.* Colorado Springs: NavPress: 1992.

Wagner, Peter. *Your Spiritual Gifts Can Help Your Church Grow.* Ventura, Calif.: Regal, 1979.

Wilson, Earl and Sandy Wilson; Friesen, Paul and Virginia Friesen; Paulson, Larry and Nancy Paulson. *Restoring the Fallen.* Downers Grove, Ill: InterVarsity Press, 1997. A team approach to caring, confronting, and reconciling.

Wilson, Sandra. *Released from Shame, Recovery for Adult Children of Dysfunctional Families.* Downers Grove, Ill.: InterVarsity, 1990.

Woititz, Janet G. *Adult Children of Alcoholics*. Deerfield Beach, Fla.: Health Communications, 1983.

Worthen, Anita and Bob Davies. *Someone I Love is Gay: How Family and Friends Can Respond*. Downers Grove, Ill.: InterVarsity, 1996.

⚬ OTHER RESOURCES FOR THOSE WHO MINISTER:

Called Together Ministries. Linda Riley, newsletters, pastor's wives retreats, excellent resource network.

Just Between Us. Quarterly magazine edited by Jill Briscoe, 777 S. Barker Rd. Brookfield, WI 53045-3764, 1-800-260-3342.

The Pastor's Helpmate. Newsletter by Jean Coleman, The Tabernacle, 11601 S. Laurel Drive, Laurel, MD 20708.

Retreat Centers

Fairhaven Ministries. Charles Shepson, Director, Rt. 2, Box 1022, Roan Mountain, TN 37687, 615-542-5332.

Life Enrichment. Wes Roberts, President, 14581 E. Turts Ave., Aurora, CO 80015, 303-693-3954, Compuserve:73743,673.

Marble Retreat. Louis and Melissa McBurney, Directors, 139 Bannockburn, Marble, CO 81623, 303-963-2499.

Paraklesis Ministries. Dr. Sidney Draayer, Director, 1550 East Beltline SE, Suite 340, Grand Rapids, MI 49506, 616-957-9709 or 800-421-8352.

SonScape Ministries. Bob Sewell, Director, P. O. Box 7777, Pagosa Springs, CO 81147, 303-264-4777.

The Leadership Center. David Morgan, Director, 112 Lakeview Terrace, Wolfeboro, NH 03894, 603-569-3922.

Other Books by Gail MacDonald

A Step Farther and Higher. Sisters, Ore: Questar, 1989. Presently out of print.

Heart Connections. Coauthored with her husband. Old Tappan, N.J.: Revell, 1997. Formerly titled, *'Til the Heart Be Touched*.

Parenting: Questions Women Ask. 1992. Coauthored with Karen Mains and Kathy Peel.

Other Books by Gordon MacDonald

The Effective Father. Wheaton, Ill. Tyndale, 1977.
Ordering Your Private World. Nashville: Oliver/Nelson, 1984.
Renewing Your Spiritual Passion. Nashville: Oliver/Nelson, 1986.
Rediscovering Yourself: Grasping the Opportunities of Midlife. Old
        Tappan, N.J.: Fleming H. Revell, 1987.
Rebuilding Your Broken World. Nashville: Oliver/Nelson, 1988.
Christ Followers in the Real World. Nashville: Oliver/Nelson, 1989.
The Life God Blesses. Nashville: Oliver/Nelson, 1994.
When Men Think Private Thoughts. Nashville: Oliver/Nelson, 1996.

STUDY GUIDE

for *High Call, High Privilege*

INTRODUCTION

1. What do Paul's comments about the "treasure within" mean to you (2 Cor. 4:7)? See page xi.

2. Discuss the following verses about the "treasure" within. Why is it so easy for us to dwell on the "clay pot" instead of the treasure?

   Isaiah 61:10
   1 Corinthians 2:16
   2 Corinthians 6:4–7
   Galatians 2:20
   Colossians 1:27

3. Recall some experience this month that is a memory of God working through you because of the "treasure" within.

4. List the five key relationships the author mentions in priority order. See page xi. Does the order seem significant to you? Look at the order in which relationships were shattered at the time of the fall in Genesis 3:8–13. Can you illustrate from your own life or from Scripture how topsy-turvy priorities can get us into dilemmas?

5. Pray Isaiah 43:18–19 together, offering to the Lord all the priorities in your lives. If you mean it, tell the Lord you desire that he do a new thing in the weeks to come. Expect it!

Chapter One
The Journey Begins: Come to the Fire

1. Does anyone in the group relate to needing easy answers? If so, how have you grown beyond them to allow for mystery in your faith as well as for the unpredictability of God's ways?

2. Discuss what the concept of the *inner fire* means to you after reading this chapter.

3. List and talk about obstacles that tend to keep you from your fire-time with Christ.

4. Name the four things that happened to the disciples around the camp-fire Christ made for them (John 21:4–23).

5. Has there been a time when a woman has repeatedly tried to draw strength from your fire instead of maintaining her own? What did you do to help her begin her own fire?

6. Take your "fishbowls" to God in prayer. Ask for nothing but openness and willingness of spirit. Admit your inadequacies and need for his empowering love.

Chapter Two
The Journey Continues: Sainty

1. Do any of you relate to the youth-pastorate experience the MacDonalds had and the bewilderment that followed? How did you and your husband grow through it?

2. List some of the principles the author learned during the Sainty years. Which struck you as most important for your own life? Illustrate, if possible.

3. Study Numbers 12 and discuss why it is so important to nip the sin of jealousy in the bud.

4. Are there Scriptures that you might mention to remind each other to live today to the fullest instead of falling prey to the attitude that suggests that things will be better when we get out of seminary . . . or when we are able to have a baby . . . or when we have a church . . . ? Add other categories of "if onlys" you are tempted to use.

5. Look at the following Scripture from Eugene Peterson's *The Message*. Discuss what it means to each of you as you look at your present situation. After each has had opportunity to add her perspective, pray through the passage.

> Do you see what this means—all these pioneers who blazed the way, all these veterans cheering us on? It means we'd better get on with it. Strip down, start running—and never quit! No extra spiritual fat, no parasitic sins. Keep your eyes on *Jesus,* who both began and finished this race we're in. Study how he did it. Because he never lost sight of where he was headed—that exhilarating finish in and with God—he could put up with anything along the way: cross, shame, whatever. And now he's *there,* in the place of honor, right alongside God. When you find yourselves flagging in your faith, go over that story again, item by item, that long litany of hostility he plowed through. *That* will shoot adrenaline into your souls! (Hebrews 12:1–2)

CHAPTER THREE
THE JOURNEY CONTINUES: LEARNING TO LOVE, LOVING TO LEARN

1. Do you agree with the author's statement on page 32, "Anyone—regardless of talent or gift—can love if she asks God for the power and the will"? Why or why not? (1 John 4:7,12). Recall your history. Have you ever been in a congregation like Collinsville? Would the strategy God gave to the MacDonalds to love people and not make changes have helped? What difference has reading this chapter made in your thinking?

2. Compare and contrast hospitality and entertaining, as on pages 35–36. Add any ideas you may have for inexpensive, yet creative hospitality.

3. The MacDonalds found it difficult when they were no longer able to work side by side. What have been the areas where you have found adapting to changes in ministry most challenging?

4. How do you relate to the author's comments on pages 39–40 concerning her tendency to say yes too much? Do you have other suggestions that have been helpful concerning how you have dealt with expectations, both yours and others?

5. Discuss Brigid Herman's quote on page 43. How have you balanced this tension that exists in all of us?

6. Dialog about your responses to the author's comments concerning how to handle criticism and slander. Support your opinion with Scripture (see pages 43–46).

7. Going back over the *lessons* cited in this chapter, which one is most germane to where you are today?

8. Before coming together as a group next week, read the story of Hannah in 1 Samuel.

CHAPTER FOUR
SERVING AN AUDIENCE OF ONE

1. Discuss the different Scriptures the author mentions from St. Paul concerning who he was trying to please (2 Cor. 5:9; Gal. 1:10). In 1 Corinthians 10:31–11:1, how did Paul's people-pleasing differ from what the author struggled with? Think motive.

2. Having read the story of Hannah this past week, discuss your differing perspectives on what was in the soul of this woman.

3. How does the Oswald Chambers quote on page 51 affect you?

4. Give an example of how you have seen the connection between your body and spirit over the years. Refer to pages 52–55.

5. How do you relate to Sindia and Stuart Foster's loss and comments?

6. Use either Hannah's prayer in 1 Samuel 2 or 1 Corinthians 10:31–11:1 as a basis for surrendering to your audience of One as a group.

CHAPTER FIVE
TO BE OR TO DO: THAT IS THE QUESTION

1. Are you Mrs. Inside or Mrs. Outside? What insights in this chapter have been like light bulbs coming on? Discuss the differences in your marriage, depending on if you married a person like you or opposite you.

2. Can you think of a time in recent months when you felt too many "pucks" coming at you, which resulted in inner confusion? How did solace return to your soul? Refer to page 63.

3. Which of the experiences listed on pages 64–65 have also been yours?

Encourage each other by talking through how these instances, and others your group might add, have affected you and how God has used them for *long-term* good.

4. Think of other times in the life of Mary, the mother of our Lord, when being a quiet, thoughtful, obedient person was helpful for her. In what ways has your personality been an asset in being a pastor's wife? Have you been proactive in developing the opposite, less-preferred side of your temperament? Illustrate how this brought about growth.

CHAPTER SIX
GIVING GIFTS TO EACH OTHER

1. If possible, work through this chapter with your husband, discussing what gifts each of you has brought to the other over the years. If comfortable with it, share one or two with the group.

2. How do you respond to Catherine Booth's letter to William (pp. 72–73)?

3. List the signs you look for in your husband's life when concerned about his inner health and balance (see page 73).

4. How do each of you deal with the sensuality of ministry? Did what the author suggested help? How? (see pages 74–75).

5. Read Psalm 51:1–17 together. How does it affect each of you? Is this a normal part of your walk with God? Discuss it alongside the author's comments about living a repentant lifestyle (see pages 76–77).

6. Do you and your husband know what your "sermon" is? If not, what measures will you take to discover it?

7. Together, pray through Psalm 51, asking God to press the psalmist's spirit into your hearts.

CHAPTER SEVEN
PKs CAN BE OK (PART 1)

1. Discuss the five themes the author cited as important in her family and how you relate to each of them.

2. What are some ways our culture militates against the priorities you think are important in building a strong family unit? Mention any positive steps you are taking to keep these in check.

3. In what areas of your child rearing do you find it most challenging to be consistent?

4. On page 90, the author gives six possible reasons children may give for why they turn from the gospel. Do you agree? Have you any to add?

5. Discuss how each of you has coped with the "irrational" moments that often occur in raising of children (see page 91).

6. Can you think of times when Jesus as a discipler "produced what he believed in?" Or raised the crown a few inches above their heads and watched them grow into it?

7. Pray for each other's children and grandchildren.

Chapter Eight
PKs Can Be OK (Part 2)

1. Discuss the final five themes the author cited as important in her family and how you relate to each of them.

2. Share an open-window moment in your child's life that stands out to you. How did you or your husband handle it?

3. If you were to choose a mother in Scripture for a model, who would she be and why?

4. How do you counter the tendency of some people, in and out of the church, to expect your children to be perfect?

5. Add to the author's list of the benefits of being a pastor's family.

6. Receive the promise of Deuteronomy 29:29 for your families, praying for one another in specific ways: "The things revealed belong to us and to our children forever, that we may follow all the words of this law."

Chapter Nine
The Journey Continues: Becoming Yankees

1. Read 2 Samuel 24:24 and discuss it in the context of what it has cost you to follow Christ (see page 109–110).

2. Why is it important to share the ministry with others? Are there reasons why you fail to delegate?

3. Which *shepherd's instincts* relate most to you and your husband? Why?

4. If time allows, look at the lives of Eve, Sarah, Leah, Rebecca, Lot's wife, and Hannah concerning their infertility and "move" challenges. What are your thoughts regarding the author's conclusions?

5. Name gifts and strengths which you've seen in each other over the weeks you've been meeting. Mention at least one strength or gift for each woman. Then press Ephesians 4:11–16 into each other through prayer.

CHAPTER TEN
THE JOURNEY CONTINUES: FORGIVING AND BEING FORGIVEN

1. What is your response to the T. C. Upham quote at the beginning of the chapter? Are there Scriptures that come to mind that support this conviction?

2. Have there been times when the Scriptures the author gives have also been encouraging to you? Be specific. Perhaps you can add your own.

3. If each of us fears the condemnation of other Christ-followers should we fail, how can the church ever hope to be a safe place for sinners to repent?

4. Discuss the Larry Crabb quote and the realization that the author had of her own sinfulness (see pages 133).

5. Can you think of a trial in your life that showed you something about yourself that you had not known before? Are the seven things Paul Modesto suggests (page 135) useful? How?

CHAPTER ELEVEN
THE JOURNEY CONTINUES: GETTING LOST IN NEW YORK CITY

1. As you read this chapter, in what ways did you see God using the MacDonalds' brokenness for the good of the people of Trinity Baptist?

2. Would you be open to going to a place like New York? Respond to this statement: *The will of God will never lead you where God's grace cannot keep you.* Has this been your experience? Support with Scripture if possible.

3. How does their city church experience vary from your congregation?

4. Discuss the Fenelon quote in the context of whether a couple should ever return to a former congregation. How would you expect God to show you his will in such a circumstance? Support with Scripture.

5. God loves cities. He is taking us to one someday. Read Revelation 21:2–7, using it as a basis for prayer.

Chapter Twelve
Friends: The Difference They Make

1. How important is it to you to cultivate a few strong friendships? Tell each other some of your friendship history since being in ministry.

2. Do you relate to the author's temptation to lead with strength instead of weakness? Explain.

3. Talk about the questions on pages 156–157 that we need to ask ourselves before we commit to friendships.

4. Discuss the last days of Jesus' life as the author has presented them. What are your responses to his choice and ability to love without condition, share with vulnerability, and lean on weak people? (see pages 157–158).

5. Pray that such friendships will come to pass for each other.

Chapter Thirteen
Protecting the Permanency of Your Marriage

1. Think of an older ministry-couple you would wish to be like when you "grow up." What character traits stand out? Make a list together of what is most important to you as a group.

2. After reading through this chapter with your husband, where are your strengths and/or challenge areas when it comes to the author's non-negotiables?

3. Discuss your response to comments about a ministry-marriage. Can you relate? If so, how?

4. How have you found it easiest to maintain a soothing, rather than a scolding voice? (see page 201).

5. Can you reflect on a time in your life like the author or the Conways had, when your response showed there was something far deeper going on? (see pages 170–171).

6. How have you and your husband brought time under control? Do you find any of the suggestions in this chapter helpful? If so, which ones?

7. Look at 1 Corinthians 2:1–5; 4:8–13; 2 Corinthians 1:8–9; 11:16–30; 12:5–10; and Romans 7:14–25. Discuss how often Paul felt weak and talked about it. Do you have the freedom to do so? In your marriage, what difference would it make if you and your husband allowed one another room to be weak?

8. Press the power of these Scriptures into each other through prayer.

Chapter Fourteen
In Retrospect: What Matters Most

1. Discuss the quote from E. Stanley Jones regarding prayer as cooperation with God (page 180). How do we move from insisting on "our way" to "attunement?"

2. Read Romans 1. How has the importance of honoring and thanking God changed for you since reading this chapter?

3. Do any of you have anything like a personal Thanksgiving Day? If so, explain what it means to you and why.

4. Study Jeremiah 5:21–25 together, citing themes from this chapter.

5. Contrast our "hurried sickness" in today's society to Brigid Herman's comments. Is such a life possible today? Why or why not? What one step can we take to "hit the mark?"

6. Has repentance come easily to you? Why or why not?

7. Discuss the *grace of silence* on pages 189–190.

8. Are you drawn to the intercessory gifts in Moses? Have you had a time in your life when God taught you how to be an advocate for others? Explain (see the William Law quote on page 191).

9. If you and your husband do not have a prayer covering, seek prayer from this group that you might see the importance of this, and begin to find those who will join such a team.

10. Pray Exodus 33:14–18 into each other.

Chapter Fifteen
The Journey Continues: Going Home

1. What is your response to the author's awareness that she needed to embrace her brokenness instead of trying to run from it?

2. Discuss some experience in your life when you did what Amy Carmichael suggested, or wish you had (see page 195).

3. Study Acts 14:19–20, 16:1–2. Have there been times and places that you have found it difficult to return to because of the former pain? How does Paul's willingness to forgive Lystra and its people affect you? In what ways will this insight hopefully change future "stoning" situations?

4. What does it do to you when people in your congregation simply want to repeat all that has happened in the past? In what ways can we as leaders infuse the spirit that C. S. Lewis has in the quote on page 196?

5. Have there been times in your ministry journey when your lifestyle changed as much as the author's did in the eight years she was gone from Grace Chapel? Were you able to get the people to accept these new realities? How? (see page 197).

6. Going back over your notes from all sixteen weeks, share two or three insights, quotes, or Scriptures that have been life-altering for you.

7. Reread 1 Samuel 1:1–2:26, making note of what impresses you most about Hannah. Pray her prayer into each other as you close.